Learner English

CAMBRIDGE HANDBOOKS FOR LANGUAGE TEACHERS

This is a series of practical guides for teachers of English and other languages. Illustrative examples are usually drawn from the field of English as a foreign or second language, but the ideas and techniques described can equally well be used in the teaching of any language.

In this series:

Drama Techniques in Language Learning – A resource book of communication activites for language teachers
by Alan Maley and Alan Duff

Games for Language Learning
by Andrew Wright, David Betteridge and Michael Buckby

Discussions that Work – Task-centred fluency practice *by Penny Ur*

Once Upon a Time – Using stories in the language classroom
by John Morgan and Mario Rinvolucri

Teaching Listening Comprehension *by Penny Ur*

Keep Talking – Communicative fluency activities for language teaching
by Friederike Klippel

Working with Words – A guide to teaching and learning vocabulary
by Ruth Gairns and Stuart Redman

Learner English – A teacher's guide to interference and other problems
edited by Michael Swan and Bernard Smith

Testing Spoken Language – A handbook of oral testing techniques
by Nic Underhill

Literature in the Language Classroom – A resource book of ideas and activities
by Joanne Collie and Stephen Slater

Dictation – New methods, new possibilities
by Paul Davis and Mario Rinvolucri

Grammar Practice Activities – A practical guide for teachers
by Penny Ur

Testing for Language Teachers *by Arthur Hughes*

Pictures for Language Learning *by Andrew Wright*

Five-Minute Activities – A resource book of short activities
by Penny Ur and Andrew Wright

The Standby Book – Activities for the language classroom
edited by Seth Lindstromberg

Lessons from Nothing – Activities for language teaching with limited time and resources *by Bruce Marsland*

Beginning to Write – Writing activities for elementary and intermediate learners
by Arthur Brookes and Peter Grundy

Ways of Doing – Students explore their everyday and classroom processes
by Paul Davis, Barbara Garside and Mario Rinvolucri

Using Newspapers in the Classroom *by Paul Sanderson*

Learner English

A teacher's guide to interference and other problems

Michael Swan and Bernard Smith

 CAMBRIDGE
UNIVERSITY PRESS

PUBLISHED BY THE PRESS SYNDICATE OF THE UNIVERSITY OF CAMBRIDGE
The Pitt Building, Trumpington Street, Cambridge, United Kingdom

CAMBRIDGE UNIVERSITY PRESS
The Edinburgh Building, Cambridge CB2 2RU, UK   http://www.cup.cam.ac.uk
40 West 20th Street, New York, NY 10011–4211, USA   http://www.cup.org
10 Stamford Road, Oakleigh, Melbourne 3166, Australia
Ruiz de Alarcón 13, 28014 Madrid, Spain

First published 1987
Fourteenth printing 1999

Printed in the United Kingdom at the University Press, Cambridge

British Library Cataloguing in Publication Data
Swan, Michael, 1936–
Learner English: a teacher's guide to
interference and other problems.
1. English language — Spoken English
2. English language — Study and teaching —
Foreign students
I. Title   II. Smith, Bernard, 1937–
428.3   PE1128.A2

Library of Congress Cataloguing in Publication data
Swan, Michael.
Learner English.
(Cambridge handbooks for language teachers)
1. English language — Study and teaching — Foreign speakers.
2. Interference (Linguistics)
I. Smith, Bernard, 1937–   II. Title.   III. Series.
PE1128.A2S9   1987   428'.007   86–24482

ISBN 0 521 26910 5 paperback
ISBN 0 521 32442 4 cassette

CE

Contents

Notes on contributors

Alexander Burak (Russian) is a lecturer in English attached to the Philosophy and Scientific Communism Department of Moscow State University.

Jung Chang (Chinese) teaches at the School of Oriental and African Studies, University of London.

Norman Coe (Spanish and Catalan) is a teacher and teacher-trainer at the British Institute in Barcelona.

Niels Davidsen-Nielsen (Scandinavian) is Professor of English at the Copenhagen School of Economics, Business Administration and Modern Languages.

Xavier Dekeyser (Dutch) teaches English language and linguistics at the University of Antwerp.

Betty Devriendt (Dutch) teaches English language and linguistics at the University of Antwerp.

Alison Duguid (Italian) works as a teacher-trainer with the British Council in Naples.

Steven Geukens (Dutch) teaches English language and linguistics at the University of Antwerp.

Neville Grant (Swahili) is a writer, educational consultant and teacher-trainer. He has written textbooks for English students in Africa and elsewhere.

Peter Harder (Scandinavian) is Senior Lecturer in English at the University of Copenhagen.

P. J. Honey (Vietnamese) was formerly a lecturer at the School of Oriental and African Studies, University of London.

Bruce Monk (Russian) teaches at International House, London, and is carrying out research on specialised language schools in the Soviet Union.

Sophia Papaefthymiou-Lytra (Greek) is a teacher-trainer and teacher of applied linguistics at the University of Athens.

Christopher Shackle (Indian) is Professor of Modern Languages of South Asia at the University of London.

David Shepherd (Portuguese) has been working for many years as an EFL lecturer and teacher-trainer in Brazil, where he is now a lecturer in English at the University of Paraná.

Bernard Smith (Arabic) specialises in the teaching of English to Arabic speakers, and has written an English course for the Sultanate of Oman.

David Smyth (Thai) teaches at the School of Oriental and African Studies, University of London.

Michael Swan (German) writes English-language teaching and reference books.

Ian Thompson (Japanese, Turkish) has taught English in Britain, Japan, Turkey and South America, and has a special interest in contrastive studies.

Guy Tops (Dutch) teaches English language and linguistics at the University of Antwerp.

Philip Tregidgo (West African) specialises in the practical description of English grammar, and has written English textbooks for schools in various parts of Africa.

Catherine Walter (French) has taught and trained teachers in Britain, France and the USA. She is currently working on an English course for adults.

Martin Wilson (Farsi) taught English in Iran and is now a senior lecturer at the Brighton Polytechnic, involved in teaching English as a foreign language and training EFL teachers.

Lili Wilson (Farsi) taught English in Iran and is currently a lecturer at the Brighton Polytechnic, specialising in Computer Assisted Language Learning.

Introduction

Purpose and scope of the book

This book is a practical reference guide for teachers of English as a foreign language. It will help teachers to anticipate the characteristic difficulties of learners who speak particular mother tongues, and to understand how these difficulties arise.

It is obviously not possible, in one book, to deal exhaustively with the problems of speakers of all the world's languages. We hope, however, that in the nineteen chapters that follow most teachers will find information about the more common problems encountered by most of their students. Generally a chapter discusses the typical 'interlanguage' of speakers of a particular mother tongue. (By 'interlanguage' we mean the variety of a language produced by non-native learners.) In some cases (e.g. Swahili, Russian), the language focused on can be taken as broadly representative of a whole group, in that speakers of related languages are likely to share a number of the problems described. In three chapters (those on West African, Indian and Scandinavian learners), the description relates to the English of speakers of a whole group of languages.

The book is accompanied by a cassette with recordings of learners of various nationalities, to illustrate the pronunciation problems described in the different chapters.

Approach

The book is written especially for the practising non-specialist teacher who needs an introduction to the characteristic problems of a particular group of learners. Technical linguistic terminology has been kept to a minimum, and contributors have in general aimed at clear simple descriptions of usage rather than detailed scholarly studies. This is particularly the case in the area of pronunciation, where excessive detail can be confusing and counterproductive. Within these limits, however, we believe that the descriptions given here are valid and reasonably complete.

British and other varieties of English

Learners' problems are described in terms of the way their typical 'interlanguages' deviate from a standard British variety of English. (No value judgement is implied in this choice.) Not all the comparisons are valid for all other varieties of English. Certain uses of the present perfect tense, for instance, or particular pronunciations of the vowel /əʊ/, count as mistakes in standard British English but are perfectly acceptable in American English. Similarly, there may be 'typical mistakes' in certain learners' use of non-British kinds of English which are not wrong from a British point of view. Teachers of other varieties will therefore need to be selective in their use of the information given here, particularly as far as pronunciation is concerned (see note below for teachers of American English).

Editorial conventions

In the 'distribution' sections, capitals are used for the names of countries in which the language concerned has official or quasi-official status. Small letters are used for other countries in which substantial numbers of native speakers of the language may be found. Thus the distribution of Italian is given as: ITALY, REPUBLIC OF SAN MARINO, VATICAN, SWITZERLAND, Malta, Somalia.

Pronunciation is shown by the use of common phonetic symbols between slashes, thus: /ðʌs/. The context should make it clear whether the transcription is intended to show a correct English pronunciation, a characteristic learner's mistake, or a sound in a foreign language. We have not tried to distinguish between phonetic and phonemic levels of description.

Except in the sections on pronunciation, an unacceptable or doubtfully acceptable form or usage is preceded by an asterisk (*).

All foreign words are in a different typeface, e.g. wat.

Note: 'interference' mistakes and others

In recent years there has been considerable controversy about how far a learner's 'interlanguage' is influenced by his or her mother tongue. Some linguists have claimed that the large majority of typical learners' errors are shared by speakers of widely different first languages, that mother-tongue interference is not an important factor in interlanguage, and that learners of a given foreign language tend to follow the same kind of 'route' through its difficulties regardless of their first language. For those interested in such matters, it is worth noting that the following descriptions do not appear to support this view. The specialist contributors do not, it is true, set out to distinguish systematically between 'interference' mistakes and others; nor do they concern themselves with the relative frequency of different types of error. However, they are all clearly convinced that the interlanguages of the learners they are discussing are specific and distinct (so that it makes sense to talk about Thai English, Japanese English, Greek English and so on); and they all obviously see mother-tongue influence as accounting for many of the characteristic problems they describe.

Comments

We would be glad to hear from readers who discover errors or important omissions in the descriptions of the various kinds of learner English. Please write to us c/o Cambridge University Press, The Edinburgh Building, Shaftesbury Road, Cambridge CB2 2RU, England.

Michael Swan
Bernard Smith

Note for teachers of American English*

Pronunciation

The British vowel charts given in some of the chapters will appear complicated to Americans. This is mainly because of the diphthongs (/eə/, /ɪə/, etc.) which have replaced 'vowel + *r*' in standard British English.

British English also has an 'extra' pure vowel as compared with American English. This is the rounded short o (/ɒ/) used in words like *dog, got, gone, off, stop, lost.* (*Cot* and *cart* have quite different vowels in British English, whereas in American English the main difference is the absence versus presence of an *r* sound.)

Many words written with '*a* + consonant' (e.g. *fast, after*) are pronounced with /ɑː/ in standard southern British, while American and most other varieties of English have /æ/.

Because of differences between British and American pronunciation, some of the 'mistakes' described in the various chapters may not sound wrong to an American ear. Note in particular:

1. The standard British vowel /əʊ/ (as in *boat, home*) is rather different from the American equivalent. Some learners' approximations are wrong in British English but acceptable in American English.
2. Faulty pronunciations of British /ɒ/ as in *dog, cot* (see above) may sound all right in American English.
3. Pronunciation of *r* after a vowel (as in *turn, before, car*) is a common mistake among learners of British English. It is of course perfectly correct in American English, assuming the *r* is pronounced in the right way.
4. Some learners pronounce intervocalic *t* like *d* in words like *better, matter.* Again, this produces a mistake in British English but not in American.

Grammar

There are few differences between British and American English grammar, and almost all the descriptions of learners' grammar problems

---

* In compiling these notes, we have been greatly helped by information supplied by Professor J. Donald Bowen and Professor Randall L. Jones.

are valid for both varieties. Note, however:

1. The present perfect tense is used in British English in some cases where Americans tend to prefer a past tense (e.g. BrE *He's just gone out* / AmE *He just went out*). This can lead to differences in the acceptability of learner usage.
2. Pre-verb adverbs are often placed earlier in the verb phrase in American English than in British English (e.g. BrE *He would probably have agreed* / AmE *He probably would have agreed*). Again, this can mean that a 'mistake' in British English is a correct American form.

Spelling, punctuation and vocabulary

The problems described in these areas, with very few exceptions, are common to learners of both varieties of English.

List of phonetic symbols used in English

/ɪ/	as in 'pit' /pɪt/		/iː/	as in 'key' /kiː/
/e/	as in 'pet' /pet/		/ɑː/	as in 'car' /kɑː/
/æ/	as in 'pat' /pæt/		/ɔː/	as in 'core' /kɔː/
/ʌ/	as in 'putt' /pʌt/		/uː/	as in 'coo' /kuː/
/ɒ/	as in 'pot' /pɒt/		/ɜː/	as in 'cur' /kɜː/
/ʊ/	as in 'put' /pʊt/			

/ə/   as in 'about', 'upper'
/əbaʊt/, /ʌpə/

/eɪ/	as in 'bay' /beɪ/		/əʊ/	as in 'go' /gəʊ/
/aɪ/	as in 'buy' /baɪ/		/aʊ/	as in 'cow' /kaʊ/
/ɔɪ/	as in 'boy' /bɔɪ/			

/ɪə/	as in 'peer' /pɪə/
/eə/	as in 'pear' /peə/
/ʊə/	as in 'tour' /tʊə/

/p/	as in 'pea' /piː/		/b/	as in 'bee' /biː/
/t/	as in 'toe' /təʊ/		/d/	as in 'doe' /dəʊ/
/k/	as in 'cap' /kæp/		/g/	as in 'gap' /gæp/
/f/	as in 'fat' /fæt/		/v/	as in 'vat' /væt/
/θ/	as in 'thing' /θɪŋ/		/ð/	as in 'this' /ðɪs/
/s/	as in 'sip' /sɪp/		/z/	as in 'zip' /zɪp/
/ʃ/	as in 'ship' /ʃɪp/		/ʒ/	as in 'measure' /meʒə/
/h/	as in 'hat' /hæt/			

/m/	as in 'map' /mæp/		/l/	as in 'led' /led/
/n/	as in 'nap' /næp/		/r/	as in 'red' /red/
/ŋ/	as in 'hang' /hæŋ/		/j/	as in 'yet' /jet/
			/w/	as in 'wet' /wet/
/tʃ/	as in 'chin' /tʃɪn/		/dʒ/	as in 'gin' /dʒɪn/

/i/   as in 'react', 'happy' /riækt/, /hæpi/

/u/   as in 'to each' /tu iːtʃ/

/ʔ/   glottal stop

/ʰ/   aspiration, as in 'pin' /pʰɪn/

/'/   primary stress, as in 'open' /ˈəʊpən/

/ˌ/   secondary stress, as in 'ice cream' /ˌaɪsˈkriːm/

The International Phonetic Alphabet

	Bilabial	Labiodental	Dental, or Alveolar, or Post-alveolar	Retroflex	Palato-alveolar	Palatal	Velar	Uvular	Labial-Palatal	Labial-Velar	Pharyngeal	Glottal
Nasal	m	ɱ	n	ɳ		ɲ	ŋ	ɴ				
Plosive	p b		t d	ʈ ɖ		c ɟ	k ɡ	q ɢ		k͡p ɡ͡b		ʔ
(Median) Fricative	ɸ β	f v	θ ð s z	ʂ ʐ	ʃ ʒ	ç ʝ	x ɣ	χ ʁ			ħ ʕ	h ɦ
(Median) Approximant		ʋ	ɹ			j			ɥ	w		
Lateral Fricative			ɬ ɮ									
Lateral (Approximant)			l	ɭ		ʎ	(ʟ)					
Trill	ʙ		r					ʀ				
Tap or Flap			ɾ	ɽ				ʀ				
Ejective	p'		t'				k'					
Implosive	ɓ		ɗ									
(Median) Click	ʘ		ʇ									
Lateral Click			ʖ									

(rows above the Ejective are **pulmonic air-stream mechanism**; Ejective, Implosive, Click and Lateral Click are **non-pulmonic air-stream**)

DIACRITICS

- ˳ or ˌ Voiceless n̥ d̥
- ˬ or ˌ Voiced s̬ ţ
- ʰ Aspirated tʰ
- ̤ Breathy-voiced b̤ a̤
- ̪ Dental t̪
- ̫ Labialized t̫
- ̡ Palatalized t̡
- ̴ Velarized or Pharyngealized ɫ, t̴
- ˌ Syllabic n̩ ḷ
- ˟ or ͡ Simultaneous ʃʃ (but see also under the heading Affricates)

- ˙ or ˙ Raised e̝, e̝, ẇ
- ˎ or ˬ Lowered e̞, e̞, β̞
- ˔ Advanced u̟+, ṭ
- ˍ or ˍ Retracted i̠, i-, ṭ
- ¨ Centralised ë
- ~ Nasalized ã
- ˞ r-coloured aʴ
- ː Long aː
- ˑ Half-long aˑ
- ˘ Non-syllabic ŭ
- ˒ More rounded ɔ̹
- ˓ Less rounded y̜

OTHER SYMBOLS

ɕ, ʑ Alveolo-palatal fricatives
ʃ, ʒ Palatalized ʃ, ʒ
ʀ Alveolar fricative trill
ɺ Alveolar lateral flap
ɧ Simultaneous ʃ and x
ʮ Variety of ʃ resembling s, etc.
ɪ = i
ʊ = u
ɘ = Variety of ə
ɚ = r-coloured ə

VOWELS

	Front		Back
	Unrounded	Rounded	

Close: i y / ɨ ʉ / ɯ u
Half-close: e ø / ɘ ɵ / ɤ o
Half-open: ɛ œ / ɜ ɞ / ʌ ɔ
Open: a ɶ / ɐ / ɑ ɒ

STRESS, TONE (PITCH)

- ˈ stress, placed at beginning of stressed syllable:
- ˌ secondary stress:
- ˉ high level pitch, high tone:
- ˍ low level:
- ˊ high rising:
- ˏ low rising:
- ˋ high falling:
- ˎ low falling:
- ˆ rise-fall:
- ˇ fall-rise:

AFFRICATES can be written as digraphs, as ligatures, or with slur marks; thus ts, tʃ, dʒ: t͡s t͡ʃ d͡ʒ: t͜s t͜ʃ d͜ʒ:
c, ɟ may occasionally be used for tʃ, dʒ.

Dutch speakers

Guy A. J. Tops, Xavier Dekeyser, Betty Devriendt and Steven Geukens

Distribution

THE NETHERLANDS, BELGIUM, Surinam, Dutch Antilles; about 20 million people. (Its descendant Afrikaans, spoken by about 3.5 million people in South Africa and Namibia, is now officially considered a separate language.)

Introduction

Dutch is a member of the (West) Germanic branch of Indo-European, and as such is closely related to Frisian, English, German and the Scandinavian languages. It is the standard language in the Netherlands and the northern parts of Belgium (Flanders). In the Netherlands, there are many native speakers of Standard Dutch and most people know it as a second 'dialect'; there is, however, great variation throughout the Dutch language area, especially in Belgium, and some dialects are so different as to be mutually unintelligible. The type of Southern Dutch spoken in Belgium is often called 'Flemish'.

Dutch and English being so closely related, they have many similarities in all areas of their grammars, and Dutch speakers regard English as easy to learn, at least initially, when they make rapid progress.

Phonology

General

The Dutch and English phonological systems are broadly similar, so that speakers of Dutch do not normally have serious difficulties in recognising or pronouncing most English sounds.

Many learners may use strong regional accents in their Dutch, and their problems with English tend to vary accordingly. Universal features of Dutch giving rise to a Dutch accent in English are:
- Absence of word-final lenis ('voiced') consonants and corresponding variations in length of preceding vowels.
- A much narrower intonation range, not reaching the same low pitch areas as English.
- Pronunciation of r whenever it occurs in the spelling.

Vowels

iː	ɪ	e	æ	eɪ	aɪ	ɔɪ
ɑː	ɒ	ɔː	ʊ	aʊ	əʊ	ɪə
uː	ʌ	ɜː	ə	eə	ʊə	aɪə / aʊə

Shaded phonemes have equivalents or near equivalents in Dutch, and should therefore be perceived and articulated without serious difficulty, although some confusions may still arise. Unshaded phonemes may cause problems. For detailed comments, see below.

1. Depending on the learners' region of origin, /ɪ/ may be pronounced too close (leading to confusion between pairs like *sit* and *seat*), or too open (with confusion between pairs like *sit* and *set*).
2. Standard Dutch /e/ is somewhere between English /e/ and /æ/. This results in confusion of the latter two (in pairs like *set* and *sat* or *then* and *than*), especially since Dutch has no vowel corresponding to /æ/.
3. Many learners pronounce English /ɑː/ very far back; it may sound similar to /ɔː/ (which is often very open), leading to confusion between pairs like *part* and *port*.
4. /ɒ/ and /ʌ/ may not be distinguished, leading to confusion in pairs like *not* and *nut*. Some learners may also pronounce /ʌ/ rather like /ə/.
5. Dutch speakers find English /ɔː/ and /əʊ/ difficult, and may confuse pairs like *caught* and *coat*.
6. Dutch has no equivalent of /ʊ/, as in *book*. It may be pronounced rather like /ʌ/ (with confusion between *look* and *luck*, for example), or like /uː/ (making *pool* similar to *pull*).
7. /ɜː/ (as in heard, turn) is usually pronounced with lip-rounding by Dutch learners.

Consonants

p	b	f	v	θ	ð	t	d
s	z	ʃ	ʒ	tʃ	dʒ	k	g
m	n	ŋ	l	r	j	w	h

Shaded phonemes have equivalents or near equivalents in Dutch, and should therefore be perceived and articulated without serious difficulty, although some confusions may still arise. Unshaded phonemes may cause problems. For detailed comments, see below.

1. The lenis ('voiced') consonants /b/, /d/, /v/, /ð/, /z/, /ʒ/ and /dʒ/ do not occur at the ends of words in Dutch. Learners will replace them by their fortis ('unvoiced') counterparts: *Bop* for *Bob*; *set* for *said*; *leaf* for *leave*; *cloth* for *clothe*; *rice* for *rise*; '*beish*' for *beige*; *larch* for *large*. (Most learners also fail to make the English distinction in the length of vowels before lenis and fortis consonants.)
2. In other positions in words, too, many Northern Dutch learners pronounce /f/ instead of /v/, /s/ instead of /z/, and /ʃ/ instead of /ʒ/: *file* for *vile*; *sue* for *zoo*; '*mesher*' for *measure*.
3. Dutch lacks the phoneme /g/ as in *get*. Learners will use either /k/ or the fricatives /x/ (as in Scottish *loch*) or /ɣ/.
4. /p/, /t/ and /k/ are not aspirated at the beginning of a word in Dutch; this can make them sound rather like /b/, /d/ and /g/: *bay* for *pay*; *den* for *ten*; *goat* for *coat*.
5. /tʃ/ is often reduced to /ʃ/ and /dʒ/ to /ʒ/ (or /ʃ/): *shop* for *chop*; /ʒæm/ or *sham* for *jam*.
6. /θ/ is usually pronounced /s/ or /t/: *sank* or *tank* for *thank*. /ð/ is usually pronounced /z/ or /d/: *zen* or *den* for *then*.
7. Northern Dutch speakers may make /s/ rather like /ʃ/: *sheet* for *seat*.
8. Learners may make /w/ with teeth and lip, leading to confusion with /v/: *vile* for *while*.
9. Dutch /r/ exhibits a lot of variety; none of the versions are like English /r/.
10. Dutch 'dark' /l/ is very 'dark', with the tongue further back in the mouth than in English, especially after /iː/, /ɪ/ and /e/. Some Dutch accents have 'dark' /l/ where English has 'clear' /l/.
11. /h/ can be a problem for learners with a dialect background from the coastal provinces of Belgium: they produce a /x/-like fricative.

Consonant clusters

English clusters are not in general difficult for Dutch speakers. Students may insert /ə/ between /l/ and certain other consonants: '*fillum*' for *film*; '*millock*' for *milk*.

Influence of spelling on pronunciation

1. The Dutch system for spelling vowels and diphthongs is fairly simple and consistent. Learners have great difficulty therefore in dissociating a word's spelling from its pronunciation.

Dutch speakers

2. Learners tend to pronounce the letter *r* whenever it occurs, leading to mistakes if they are aiming at standard British English.
3. The combination *ng* is always pronounced /ŋ/ in Dutch. This leads to problems with words like *finger, hunger*, etc.
4. Even very advanced learners will pronounce the letter *o* in words like *front* and *mother* as /ɒ/ instead of /ʌ/.
5. The letters *u* and *w* in words like *caught* and *saw* lead many speakers to use an /əʊ/-like sound instead of /ɔː/.
6. Final *-w* is often pronounced as /w/: *how* pronounced /haʊw/; *saw* pronounced /sɔːw/; *draw* pronounced /drɔːw/, etc.
7. Learners will tend to pronounce the silent letters in words like *knot, gnaw, comb, bomb, half, sword, psychiatrist*, etc.

Stress

Dutch and English stress patterns in words and sentences are quite similar. There are some problems, though.
1. Dutch compounds have stress on the first element: hence * 'appletart* for *apple 'tart* (Dutch 'appeltaart).
2. Dutch stress patterns are not susceptible to variation depending on grammatical category, as in *con'vict* (verb) vs *'convict* (noun). This leaves learners very uncertain about the stress patterns of many words.
3. Dutch does not have as many weak forms as English, nor does it use them so consistently. Many speakers will overstress words like *and, but, than*, etc., using strong forms throughout.

Intonation

Dutch intonation moves within a much narrower range than English. The Dutch intonation range is on the whole relatively high and does not reach the same low pitches as English. Learners trying to widen their voice range often do it upwards rather than downwards.

Juncture and assimilation

1. Dutch does not have final lenis ('voiced') obstruents. Learners who have acquired them will still tend to make them fortis if the next word begins with a fortis sound. Conversely, Dutch word-final fortis sounds will often become lenis before a word beginning with a lenis stop or a vowel. This leads to problems in English. For example:
  if it is Tom pronounced '*iv id iss Tom*'
  this is Kate pronounced '*thiz iss Kate*'
  back door pronounced '*bag door*'
  Dad comes pronounced '*Dat comess*'

4

2. In Dutch, a sequence of two identical or similar stop consonants is usually reduced to one:

> *sharp pins* pronounced '*sharpins*'
> *hard times* pronounced '*hartimes*'

Punctuation

Dutch puts a comma after restrictive relative clauses; hence mistakes like:

> **The concern they show, is by no means exaggerated.*

Commas may be used between unlinked clauses:

> **This is somewhat surprising, as they are forbidden in Dutch too, they nevertheless occur regularly.*

Quotation marks are written like this:

> **„I am thirsty”, he said.*

Grammar

General

Typologically speaking, the Dutch language occupies a position midway between English and German. Word order is virtually the same as in German; Dutch still has grammatical gender, and a high percentage of its vocabulary betrays its Germanic origin.

However, Dutch is not a variety of German. Apart from a fair number of language-specific differences, its morphology comes close to the English system. The inflectional system is relatively simple; neither verbs nor prepositions govern 'cases'; there are only a few relics of the old subjunctive.

Interrogative and negative structures

1. Dutch has no *do*-support. Interrogatives are formed by simple inversion; negatives by placing niet (= *not*) after the verb or before the first non-finite verbal element:

   > **What mean you?*
   > **Thank you, I smoke not.*
   > **I have her yesterday not seen.*

2. Dutch has no construction comparable with the English question tag; instead it uses particles and adverbs:

   > **She is your best friend, eh?* (for *She is your best friend, isn't she?*)

3. Unlike English, Dutch does not have such a stereotyped 'grammar of conversation'; hence the English of a speaker of Dutch may sometimes seem rather unidiomatic and at times even rude or ill-mannered:

'*Your glass is empty.*' '*Oh yes?*' (for '*So it is.*')
'*They never listen to good advice.*' '*No.*' (for '*No, they don't.*'
or '*No, they don't, do they?*')
'*You can't speak without a regional accent.*' *'*Yes!*' (for '*Yes, I can.*' or '*But I can.*')

Auxiliaries

The general perfective aspect-marker, in Dutch as in English, is hebben
(= *have*). However, zijn (= *be*) is used to form the perfect tenses of verbs
of movement:
He is left ten minutes ago.
The Dutch marker of the passive voice is worden (= *become*) in the
simple tenses, zijn in the perfect forms (in Southern Dutch also occasionally worden):
*He is seen in the neighbourhood. (Southern Dutch also *He is
been seen ...) (for He has been seen ...)*

Time, tense and aspect

A. PAST TIME

To refer to a past event Dutch can use both a past tense and a perfect
tense, without much difference in meaning. The latter is the more usual
form. Conversely, Dutch can use a past tense where English would use a
present perfect:
I have seen him yesterday.
All my nineteenth-century ancestors have lived here.
Since I made my report last year, there was a steady improvement in the company's trading position.

B. PRESENT TIME

To express how long a present state of affairs has been going on, Dutch
normally uses a present tense, not a present perfect:
I know him for five years.
I live in Amsterdam since I was a child.

C. FUTURE TIME

1. Even though Dutch has a future tense formed with an auxiliary
   (roughly equivalent to the *shall/will* future of English), it often uses the
   present tense to refer to the future:
   I promise I give it to him tomorrow.

2. To express how long a future state of affairs will have been going on, Dutch often uses a simple future:
   > *In 1990 I will work here for seventeen years.*
3. Dutch can freely use the future tense in a subclause of time:
   > *I'll be old when this will happen.*

D. ASPECT

Dutch does not have progressive verb forms:
> *I lived in London at that point in my life.*
> *I have a lot of trouble with John at the moment.*

'Progressive' meanings can however be expressed, if necessary, by the use of certain adjectives and adverbs:
> *What were you busy with yesterday?* (for *What were you doing yesterday?*)
> *You have seen each other continually this last fortnight, haven't you?* (for *You've been seeing ...*)

Some beginners over-generalise the English progressive:
> *The house is belonging to my father.*

Conditionals

1. There is no such sharp distinction between the use of verbal forms in the Dutch subclause and main clause as there is in English:
   > *If I shall see him, I shall tell him.*
   > *If you would know him, you wouldn't* (or even *didn't*) *say such things.*
   > *If he would have worked harder, he had succeeded.*
2. Inversion in the subclause is much more widely used in Dutch than in English. This is the reason why the adverb *then* is often used in the main clause:
   > *Had I known in time, then I would have come along.*

Modal verbs

On the whole, the Dutch and English systems of modal auxiliaries are similar. But:
1. English *must* is deceptively like Dutch **moeten**; hence the frequent use of *must* where this is not the appropriate modal:
   > *When must you take up your new appointment?* (for *When are you to ...?*)
   > *In Venice people must go everywhere by boat.* (for *... have to ...*)

Dutch speakers

2. More specifically, learners may take *must* to be the equivalent of the Dutch past tense **moest** (= *had to* or *was to*):
   * *I must go to London yesterday.*
   * *It must have been yesterday.* (for *It was to have been yesterday.*)
3. In Southern Dutch **moet niet** means *don't have to*, *needn't*, and is therefore completely different from *must not*:
   * *I mustn't, but I may if I want to.*
4. In Northern Dutch especially, **moest** niet means *should not*, *ought not to*:
   * *You mustn't smoke so much, if I may say so.*
5. Dutch **kan** (infinitive **kunnen**) denotes all types of possibility; there is no equivalent of English *may*:
   * *It can rain tonight; don't forget your umbrella.*
6. Permission is mostly sought and granted in Dutch by means of the modal **mag** (infinitive **mogen**), even in informal registers, leading students to overuse *may* and avoid *can*. English *might* looks like the past tense of **mag** which is **mocht** (= *could*, *was allowed to*):
   * *She might go out every week when she was sixteen.*
7. Dutch **zou** (past future or conditional *should/would*) is sometimes mistranslated as *should*:
   * *Little did they know that they should never see each other again.* (for ... *were never to* ...)

Non-finite forms

1. In Dutch, infinitives and participles occur less often than in English as the complements of verbs. Instead, Dutch makes frequent use of *that*-clauses:
   * *He wants that I go.*
   or it will prefer adverbial or adjectival constructions:
   * *I've always gladly gone there.* (for *I've always loved going there.*)
2. Dutch has no equivalent of the English gerund:
   * *I really must stop to smoke.*
   * *Instead of to fight, they started to laugh.*
   * *It's no use to ask her.*
3. Present participle constructions in postposition are rare in Dutch. So, for instance, instead of talking about *the girl sitting in the corner*, a Dutch learner is likely to say *the girl who is sitting in the corner*.
4. There is no Dutch equivalent of the structure 'verb + object + past participle':
   * *I hear my name call.*

8

* I like that it is done quickly.
* It's no use to try to make yourself understandable.

Word order

Word order in Dutch is less simple than in English. Some of the most striking differences will only interfere at an elementary level, but other Dutchisms may be so deeply rooted that they will yield problems at a more intermediate or even advanced level.

A. MAIN CLAUSE

1. In Dutch, the subject and the finite form of the verb are not separable:
   * He works sometimes on Sundays.
2. The Dutch finite verb group tends to be separated from the rest of the verbal group (infinitives, past participles):
   * I must at once my sister see.
   * They were of everything robbed.
3. In contrast to English, Dutch can have its verb and (simple) objects or complements separated by adverbials:
   * I hear every day the bells ring from my bedroom.
   * Bill loved passionately his wife.
   * She kept fortunately her mouth shut.
4. Invariably, there is inversion in Dutch if the sentence opens with a constituent other than the subject:
   * Tomorrow shall I see him.
   * Incredible is that!
   * This have we already examined.
5. The internal order of adverbials is also different, time adverbials tending to precede those of place:
   * She has already been living for two years in London.
6. The adverb particle tends to come at the end of the clause:
   * He got quickly up.
7. In Dutch, the article can be separated from its noun by a complex participial clause or by an adjective and its complement:
   * the by the Senate with unanimity voted down proposal
   * He is a hard to convince man.
8. For word order in interrogative clauses, see the section 'Interrogative and negative structures'.

B. SUBCLAUSE

A verb or verbal group comes at the end of a subordinate clause:
   * He asked whether we John had seen. (or even * ... seen had.)

Articles

The Dutch system of definite and indefinite articles is basically the same as in English. Apart from a number of differences of an idiomatic nature, the main points to note are:

1. Dutch sometimes uses a definite article with uncountable and plural nouns referring to something/things/people in general:
   > *The wages have been rising recently.*
   > *the life in modern Britain*
2. There is usually no indefinite article in subject complements:
   > *She is widow.*
   > *He would like to be engineer.*
3. Though Dutch also has collocations without overt articles like naar bed/school gaan (= *go to bed/school*), aan tafel zitten (= *be at table*), etc., it is not as systematic as English in this respect:
   > *go to the church* (for *go to church*)
   > *be sent to the prison*

Adjectives and adverbs

Adverbs are identical with the uninflected form of the adjective. This use of unmarked adverbial forms is so deeply rooted in the Dutch speaker's competence that even advanced learners tend to make mistakes like:
   > *She drives very careful.*
   > *You speak English very good.*
or in noun phrases:
   > *an economic weak theory*

Quantifiers and determiners

1. Dutch does not use different quantifiers with countable and uncountable nouns; hence mistakes like *much books* and, less often, *little persons* (for *few persons*).
2. The distinction between *some* and *any* will have to be taught explicitly, as there is nothing that comes close to these quantifiers in Dutch. The same holds for *either/each/every*:
   > *Take a ball in every hand.*

Interrogative pronouns

Here the only problem is the appropriate use of *which*, there being no exact equivalent for this in Dutch; hence:
   > *What is your second language, English or French?*

Relative pronouns

1. Dutch does not have different relative pronouns for people and things. The use of *which* with a personal antecedent (*A person which ...*) is difficult to eradicate.
2. There being no distinction between restrictive and non-restrictive clauses as far as the choice of pronouns is concerned, beginners often do not understand why structures like *My parents, that were born in France ...* or *My father, you met in Amsterdam ...* are ungrammatical.
3. *Wat* has a much wider coverage than English *what*: it is used with clause antecedents, with quantifier antecedents, and in very recent usage also with neuter nouns. This explains the use of *what* in a number of cases where English requires *which*:
     John went to Brussels, what explains everything.
     This is all what I know.
   Occasionally also:
     The picture what I was drawing ...
4. Contact clauses (clauses without overt relative pronouns) and preposition stranding are totally unknown in Dutch syntax; therefore beginners tend to make excessive use of structures like:
     the woman whom I met in Glasgow the other day
     the pen with which Jane was writing yesterday

Gender

The natural gender system of English has no match in Dutch: Southern Dutch speakers have mostly preserved the tripartite Germanic system (just like the Germans), while speakers of Northern Dutch now use a binary system (masculine and neuter) with a limited and shrinking number of feminine nouns. Whichever system is adhered to, Belgian and Dutch students are often inclined to treat certain inanimate nouns as either masculine or feminine, in agreement with their Dutch equivalents:
     The English language ... she ...
     The state ... he ...

Conjunctions

The only real problem here is the common confusion between *if* and *when*:
     When it rains the trip will have to be cancelled.

Prepositions

(See also 'Vocabulary: complementation'.)

Though it is possible to indicate rough equivalences between Dutch and English prepositions, there are so many instances where there is no match that students will have to learn many prepositions in their collocations. A few common mistakes, by way of example:

> *on the party*
> *he lives on number 9*
> *with/*by my aunt* (for *at my aunt's*)
> *good in games*
> *on the meadow*
> *on sea*

The list is endless. However, a few systematic remarks can be made.

1. **Sinds** translates as either *for* or *since*; students tend to use *since* only:
   > *I've lived here since four years.*
2. **Achter** translates as either *after* or *behind*; students confuse them:
   > *He stood after me.*
3. **In** translates as either *in* or *into*; students tend to use *in* only:
   > *Go in the room.*

Vocabulary

Dutch and English share the basic Germanic vocabulary (e.g. **voet** = *foot*, **groot** = *great*, **zien** = *see*, **mij** = *me*, **in** = *in*), which greatly facilitates learning, in spite of the numerous false friends. Learning the Romance part of the vocabulary is facilitated by the fact that Dutch has borrowed fairly extensively from Romance and that many educated people know French (especially in Belgium) and even some Latin.

False friends

The list of false friends is endless; the German list (p. 39) applies in its entirety to Dutch as well as to German (except for the remarks pertaining to *mean* and *who/where*).

Some typical mistakes with high-frequency words

make vs *do*	*I still must make my homework.*
what vs *how*	*How do you call that?*
there /ðə/	*There happened a strange thing.*
used	*I am used to do this.*
own	*She has an own room.*
also	*... the Smiths. Also they were shocked.*
please	'Can I have your book?' (handing it over) *'Please.'*

Compounding

English compounds less freely than Dutch and students will make such odd compounds as *life-habits*.

Complementation

Students often fail to realise that the complementation of an English word (that is to say, the type of structure that can follow it) is quite arbitrary, and needs to be learnt along with the word if it differs from Dutch. This is especially true of verbal complementation (a) and of prepositional complementation of adjectives and nouns (b). A few typical mistakes:

a) *I don't mind to do it.*
If you can't avoid to go, you risk to upset your Dad.
I suggest to go to the pictures tonight.
I object against that word.
b) *That is typical for someone who is bad in chess.*
There is no proof for that.

Multi-word verbs

They exist in Dutch, too, but they are used far less than in English, and it will often be necessary explicitly to draw the students' attention to everyday prepositional verbs that they will otherwise fail to notice and use:

Dutch	Simple verb	Multi-word verb
zoeken	seek, search for	look for
beschouwen	consider	look on
verdragen	bear	put up with

(Many multi-word verbs fortunately pose no problem, as they are matched by similar or compound but separable verbs in Dutch.)

A sample of written Dutch with a word for word translation

Ik had reeds   veel van de moderne dichter gelezen; maar
I   had already much of   the modern   poet   read;   but

na   zijn laatste bundel: *Het Hart   op de Pijnbank* werd
after his latest   volume *The Heart on the Rack*   became

het mij te   machtig: deze man
it   me too mighty [= I could stand it no longer]: this man

moest geholpen worden. Toch aarzelde ik nog. Iedereen
had-to helped   be.   Yet   hesitated I still. Everyone

weet, dat ik een onbenullig man ben, die   onder de
knows, that I an insignificant man am, who under the

dekmantel van misselijke scherts zijn totale leegheid
cover   of miserable jest   his total emptiness

van geest tracht te bemantelen. Wat   moest ik   bij
of mind tries   to cover.   What had-to I [to do] at

die man?   Zou   hij, die dagelijks zijn ontzettende
this man['s]? Would he, who daily   his terrifying

zieleworstelingen op rijm   zette, niet in lachen   uitbarsten
soul-wrestlings   on rhyme put,   not in laughing out-burst

wanneer mijn stompzinnig hoofd in zijn deuropening verscheen?
when   my dumb-minded head in his door-opening appeared?

Maar na   zijn allerlaatste bundel *De Naakte Man* (uit de
But   after his very-latest   volume *The Naked Man* (out the

hand gezet in de Lutetia-letter op oud-Hollands wormvrij
hand set   in the Lutetia-letter on old-Dutch   wormfree

papier in 150 exemplaren, waarvan 75 jammerlijk genoeg niet
paper in 150 copies,   whereof 75 sadly   enough not

in de handel)   gaf de doorslag:
in the trade [not commercially available]) gave the punch

              hier mocht   niet langer geaarzeld
[= clinched it]: here might [could] not longer hesitated

worden. Hier diende   ingegrepen.
be.   Here [it] behoved to interfere [past participle].

Ik kocht   derhalve een pakje   boter, een
I bought therefore a   packet [diminutive] [of] butter, an

ons   Versterkende Middelen, een stuk
ounce [100g] [of] Fortifying   Substances, a   piece [of]

spek,   een borstrok, wat   eieren en   een bos
bacon, a   singlet,   what [a few] eggs   and a   bunch [of]

bloemen en begaf mij   onverwijld naar het huis
flowers   and betook me [reflexive] immediately to   the house

van de moderne dichter.
of   the modern   poet.

('De Moderne Dichter' by Godfried Bomans from *Kopstukken*)

Speakers of Scandinavian languages: Danish, Norwegian, Swedish

Niels Davidsen-Nielsen and Peter Harder

Distribution

DENMARK, NORWAY, SWEDEN, FINLAND (Swedish), Germany (Danish).

Introduction

The Scandinavian languages are Indo-European languages belonging, like English, to the Germanic branch. Considerable contact in past and present between the English and Scandinavian languages, as well as common outside influences, have served to keep up and reinforce the close relationship between the languages. English is therefore relatively easy for Scandinavians to learn.

For the sake of simplicity, the following description concentrates on the major problems which Danish, Norwegian and Swedish learners of English have in common. Less attention has been paid to issues which require cross-Scandinavian comparisons (though it has been necessary to deal with some points of this kind in the sections on phonological problems). And, for reasons of space, it has not been possible to include the difficulties of Icelandic and Faroese learners.

Phonology

General

All three Scandinavian languages are phonologically broadly similar to English, and most features of English pronunciation do not present serious difficulty to speakers of these languages. The phonological systems of Danish, Norwegian and Swedish are characterised by considerable similarity, both with respect to sound segments (for example the rounded front vowels) and to prosody, and as will appear below there are many common Scandinavian errors in English. Nevertheless, several pronunciation features do exist which separate the Scandinavian languages from each other, and it is therefore only from a bird's-eye view that it makes sense to speak about English pronounced with a 'Scandinavian accent'. In the vocalic and consonant charts below inter-Scandinavian differences have not been marked, but some differences of this type are described in the text.

Vowels

	ɪ		æ	eɪ	
			ʊ	əʊ	ɪə
uː	ʌ	ɜː	ə	eə	ʊə

Shaded phonemes have equivalents or near equivalents in all three Scandinavian languages and are perceived and articulated without serious difficulty, although some confusions may still arise. Unshaded phonemes may cause problems to speakers of Danish, Swedish and/or Norwegian. For detailed comments, see below.

1. /ɪ/ is often pronounced as a close vowel /iː/: *seat* for *sit*.
2. /æ/ is often pronounced by Swedish speakers as /e/: *bed* for *bad*. Conversely, some Norwegians tend to pronounce /e/ as /æ/: *bad* for *bed*.
3. /ʊ/ is often pronounced as a close and clearly rounded vowel by Danes and Swedes. Norwegians tend to substitute a more advanced, less closely rounded vowel.
4. /uː/ is often pronounced as a central vowel by Norwegians, and as a strongly advanced and somewhat lower vowel by Swedes.
5. Swedes and Norwegians frequently replace /ʌ/ by a more rounded front vowel.
6. Danes characteristically replace /ʌ/ by a vowel intermediate between English /ʌ/ and /ɒ/. They also tend to partly unround /ɒ/, and consequently find it very difficult to keep *hut* apart from *hot*, *luck* from *lock*, etc.
7. /ɜː/ (as in *turn*) is typically rounded and advanced by Swedes and Danes.
8. /ə/ is not always sufficiently reduced ('unstressed').
9. Norwegians may pronounce /eɪ/ (as in *take*) too open: /æɪ/.
10. /əʊ/ is often pronounced by Swedes as /uː/ (*soup* for *soap*), by Danes as /ɔu/ or /œu/, and by Norwegians as /au/ or /ɒu/. Norwegians typically find it difficult to distinguish between English /əʊ/ and /au/ and, at a more advanced level, to distribute them correctly.

17

11. /ɪə/, /eə/ and /ʊə/ are usually pronounced with /r/ instead of /ə/ by Norwegians and Swedes. Danes typically replace them with the diphthongs /ɪɒ/, /eɒ/ and /uɒ/ respectively.

Consonants

p	b	f	v	θ	ð	t	d
s	z	ʃ	ʒ	tʃ	dʒ	k	g
m	n	ŋ	l	r	j	w	h

Shaded phonemes have equivalents or near equivalents in all three Scandinavian languages and are perceived and articulated without serious difficulty, although some confusions may still arise. Unshaded phonemes may cause problems to speakers of Danish, Swedish and/or Norwegian. For detailed comments, see below.

1. /θ/ does not occur and is typically pronounced as /t/ or (by Danes) as /s/: *tank, sank* for *thank*; *tree* for *three*.
2. /ð/ does not occur in Norwegian and Swedish and is often pronounced as /d/: *den* for *then*; *udder* for *other*. Danes tend to replace it with a much more loosely articulated /ð/.
3. /z/ does not occur and is typically replaced by /s/: *racer* for *razor*.
4. /ʒ/ does not occur and is typically replaced by /ʃ/: '*mesher*' for *measure*.
5. /tʃ/ does not occur and is often pronounced as /tj/.
6. /dʒ/ does not occur. It is often pronounced as /dj/ by Danes and Norwegians, and as /j/ by Swedes: *year* for *jeer*.
7. /r/ is pronounced with the back of the tongue by Danes and some (southern) Swedes. Norwegians and most Swedes replace it by other non-English tip-of-the-tongue *r*-sounds.
8. /w/ does not occur and tends to be replaced by a lax /v/: *vine* for *wine*.
9. 'Dark' /l/, as in *full, fill*, occurs only in some Swedish and Norwegian dialects; students tend to replace it by 'clear' /l/, as in *light*.
10. Danes tend to replace word-final /b/, /d/ and /g/ with /p/, /t/ and /k/: *pup* for *pub*; *set* for *said*; *dock* for *dog*. Between vowels, the opposite may happen: *rabid* for *rapid*; *ladder* for *latter*; *bigger* for *bicker*.
11. In Swedish and Norwegian, consonants are pronounced very long after short vowels; this may be carried over into English words like *coffee, letter*.

Influence of spelling on pronunciation

Spelling and pronunciation are more closely related in the Scandinavian languages (especially Swedish and Norwegian) than in English, and there are fewer ambiguities. Mistakes may be made in cases where a letter has different values in English and the mother tongue; or where English orthography lets the learner down after he or she has worked out the basic rules for correspondences between letters and sounds in English. Note particularly:

1. Beginners may pronounce the letter *i* as /iː/, *y* as /y/ (like German ü or French u), *a* as /ɑː/, and (depending on nationality) *u* as /ʊ/ and *au* as /aʊ/, leading to mistakes in words like *ride, symbol, parade, rush, automatic*.
2. /ə/ is always spelt *e* in Scandinavian languages. When /ə/ is spelt with another letter in English, students may use an unreduced vowel, pronouncing for example /ɒ/ in *commercial*, /æ/ in *alliance* and /ɑː/ in *particular*.
3. Even after Scandinavian students have learnt to pronounce English /z/, they commonly mispronounce the letter *s* as /s/ in words such as *cousin, trousers, reserve, president*.
4. Even after Scandinavian students have learnt to pronounce English /ð/ (as well as /θ/), they may mispronounce *th* as /θ/ in *smooth, with*, etc.
5. The *r* may be pronounced in words like *mattered, murdered, wondered*, leading to mistakes in British English.

Rhythm and stress

Patterns of word and sentence stress are quite similar in English and the Scandinavian languages, so there are relatively few problems in this area. Note, however:

1. Scandinavian compound nouns are usually stressed on the first element. Mistakes are common in English compounds which do not follow this pattern:
   *'prime minister (cf. 'statsminister)
   *'town hall
   Conversely, compound nouns made up of 'verb + adverb' combinations tend to be stressed on the second element:
   *break'down
   *come-'back
   *hang'over
   *hold-'up
2. The Scandinavian languages have fewer 'weak forms' than English, so students characteristically overstress words like *and, but, a(n), the*,

than, *as*, *have*, *was*, giving them their 'strong' pronunciations in too many cases. This prevents learners from acquiring a natural sentence rhythm. Beginners may have difficulty in perceiving weak forms.

Intonation

1. Unstressed syllables in Danish (and very often in Norwegian and Swedish) are pronounced on a higher pitch than a preceding stressed syllable. This is often transferred to English, together with a tendency to pronounce the first stressed syllable of a tone unit on too low a pitch:

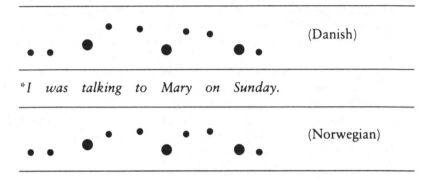

*I   was   talking   to   Mary   on   Sunday.

2. Danes are inclined to use a pitch range which is too narrow, and to a lesser extent this also applies to Swedes and some Norwegians.
3. The fall–rise tone is difficult for Scandinavian learners.
4. Norwegians (and some Swedes) tend to use too many rising tone units and to make their upglides too long and too high.

Orthography and punctuation

Spelling

Those who have become aware of the distinction between /v/ and /w/ but do not fully control it tend to replace *v* by *w* (**wery*, **wolley ball*), probably because this spelling is assumed to be the more 'English'. Influence from German may make some students write *sch* instead of *sh* (**schoot*, **schut up*). The letter *k* is used much more frequently than *c* in the Scandinavian languages, and this may lead to errors like **kapitalism*, **kannibal*.

Punctuation

1. As most Scandinavian compounds are written as one word, the use of the hyphen in words like *fire-alarm* (**brandalarm**), and of spacing in words like *front door* (**ytterdør**) create difficulty.
2. Scandinavian students sometimes use a comma instead of a semi-colon between main clauses which are not separated by a co-ordinating conjunction, but are felt to be closely related:
   That's the way it had to be, he was not ashamed of it.
3. Danes tend to use commas before object clauses and restrictive relative clauses:
   I think, there has been a mistake.
   What's the worst thing, that could happen to you in that minefield?

Grammar

Order of constituents

In the Scandinavian languages, it is easy to begin a sentence with something other than the subject – which is then placed after the verb. In English, only adverbials are regularly 'fronted', and this does not generally cause verb–subject inversion. To give prominence to objects, complements, etc., English tends to use intonation. Typical mistake:
   That have I not seen.

Position of adverbs

In the Scandinavian languages, mid-sentence adverbs are generally placed after the finite verb. This leads to mistakes in English sentences with one-word verbs:
   Children leave often home nowadays.
However, in subordinate clauses adverbs are placed *before* finite verbs in Scandinavian languages. This leads to mistakes in English sentences with complex verb phrases:
   ... that children often will leave home nowadays.
This can happen with quite long adverbials:
   He said that they in the northern part of Jutland speak a special dialect.

Constructions with it *and* there

1. In Norwegian and Swedish, the equivalent of the *there is* construction

21

uses the pronoun **det**, which also means *it*. Beginners tend to overuse *it* as a consequence:

> **It is somebody at the door.*

2. In all three languages, the *there* construction is used with a wide range of verbs (whereas in English it is only common with *be* used as a main verb). This results in mistakes like:

> **It/There was shot a man here yesterday.*
> **It/There happens something strange here quite often.*
> **It/There left a lot of tourists because of the epidemic.*

3. Scandinavian languages tend, more often than English, to avoid having indefinite noun phrases in subject position. This may result in overuse of sentences like *There was someone who told me that ...* instead of the less cumbersome *Someone told me that...*

Nouns: countability and number

1. The countable/uncountable distinction is found in Scandinavian languages, but there are some differences of distribution which give rise to problems:

> *informations   *an advice   *a work (for *a job*)

2. The Scandinavian counterparts of *money* are plural:

> **How many money have you got?*

3. Collective nouns as a special group do not exist in the Scandinavian languages. Pronominal reference like *The government ... they ...* occurs, but is felt to be colloquial.

Articles

1. The definite article occurs in Scandinavian languages before uncountable and plural nouns used in a general sense. In English it is normal to use no article in these cases. This leads to errors like:

> **Some people always blame the society for everything.*
> **The horses were introduced into America by Spanish soldiers.*

2. In subject or object complement position, and similarly after *as*, the Scandinavian languages often drop the indefinite article, which leads to errors like:

> **He has been teacher for many years.*
> **As member of the family he wanted to come.*

3. In a large number of more or less idiomatic cases the same tendency is found, particularly when the noun is in object position and can be seen as forming more or less a semantic whole together with the verb. Thus phrases like *get an answer, take a seat, drive a car* would have no article in the Scandinavian languages. Articles are also commonly left out after the words for *with* and *without*:

> *a man with hat   **a cat without tail*

Premodification

1. The *'s* genitive is found in the Scandinavian languages, and is not subject to the restrictions that limit its use in English. This may lead to errors:
   > *the car's driver   *the water's temperature
2. Nouns can be used to modify other nouns, as in English. However, in the Scandinavian languages the two nouns form a compound, written as one word and stressed on the first element (see earlier sections on stress and punctuation).
3. In official styles, attributive adjectives or participles can have sentence elements attached to them, as in Danish:
   > den i de gamle regler beskrevne måde (= the in the old rules described manner)

   Learners may occasionally try to transfer this type of construction to English.
4. The rules for using adjectives without a head noun in the Scandinavian languages are considerably less restrictive than in English, which leads to errors like:
   > *A poor never gets the chance to have a good life.*

Postmodification

1. The Scandinavian languages often use full relative clauses in cases where English uses less cumbersome participle constructions, like *the house built to accommodate the library* or *a man waiting to join.*
2. In some cases English uses a prepositional phrase with *of* as a postmodifier, where the Scandinavian languages use an apposition. This leads to a common mistake in the use of the words *sort* and *kind*:
   > *this sort cheese*

Adjective or adverb?

1. Scandinavian adverbs of manner tend to be similar in form to adjectives, which leads to frequent mistakes:
   > *She spoke to me quite polite.*
   > *You don't sing very good.*
2. The opposite mistake can occur in sentences with the verbs *look, sound, smell, taste, feel,* which in most cases take adverbs, not adjectives, in Scandinavian languages:
   > *I feel terribly.*

Pronouns and determiners

1. The *who/which* distinction has no counterpart in Scandinavian languages:
     **the man which I told you about*
2. *Some* and *any* have a single equivalent:
     **Sorry, I haven't got some.*
3. In front of a noun followed by a relative clause, Scandinavian languages put a type of demonstrative determiner:
     **That man we're talking about is sitting in the next room.*
4. The Scandinavian languages have a completely unspecific personal pronoun *man*, which corresponds to the English 'general' use of *you*, *they* and *one*, and may be used where English has a passive in cases like *It isn't done*. Many learners tend to use *you* as an equivalent in all cases.

Verb forms

There is no inflection for person or number in Scandinavian languages. Consequently learners tend to drop the third-person *-s*; even very advanced speakers slip up in their speech on this point occasionally:
     **He fly to Copenhagen twice a week.*
Are (the form of *to be* most similar to the single Scandinavian present-tense verb form) tends to be used for *am*, *are* and *is*:
     **I don't know if she are ready yet.*

Do

Scandinavians have the same problems with the *do* construction as other types of learners, and need practice to get used to the formation of questions and negatives. Negatives are especially difficult in subordinate clauses:
     **They asked why he not came.*
Note the common use of 'double' past/present forms:
     **He didn't came.*
     **She do(es)n't listens.*

-ing forms

1. The Scandinavian present participle plays a very limited role as compared with English, being used mainly as an attributive adjective (as in *a sleeping child*), and with certain verbs (as in *he came running*). Consequently learners have problems with the present participle in a number of cases, for example in adverbial clauses (as in *Going home that evening, I called at the chemist's for some razor blades.*).

2. The absence of the gerund in their own language tends to make Scandinavians use the infinitive in cases like:
> *I really must stop to smoke.*
> *Instead of (to) get on with his work he slept all afternoon.*

Progressive aspect

Scandinavian languages have no progressive verb forms. Elementary students often generalise the English 'simple' forms:
> *The band plays now.*

Intermediate students may overwork progressive forms as the result of intensive practice in their use:
> *In Scandinavia we're putting people in prison if they have struck another person.*

Tense

1. In Danish, perfect tenses are commonly formed not only with the auxiliary *have* but also with the equivalent of *be*. Transfer of the *be*-perfect, which is used to express change from one state to another, is not uncommon among elementary Danish learners:
> *The prisoner is escaped.*
> *They are become famous.*

2. The Scandinavian present perfect can be used with definite past reference, leading to mistakes like:
> *Dickens has written many novels.*
> *He has left school in 1982.*

3. In Swedish, the present tense is often used in sentences constructed with **sedan** (= *since/for*):
> *I know him since a long time.*

4. In the Scandinavian languages, future tenses are not used when the sense of the verb, or accompanying adverbs, already makes it clear that the reference is to the future. This leads students to use the simple present instead of the *will* future (and the present perfect instead of the future perfect):
> *She doesn't come anyway.*
> *I don't tell you. You only forget it.*
> *We talk about it next week.*
> *By this time tomorrow I've finished sorting out the replies.*

The simple present is also used instead of the present progressive or *going to* form:
> *Jane moves to the States.*
> *I think I faint.*

25

Voice

In the Scandinavian languages the passive voice is expressed in either of two ways: with the suffix -s or with the auxiliary blive/bli (which can also mean *become*). Both of these structures result in occasional transfer mistakes:
> *It finds not. (for It is not found.)*
> *He became killed.*

The passive may also be under-used in favour of the impersonal structure with *you* (see the section 'Pronouns').

Modal verbs

Although a number of the English modals have rough Scandinavian equivalents, there are various differences in the use of modals, with consequent learning problems. Some of the most important are as follows.

1. Kan, unlike *can*, is used in affirmative sentences to talk about whether things are the case, or may happen in the future:
   > *Peter can be in London now.*
   > *The time can come when the educational system is mixed.*
2. Skal is used to express compulsion or command. The similarity with *shall* leads to confusion:
   > *You shall lie down quietly now.*
3. Skal can also express the idea of *report* or *rumour* (like English *is said to* or *is supposed to*):
   > *He shall be a poor researcher.*
4. Another use of skal is to talk about arrangements (English *is to* or *is going to*):
   > *My daughter shall start school in August.*
   > *John shall play football tonight.*
5. In Swedish and Norwegian, the past tense form skulle corresponds to a number of English verbs besides the apparent equivalent *should*. This leads to mistakes:
   > *She said she should do it. (for She said she would ...)*
   > *She looks as if she should be ill. (for ... might ...)*

Complementation

1. Problems arise where a Scandinavian verb is used in different patterns from its English equivalent:
   > *She told that she was fed up with her job.*
2. Scandinavian prepositional verbs can be followed by the equivalent of a *that*-clause. In English, either the preposition is dropped or a

different complement structure is used (e.g. an -*ing* form or a clause introduced by *the fact that*):

> *It results in, that people don't care.*
> *He spoke about, that unemployment was going up.*
> *She was delighted about, that he was home again.*
> *They believe in, that they will succeed.*

3. Verbs with obligatory reflexive pronouns are much more common in the Scandinavian languages than in English:

> *Hurry yourself!*

4. The 'object + infinitive' structure is rare in Scandinavian languages, and students will tend to avoid it:

> *He caused that the prisoners were put to death.* (for *He caused the prisoners to be ...*)
> *I don't want that there is any misunderstanding.*

Vocabulary

The close relationship between the Scandinavian languages and English makes a large proportion of English vocabulary easily accessible to Scandinavians. Words like *can, have, good, man* are virtually 'the same'; and in a number of cases the spelling, which reflects older stages of the language, helps to establish familiarity where the pronunciation differs markedly, e.g. in cases like *side*. Some of the similarities, of course, are deceptive; below will be found a list of English 'false friends' that are problematic for speakers of all three languages.

False friends

In the following list, common meanings of Scandinavian cognate words are shown in brackets. For instance, '*announce* (S = *advertise*)' means that there are Scandinavian words that look like *announce* but which actually mean *advertise*. (The words in this case are Danish annoncere, Norwegian annonsere and Swedish annonsera.) In some cases, Scandinavian words listed may have not only the 'false friend' meaning but also, in some contexts, the same meaning as the English cognate. For instance, komme/komma corresponds to *come* as well as to *get (somewhere)* and *arrive*.

> *actual* (S = *of current interest, topical*)
> *announce* (S = *advertise*)
> *bear* (S = *carry, wear*)
> *blank* (S = *shiny*)
> *branch* (S = *trade, line of business*)
> *come* (S = *arrive, get (somewhere)* as well as *come*)

cook (S = *boil*)
control (S = *check*)
critic (S = *criticism*)
delicate (S = *delicious*)
eventual(ly) (S = *possible, if any, if the situation arises*)
fabric (S = *factory*)
first (S can mean *not until*, as in Danish Han kom først kl. 10 =
   He didn't arrive until 10.)
genial (S = *brilliant*)
gift (S = *poison*)
history (S = *story*)
lame (S = *paralysed*)
luck (S = *happiness*)
lucky (S = *happy*)
mean (S = *think, be of the opinion*)
meaning (S = *opinion*)
motion (S = *physical exercise*)
novel (S = *short story*)
offer (S = *sacrifice, offering*)
overtake (S = *take over*)
place (S = *room, space, square, job*)
public (S = *audience, spectators*)
rent (S = *(rate of) interest*)
see (S = *look*)
spare (S = *save*)
sympathetic (S = *likeable*)
take place (S = *sit down*)
will, will have (S = *want*)

Some problems involving grammatical words

1. *As* and *like*, in many of their uses, have one Scandinavian equivalent. This may create problems with the distinction between, for instance, *Like a cabinet minister* ... and *As a cabinet minister* ..., as well as mistakes such as *I speak as my mother* and problems of style as in *He did like he had chosen to do.*
2. Scandinavians have one word covering *very, much* and (in affirmative sentences) *a great deal / a lot.* This may tend to produce some overuse of *much* as the most 'similar' word.
3. The word også/också covers the area of English *also, too, as well* in their main uses, as well as some uses of *so.* Apart from problems of choice this leads to considerable difficulties of word order.
4. The demonstrative adverb *there* corresponds to a Danish and Swedish word which can also be used as a relative. This occasionally leads to

the use of *there* in place of a relative. Danes use it in substantival function, as in **The man there was present* ... (for ... *who was present*); Swedes use it in adverbial function, as in **The place there I was born* ..., reflecting the usage in their respective languages.

5. The word om functions both as a conjunction (= *if, whether*) and a preposition (= *about, on*). Following verbs where both types of word are possible, mistakes like **Do you know about he has come?* can be found.

A sample of written Danish with a word for word translation

Der   holdt   mindst hundrede taxaer med dørene   på klem,
There stood-still least   hundred   taxis   with the-doors ajar,

og han havde aldrig set   så mange biler på en   gang. Havde det
and he had   never seen so many cars at one time. Had   it

stået til ham,   var han styret
stood to him [= if it had been left to him], was he   rushed

fra   den ene vogn til den anden, indtil han havde fundet en
from the one car   to the other, until he had   found a

chauffør med et ansigt, han kunne lide. Men hans far   løftede
driver   with a face,   he could like. But his   father lifted

blot en finger, en mand med kasket på hovedet så   det, stødte
just a finger, a man with cap   on the-head saw it,   blew

øjeblikkelig i en fløjte   og straks blev der   bevægelse i
immediately in a   whistle and at-once was there movement in

den yderste   bilrække.
the outermost car-row.

(From 'Johnny' by Bent William Rasmussen in *Jeanne Moreau i Middelfart*)

Acknowledgements

The authors' thanks are due to Thor Sigurd Nilsen, Nils Røttingen, Brit Ulseth and Moira Linnarud, and Stig Ørjan Ohlsson for advice on Norwegian and Swedish.

German speakers

Michael Swan

Distribution

GERMAN FEDERAL REPUBLIC, GERMAN DEMOCRATIC
REPUBLIC, AUSTRIA, SWITZERLAND, LUXEMBOURG, France,
Italy, Denmark, Poland, Czechoslovakia, Hungary,
Liechtenstein, Romania, United States.

Introduction

German is an Indo-European language, closely related to Dutch, English
and the Scandinavian languages. It exists in a wide variety of dialects,
some so different from each other as to be more or less mutually
unintelligible. The standard language of Germany (**Hochdeutsch**, or
'High German') is used for written communication throughout the
German-speaking area. It is spoken by most Germans, Austrians and
German-Swiss either as their first language or as a 'second dialect' (often
with strong regional colouring).

Because of the close family relationship between English and German,
there are many similarities between the two languages as regards
phonology, vocabulary and syntax. German speakers therefore find
English easy to learn initially, and tend to make rapid progress.

Phonology

General

The German and English phonological systems are broadly similar, and
German speakers do not have serious difficulty in perceiving or pronouncing most English sounds. Among the features of German which
give rise to a 'German accent' in English are:
- More energetic articulation than English, with tenser vowels, more
  explosive stop consonants (/p/, /t/, /k/), and more lip-rounding and
  spreading.
- Different intonation system from English (see below).
- Use of glottal stops before initial vowels, which gives a staccato
  effect.
- Tendency of some speakers to speak on a lower pitch than most British
  people.

Vowels

iː	ɪ	e	æ	eɪ	aɪ	ɔɪ
aː	ɒ	ɔː	ʊ	aʊ	əʊ	ɪə
uː	ʌ	ɜː	ə	eə	ʊə	eɪə / aʊə

Shaded phonemes have equivalents or near equivalents in German, and should therefore be perceived and articulated without serious difficulty, although some confusions may still arise. Unshaded phonemes may cause problems. For detailed comments, see below.

1. /e/ and /æ/ are often confused: *set* and *sat*.
2. /ɔː/ and /əʊ/ are often confused: *caught* and *coat*. Both may be pronounced as a close pure vowel /oː/.
3. /eɪ/ is sometimes pronounced as a close monophthong /eː/.
4. Stressed vowels may be pronounced over-long before unvoiced consonants (as in *shape, hot, like*).
5. Swiss speakers may nasalise certain vowels.

Consonants

p	b	f	v	θ	ð	t	d
s	z	ʃ	ʒ	tʃ	dʒ	k	g
m	n	ŋ	l	r	j	w	h

Shaded phonemes have equivalents or near equivalents in German, and should therefore be perceived and articulated without serious difficulty, although some confusions may still arise. Unshaded phonemes may cause problems. For detailed comments, see below.

1. /ʒ/ and /ʤ/ are rare in German. German speakers often realise them as /ʃ/ and /tʃ/ in English: '*mesher*' for *measure*; *chain* for *Jane*.
2. The voiced sounds /ʒ/, /ʤ/, /z/, /v/, /b/, /d/ and /g/ do not occur at the ends of words in German. Students tend to confuse them with or replace them by their unvoiced equivalents in this position: '*beish*' for *beige*; *etch* for *edge*; *rice* for *rise*; *leaf* for *leave*; *pup* for *pub*; *set* for *said*; *dock* for *dog*.

31

3. /θ/ and /ð/ do not occur in German; students may replace them by /s/ and /z/: *sing* for *thing*; *useful* for *youthful*; *wizard* for *withered*.
4. There is only one German phoneme in the area of /v/ and /w/: *vine* for *wine* or (less often) *wine* for *vine*.
5. /r/ may be pronounced with the back of the tongue (as in French) or as a flap (like English /r/, but more energetic), depending on the variety of German.
6. 'Dark' /l/ (as in *fill*, *full*) does not exist in standard German. Students may replace it by 'clear' /l/, as in *light*.

Influence of spelling on pronunciation

Spelling and pronunciation are closely related in German, and there are few ambiguities. Mistakes may be made (especially by beginners) in cases where a letter has different values in English and German. Note particularly:
1. In German, the letter *w* represents the sound /v/, and the letter *v* represents /f/; this can cause problems for beginners. *While* may be pronounced *vile*, for instance, or *eleven 'elefen'*.
2. In syllables ending with the letter *r*, this letter is pronounced in most varieties of German, and this may be carried over and cause mispronunciations (in British English) in words like *garden*, *early*, *shirt*.
3. The combination *ng* is almost always pronounced /ŋ/ in German (as in English *singer*), not /ŋg/ (as in *finger*). This leads to mistakes in words like *longer*, *finger*, *younger*.
4. The combination *au* is pronounced /aʊ/ in German, leading beginners to mispronounce words like *automatic*, *authority*.
5. /ə/ is represented in German only by the letter *e* (e.g. bekommen). In pronouncing English words, students may replace /ə/ by the written vowel if this is *a*, *o* or *u* (as in *America*, *photographer*, *suppose*).

Stress

Patterns of word and sentence stress are quite similar in English and German, so there are few problems in this area. Note, however:
1. German compound expressions are generally stressed on the first element; English compounds which are not may be mispronounced (e.g. '*front door*, '*chocolate cake*).
2. German has few 'weak forms', so German speakers may overstress words like *and*, *but*, *than*, *as*, *have*, *were*, giving them their 'strong' pronunciations in all contexts. Beginners may have difficulty in perceiving weak forms.

Intonation

This varies widely over the German-speaking area. North German intonation is quite like English. South German and Austrian intonation often has long rising glides in mid-sentence:

When I arrived at the house I found that Mary was out.

Swiss speakers may end sentences with a rise followed by a slight fall (*I don't know*): this sounds odd in English.

Certain features of German intonation transferred to English can make speakers sound peremptory: it is worth giving special practice in requests and *wh*-questions.

Juncture

A German word or syllable beginning with a vowel is often separated from what comes before by a glottal stop (instead of being linked, as in English). This can create a very foreign-sounding staccato effect:

ʔin ʔand ʔout (German ʔaus ʔund ʔein)

Orthography and punctuation

Spelling

German speakers do not have more trouble than other learners with English spelling. Beginners may tend to represent English sounds by the appropriate German letters, making mistakes like **raund abaut, *schopping, *wery much*. Note that German nouns are written with initial capital letters, leading to mistakes like **I bought my Car from a Friend*.

Punctuation

Punctuation conventions are roughly the same in German and English. The main difference is that commas are used before all subordinate clauses and dependent infinitives:

*I think, that there has been a mistake.
*She knew exactly, what he meant.
*I hope, to see you soon.

Semi-colons are used less than in English. Quotation marks are written differently:

* „How can I help you?" she asked.

Grammar

General

The German and English grammatical systems are very similar in most ways: there are the same 'part of speech' categories, and German has, for instance, singular and plural verb forms, definite and indefinite articles, regular and irregular verbs, auxiliary and modal verbs, active and passive forms, and past, present and future tenses. There are perfect verb forms (though the present perfect is not used in the same way as in English); however, German has no equivalent of the English progressive forms. German is a highly inflected language, so that words tend to change their endings according to their grammatical function – articles, adjectives and nouns, for example, have different forms ('cases') according to whether the noun phrase is subject, direct object, indirect object or possessor. This means that word order is somewhat freer than in English, where the grammatical function of a word is mostly indicated by its position. German has grammatical gender: nouns and pronouns are masculine, feminine or neuter. (There is little relationship between gender and meaning.) The lack of any systematic inflectional system in English sometimes leads German-speaking students to feel that English has 'no grammar'.

Questions and negatives; auxiliaries

1. The auxiliary *do* has no equivalent in German; interrogatives are made by simple inversion, and one-word verbs are made negative by putting nicht (= *not*) after the verb:
     **When started you to play the piano?*
     **Thank you, I smoke not.*
2. Perfect tenses are generally formed with haben (= *have*) + past participle, as in English. However, some verbs, (mostly common verbs of movement) form their perfects with sein (= *be*):
     **She is gone out.*
3. Because of the similarity of form, English *had* is often misused as an equivalent of German hat (= *has*) or hätte (which can mean *would have*):
     **Do you know if Andrew had telephoned yet?*
     **If I had known, I had told you.*

Time, tense and aspect

A. PAST TIME

1. German has past perfect, past and present perfect tenses, but no progressive forms:

      *I realised that somebody came slowly up the stairs.
      *I'm sorry I'm late. Have you waited long?

2. The German present perfect is not used in exactly the same way as the English present perfect: it often functions just as a conversational past tense:
      *I have seen Mary yesterday.

3. Conversely, the German simple past tense may be used where we would use a present perfect:
      *The German prison system improved a lot in recent years.

4. In reported speech, German tends to use a present subjunctive where English uses a past tense after past reporting verbs:
      *I didn't know if she is at home.

B. PRESENT TIME

1. German lack of a present progressive causes mistakes:
      *What do you look at?

2. To say how long a present state of affairs has been going on, German often uses a present tense (English present perfect):
      *How long are you in England? (meaning *How long have you been ...?*)
      *I know her since we were children.

C. FUTURE TIME

German has no equivalent of the *going to* future. There is a future tense formed with an auxiliary (roughly equivalent to the *shall/will* future). The present is used extensively to refer to the future:
      *I promise I bring it back tomorrow.

Conditionals

In spoken German conditional sentences, the auxiliary **würde** (which corresponds roughly to *would*) may be used in both clauses:
      *If he would ask me, I wouldn't tell him anything. (**Wenn er mich fragen würde, würde ich ihm nichts sagen.**)

Modal verbs

The English modals *can, must, may*, etc. have rough German equivalents. Inevitably there are differences of use which lead to mistakes. Some common problems:

1. **Ich kann** can be used with the name of a language to mean *I can speak*:
      *I can Russian.

2. English *must* looks like the German past tense **musste** (= *had to*):
      *Yesterday I must go to London.

> *Must be* may be used instead of *must have been*:
> > **Did you? That must be interesting.*
3. Muss nicht = *don't have to* or *needn't*; it is not the same as *must not*:
> > **I mustn't, but I can if I want to.*
4. German will means *want(s)*, not *will*:
> > **She doesn't know what she will.*
> This can lead to confusion between *would* and *wanted* (German wollte):
> > **I told her I would a coffee.*
5. German soll (= *is supposed to, is to, should*) is sometimes mis-translated as *shall*, and sollte (= *was supposed to, was to*) as *should*:
> > **He shall be a brilliant musician.* (for *He is supposed to be* ...)
> > **The little settlement of Londinium, which later should become the capital of a great empire* ...

Non-finite forms

There is no equivalent in German of the substantival use of the *-ing* form (gerund):
> **Instead of to fight, they started to laugh.*
> **I came here with the hope to find a job.*
> **I really must stop to smoke.*

Word order

1. Infinitives and past participles tend to come at the ends of clauses in German:
> > **I must at once my sister telephone.*
> > **He was in a road accident killed.*
2. Main verbs generally come at the ends of subordinate clauses:
> > **Did I tell you, that my mother English speaks?*
3. If the subject of a main clause is preceded by anything other than a conjunction, the subject and verb are inverted:
> > **On Tuesday have we a holiday.*
4. A sentence may begin with the direct object or complement:
> > **This car have I very cheap bought.*
> > **Fantastic is that!*
5. Adverbs may separate a verb from its object or complement:
> > **You speak very well German.*
> > **He became finally President.*
6. Adverb particles tend to come at the ends of clauses:
> > **He walked quickly in.*
7. In German, an article may be separated from its noun by quite a complex participle phrase:
> > **The in Britain with excitement awaited budget* ...

8. Vor (= *ago*) precedes an expression of time. Entlang (= *along*) follows its noun:
>   *I bought it ago three years.
>   *She was walking the road along.

Articles

1. In German, the definite article accompanies nouns which are used in a general sense:
>   *The books are very expensive these days.
>   *We all have to live in the society.
2. The indefinite article is not used when defining people's professions:
>   *My sister is doctor.
3. The indefinite article is often omitted after mit (= *with*) and ohne (= *without*):
>   *You can't get there without car.

Gender

Nouns are masculine, feminine or neuter. Nouns with a 'diminutive' ending are neuter. Pronouns are used accordingly:
>   *My watch is broken. Can you mend her?
>   *The girl (das Mädchen – diminutive) was lost. It didn't know where it was.

Number

German nouns form their plurals in various ways. Common plural endings are -en and -er; beginners sometimes drop the -s from the plurals of English nouns that end in these letters:
>   *I have three brother.

Adjectives and adverbs

1. A German adverb of manner is often identical in form with the uninflected adjective. Gut = *good/well*; schrecklich = *terrible/terribly*:
>   *She can drive very good.
>   *I was terrible impressed.
2. A noun may sometimes be dropped if it can be 'understood' after an adjective:
>   *The most important is, to tell everybody at once.

Relative pronouns

1. German **was** corresponds not only to *what*, but also to *that* (in certain cases), and to *which* when the antecedent is a clause. This leads to misuse of *what*:
   > *The only thing what he could do ...*
   > *All what we want ...*
   > *His offer was rejected, what took him by surprise.*
2. German does not distinguish *who* and *which*:
   > *Who are the people which came to see you this morning?*

Conjunctions

1. German has the same word for *as* and *like* (referring to similarity):
   > *You look as your sister.*
2. The German word **falls** (literally *in case*) is used to mean *if* in certain contexts. This can cause confusion:
   > *Give my love to John in case you see him.*

Prepositions

Most German prepositions have rough English equivalents. Problems arise in cases (too many to list) where an English expression is not constructed with the 'same' preposition as is used in German. Typical mistakes in this area:
   > *dressed with a dark suit*
   > *You remind me at/on your father.*
   > *That's typical for him.*
   > *full with water*

Other problems (easier to predict) occur when a German preposition has more than one regular English equivalent. Some common difficulties:
1. **Nach** (= *after*) can also mean *according to*:
   > *After my teacher, this is correct.*
2. **Seit** can mean *since* or *for*:
   > *I've known her since three years.*
3. **Von** = *of* or *from*; also *by* when talking about authorship:
   > *Can I have a piece from that cake?*
   > *a symphony from Beethoven*
4. **Zu** = *to* or *at*:
   > *to Easter*   *He was a student to Heidelberg.*
5. **An** = *at* or *on*:
   > *at Monday*   *on a party*
6. **Vor** = *before* or *in front of*; also *ago*:
   > *The bus stop is before our house.*
   > *I arrived before ten minutes.*

7. Während = *during* or *while*:
      *She telephoned during you were out.
8. Bei corresponds to a large number of prepositions in English, depending on the context – but rarely corresponds to *by*:
      *I spent the evening by John and Alice. (for ... at John and Alice's.)
      *By this weather no planes can fly.

Vocabulary

Very many German and English words are derived from the same roots (e.g. Haus = *house*, Schuh = *shoe*, jung = *young*, singen = *to sing*). This facilitates learning on the whole, though there are a certain number of 'false friends' (see below). German-speaking Swiss generally know some French, which helps them with that part of English vocabulary which is of French or Latin origin (though it may also lead them to make typically French mistakes of spelling or vocabulary use).

False friends

A large number of German words have meanings which are slightly or completely different in use from their English cognates. Students may misuse the following words (among others):
      come (German kommen = *come* or *go* according to context)
      go (German gehen = *go* or *walk* according to context)
      will (German will = *want(s)*)
      bring (German bringen = *bring* or *take* according to context)
      by (German bei corresponds to various English prepositions)
      mean (German meinen usually = *think* or *say*)
      actual (German aktuell = *present, current, topical*)
      actually (see above)
      sympathetic (German sympathisch = *nice)*
      Thank you (German danke can mean *No thank you*)
      when (German wenn = *if* or *whenever*)
      become (German bekommen = *obtain, get*)
      control (German kontrollieren = *check*)
Note also that *who* (German wer) and *where* (German wo) are easily confused by beginners.

Other confusions

Problems may also be caused because one German word has more than one English equivalent, or because a pair of contrasting words are not distributed in quite the same way as their apparent English equivalents. A few examples:

> *say* and *tell*
> *so* and *such*
> *yet*, *still* and *again*
> *this* and *that*
> *as* and *how*
> *as* and *than*
> *as* and *when*
> *to* and *too*
> *miss* and *lose*

Phonetically motivated confusions:

> *man* and *men*
> *prize* and *price*
> *save* and *safe*

The German word for *please* (bitte) is used when offering something, and also as a formulaic reply to thanks (rather like *not at all*). This leads students to misuse *please* in English.

Word formation

Complex nouns are common in German (Dorfschullehrer = *village school teacher*), and students may try to make similar one-word compounds in English.

A sample of written German with a word for word translation

Eines Abends   sass ich im   Dorfwirtshaus
One   evening [genitive] sat   I   in-the village-pub

vor   (genauer   gesagt, hinter) einem Glas
in-front-of (more-exactly said,   behind) a   glass [of]

Bier, als   ein Mann gewöhnlichen Aussehens
beer, when a   man   [of] ordinary   appearance [genitive]

sich   neben mich setzte und mich mit vertraulicher
himself beside me sat   placed and me   with [a] confidential

Stimme fragte, ob   ich eine Lokomotive kaufen wolle.
voice   asked, whether I   a   locomotive to-buy want

                  Nun ist es zwar   ziemlich leicht,
[present subjunctive]. Now is it indeed rather   easy,

mir   etwas   zu verkaufen, denn ich kann schlecht nein
to-me something to sell,   for   I   can   badly   no

sagen,   aber bei einer
say [I find it difficult to say no], but with a

grösseren Anschaffung dieser Art   schien mir   doch
bigger   purchase   of-this kind seemed to-me however

Vorsicht am   Platze.
caution   at-the place [caution seemed to me to be indicated].

Obgleich ich wenig von Lokomotiven verstehe,   erkundigte
Although I   little of   locomotives   understand, informed

ich mich   nach Typ und Bauart,   um   bei
I   myself after type and construction-nature, in order in

dem Mann den Anschein   zu erwecken, als   habe er es hier
the man   the impression to awake,   as [if] have he it here

mit einem Experten zu   tun, der nicht gewillt sei, die Katz
with an   expert   to   do, who not   willing be, the cat

im   Sack zu kaufen, wie man so schön   sagt.
in-the sack to buy,   as   one so beautifully says.

('Eine grössere Anschaffung' by Wolfgang Hildesheimer from *Lieblose Legenden*)

French speakers

Catherine Walter

Distribution

FRANCE (including French West Indies), BELGIUM, SWITZERLAND, CANADA, HAITI; some parts of northwestern Italy and Luxembourg; official or widespread second language in many former French and Belgian colonies in north, west and central Africa, Asia, the Pacific, and South America.

Introduction

French belongs to the Romance group of Indo-European languages, and is closely related to Italian, Spanish, Portuguese, Romanian and other less widely spoken Romance tongues. There are some differences between standard Belgian or Canadian French, for example, and the standard French of France, but the differences are not greater than those between British and American English; the different standard French dialects are certainly mutually comprehensible.

Because French is an Indo-European language, and because the Norman contribution to English was so great, there are some similarities between French and English, both in syntax and vocabulary. The phonological systems exhibit some important differences, however, and this usually presents French speakers with problems in understanding and producing spoken English, and in making links between spelling and pronunciation.

Phonology

General

French shares many phonological characteristics with English. French speakers do not have great difficulty in perceiving or pronouncing English consonants, but some of the vowel sounds present problems. Perhaps most importantly, the French and English systems of word stress and rhythm are very different, and this can lead to serious difficulties both in understanding and in producing spoken English. Among the features of French which lead to a 'French accent' in English are:

- All French words of two syllables or more are stressed in a regular way (see below), unlike the English system where the stress pattern for each group of words or individual word must be learnt. This can lead to problems of comprehension and comprehensibility.
- Unstressing a syllable in French does not involve reducing the time given to its pronunciation, as it does in English. In addition, there is little of the vowel reduction that occurs in unstressed English syllables. These two factors make it seem to French speakers that English speakers 'swallow' their words, and can make the English spoken by French speakers sound monotonous or staccato.
- French uses tenser, more rounded lips and more frequent jaw opening; the tip of the tongue is not used, and there is more use of the blade (the part behind the tip) of the tongue, giving 'softer' sounds to some consonants.

Vowels

iː	ɪ	e	æ	eɪ	aɪ	ɔɪ
ɑː	ɒ	ɔː	ʊ	aʊ	əʊ	ɪə
uː	ʌ	ɜː	ə	eə	ʊə	aɪə
						aʊə

Shaded phonemes have equivalents or near equivalents in French, and should therefore be perceived and articulated without serious difficulty, although some confusions may still arise. Unshaded phonemes may cause problems. For detailed comments, see below.

1. French has only one sound in the area of /iː/ and /ɪ/, leading to confusion between pairs like *live* and *leave*.
2. /ʌ/ is sometimes pronounced almost like /ə/, so that *much* becomes '*mirch*'.
3. French has only one sound in the area of /ʊ/ and /uː/, leading to confusion between pairs like *pull* and *pool*.
4. /ɒ/ is often unrounded, so that, for instance, *not* is realised something like *nut*.
5. Both /ɔː/ and /əʊ/ are moved towards the French /o/, leading to confusion between pairs like *naught* and *note*.
6. /æ/ often creates difficulty. Depending on how it is perceived by the French speaker, it may be realised:
   - very like an English /ʌ/, so that words like *bank* and *bunk* are confused;

- a bit like /ɑː/, so that, for instance, *hand* sounds like '*hahnd*';
- as /e/, causing confusion between pairs like *pat* and *pet*.
7. /eɪ/ sometimes becomes /e/, so that, for example, *paper* sounds like *pepper*. Since /æ/ can also be realised as /e/, this can lead to confusion in pairs like *mad* and *made*.
8. Other diphthongs are not usually too problematic, but they may be pronounced with equal force and length on the two elements: *I see now* becomes '*Ah-ee see nah-oo*'.

Consonants

p	b	f	v	θ	ð	t	d
s	z	ʃ	ʒ	tʃ	dʒ	k	g
m	n	ŋ	l	r	j	w	h

Shaded phonemes have equivalents or near equivalents in French, and should therefore be perceived and articulated without serious difficulty, although some confusions may still arise. Unshaded phonemes may cause problems. For detailed comments, see below.

1. /θ/ and /ð/ do not exist in French, and the fact that spoken French does not use the tip of the tongue makes them difficult to learn. /s/, /z/, /f/, /v/, /t/ and /d/ are common realisations of these phonemes. *Think* may be realised as *sink, fink,* or *tink*; and *that* as '*zat*', *vat* or '*dat*'.
2. /tʃ/ is often realised as /ʃ/ and /dʒ/ as /ʒ/. So *church* becomes '*shursh*' and *joke* becomes '*zhoke*'.
3. /h/ (which does not exist in French) is often dropped: '*I 'aven't seen 'enry today*'.
4. /r/ is pronounced with the back of the tongue in French, and so is likely to be pronounced the same way in English.
5. 'Dark' /l/, as in *will*, does not occur in French, and students may replace it by 'clear' /l/, as in *lay*.
6. English lengthens vowels in stressed syllables before final voiced consonants. In fact, the main way an English speaker hears the difference between words like *sat* and *sad* is by hearing the longer vowel before the *d* of the second word (the voiced/devoiced contrast between *d* and *t* is much less important for perception). French speakers do not generally lengthen these vowels, leading to confusion between pairs of words like *sat* and *sad*, *pick* and *pig*, and so on.

Consonant clusters

1. In words ending in consonant + *le*, the French speaker may reinterpret the 'dark' /l/ as /əl/. Combined with the tendency to stress multisyllabic words on the last syllable, this gives pronunciations like '*terri'bull*', '*lit'tull*'.
2. At the end of words like *realism*, French speakers may pronounce /s/ plus devoiced /m/, rather than changing the *s* to a voiced /z/ as in English. An English speaker may hear '*realiss*'.
3. One does not normally find a consonant followed by /z/ at the end of a French word. So in pronouncing English plurals, French speakers tend to drop the -*s* after voiced consonants, making mistakes like **two tin*.

Stress

1. In French words of more than one syllable, the word stress (which is somewhat weaker than in English) is on the last pronounced syllable. With the exception of /ə/, which is sometimes elided, vowels which are not stressed retain their pronunciation, rather than being shortened, or weakened to /ə/ or /ɪ/ as in English. So French speakers have great difficulty in perceiving shortened or weakened syllables when English speakers pronounce them.

   This shortening and weakening also produces problems for French speakers trying to produce spoken English, as does moving from the very regular French system of word stress to English, where the stress pattern of each word or group of words must be learnt as part of its pronunciation.
2. Where English uses stress to mark contrast, French often uses a grammatical construction. Compare French and English answers to 'Didn't you go to the grocer's?':
   English: *No, I went to the* **baker's**.
   French: Non, c'est à la boulangerie que je suis allée.
   (= *No, it's to the baker's that I went.*)

Intonation

The French and English intonation systems are similar in many respects. But movements in French tend to be steplike and avoid glides, which can in some situations give an impression of vehemence where none is intended.

Influence of spelling on pronunciation

Spelling and pronunciation are closely related in French, and with very rare exceptions a French speaker can tell how to pronounce a word from the way it is spelled. Mistakes may be made, especially by beginners, in cases where a letter or combination of letters has a different value in English and in French. Note particularly:

1. In syllables ending with the letter *r*, this letter is pronounced in French; interference here may cause problems for students of British English with words like *hard, early, garden*. In words like *sister*, French speakers may pronounce the final *e* as /e/, giving '*sistair*'.
2. *Ou* may be pronounced /uː/ and *au* may be pronounced /o/: '*pronoonce*', '*otomatic*'.
3. In regular past endings, students may pronounce final /ɪd/ or /ed/ after all consonants, or after all unvoiced consonants: *warnèd, jumpèd*.
4. Final written consonants in French (e.g. plural *-s*) are often not pronounced. This tends to be carried over into English and provoke mistakes like **differen, *She stay*.
5. There are a large number of cognates in English and French. It is very common for French students to transfer French stress patterns to these words.

Orthography and punctuation

French speakers do not have more trouble than other learners with English spelling. Note that days of the week, months, languages and national adjectives are not capitalised in French and may lead to mistakes like **I will begin german classes on the first tuesday of january*.

Punctuation conventions are roughly the same in French and English. Commas can be used in French in some cases where they would not be used in English, and may lead to mistakes like **Consonants that are doubled in writing, are usually pronounced like single consonants*.

Inverted commas are written slightly differently in French: «...» rather than '...' or "...".

Grammar

General

The French and English grammatical systems are very similar in most ways: there are the same 'part of speech' categories; word order is broadly similar; French has, for instance, singular and plural verb forms, definite and indefinite articles, regular and irregular verbs, auxiliary verbs, active and passive forms, and past, present and future tenses. There are perfect verb forms (though the tense which is constructed like the English present perfect is not used in the same way); but French has no equivalent of the English progressive forms. French verbs are inflected, so that the ending of a verb indicates both its tense and the person and number of the subject of the clause. (However, some of the inflections have disappeared from speech.) French has grammatical gender: nouns, pronouns, adjectives, articles and determiners are masculine or feminine (though only a few nouns show a relationship between gender and meaning).

Verbs

1. French speakers tend to have trouble learning to put the -s endings on third person singular present tense verbs; there are many reasons for this. English is perceived as a non-inflected language compared to French, so the one sign of inflection tends to be forgotten. Final written -s in any French word is virtually never pronounced. And although there are differences in the spellings of first, second and third person singular present tense endings of regular verbs in French, all three forms of a verb are pronounced the same.
2. Many of the concepts that are expressed in English with the verb *to be* are expressed in French with the verb **avoir**, corresponding to *to have*. This can lead to mistakes like:
   I have hunger.
   She has heat.
   You have reason. (for You are right.)

Questions and negatives; auxiliaries

1. The auxiliary *do* has no equivalent in French. French speakers can run into problems in English trying to form interrogatives as they do in French:
   - Simply by adding a question mark or by using question intonation:
     You are coming this evening?
   - By inversion:
     When think you to leave England?
   Negatives in French are formed by putting **ne … pas** around a one-word verb, or around the auxiliary of a longer verb. This can lead to omission of *do/did* and/or incorrect placement of *not*:
   She lives not in Paris.
2. French has tenses which are formed like the English perfect tenses, with the verb **avoir** (= *have*). However, some verbs (mostly common verbs of movement) form these tenses with **être** (= *be*):
   Claude is come yesterday.
3. Conjugated question tags do not exist in French; where English has the question tag agree with the main verb, French uses **n'est-ce pas?** (= *isn't it?* or *isn't that?*) after all verbs:
   You're American, isn't it?

47

Time, tense and aspect

A. PAST TIME

1. There is a tense that is formed much like the English present perfect, but it functions as a simple past in speech and informal writing:
   I have been to Japan last month.
2. It is the present tense which is used to talk about actions or states that began in the past and are continuing in the present:
   I work in Paris since August / for six months.
   She is going out with Marc since they were sixteen.
3. In writing, and occasionally in speech (especially in reporting conversations), the present tense may be used to talk about the past. In French this gives an effect of fast-moving action to a narrative:
   I phoned Eric last night. When I ask him 'Are you coming?', he says he can't.
4. French has a tense which is used in the same way as the English past progressive, to talk about an action in progress at a given point in the past. But this same tense in French is used to talk about habits or repeated actions in the past: so French speakers may use the past progressive in place of a simple past tense, *used to*, or *would* . . . (in the sense of *was/were in the habit of*):
   We were often going to the seaside when I was a child.
   I was eating here every day when I was working for IBM.
   Every Christmas my father was pretending to be Father Christmas, and we were pretending to believe him.
   This tense is also used in cases where the past perfect progressive would be used in English with *for* and *since*:
   When I arrived, they were waiting for half an hour.
   Note that all verbs, including 'state' verbs, can be put into this tense in French:
   I was knowing him when he got his first big part.
5. There is a tense in French which is formed like the English past perfect, and its usage corresponds generally to the English tense. But it can also be used when the action spoken about is separated from the present by facts that are common knowledge to the speakers – even though they may not be mentioned:
   'Here we are. Room 232.' *'But I had asked for a room with a view!'*

B. PRESENT TIME

1. French has no present progressive form:
   Julie can't come to the phone now. She has a bath.

2. French uses the present tense after expressions like *This is the first time* ... :
> * *This is the first time I come to London.*

C. FUTURE TIME

French has the same three ways of expressing future time as English: a present tense, a *going to* structure, and a future tense. In general, French and English usage of these is similar, but there are some differences.

1. Since French has no present progressive tense, the present simple may be incorrectly used for the future:
> * *I eat with Christine this evening.*

2. In French, the present tense is used to express a decision at the moment it is taken:
> (the doorbell rings) * *I'm answering it!*

The present is also used to express a promise:
> * *I'm doing / I do it this evening.*

3. French uses the future tense for future time after *when* and *as soon as:*
> * *I'll phone you when she will arrive.*
> * *Will you tell me as soon as he will have finished?*

Conditionals

French present and past conditional tenses are used in the same way as their English equivalents. However, conditionals are used (for example, in newspaper articles or news broadcasts) to indicate that the information given is not absolutely certain:
> * *The hijackers would be members of the extremist group* ...
> (instead of *The hijackers are thought to be members* ...)
> * *According to Opposition leaders, the decision would have been taken* ... (instead of ... *the decision was taken* ...)

Modal verbs

The English modals *can, must, should,* etc. have rough French equivalents. But these verbs in French are not really a class by themselves: unlike their English counterparts, they take inflections and have no special rules about questions, negatives or following infinitive. This leads to mistakes, especially for beginners, like * *He cans* ... and * *Do you must* ...

There are other differences of use which lead to mistakes. Some common problems:

French speakers

1. Since French speakers are taught that their infinitive form corresponds
   to the English *to* infinitive, it is common for them to use the *to*
   infinitive with English modals:
   > *I can to swim.
   > *You must to give way to the traffic on your right.
   > *You should to try to get there as early as you can.
2. French uses forms of the single verb **devoir** to cover the notions of
   obligation and deduction expressed in English by *must* and *should*.
   This can lead to students saying *must* when they mean *should* and
   vice versa.
3. There is no structure in French corresponding to the English use of
   shall for making and asking for suggestions. Instead, other structures
   are used: the present tense, or a special use of the 'imperfect' with *if*:
   > *I set the table?
   > *Where do we go?
   > *If I lent you part of the money?

Imperatives

1. In spoken French, the future is often used for instructions and
   directions, leading to mistakes in English:
   > *You will go straight until the lights, and then you will turn
   > left ...
2. In written French, the infinitive is often used as an imperative form:
   > *To wipe your feet, please.
   > *To break the eggs into a bowl and to beat lightly.

-ing *forms*

1. There is no equivalent in French to the English -*ing* form used as an
   adjective to refer to actions in progress:
   > *I love the sound of rain that falls.
2. French uses an infinitive, and not a gerund, when a verb form is
   needed to fill the place of a noun:
   > *I'm tired of to tell her the same thing every day.
   > *I want to talk to Susan about to change my job.
   > *He can't start the day without to have a cup of tea.

Word order

1. In French, an adverb often comes between the verb and its object:
   > *I forget always the way to his house.
   > *I like very much your dress.

       Solange speaks very well English.
       He offers never to help.

2. French can use inversion in subordinate clauses if the subject of the subordinate clause is a noun:
   I told her what wanted the others.
   Do you know how is coming John?
   The song that was singing my mother when she was putting us to bed...
   The house where lived my grandparents...

3. If the subject of the subordinate clause is a pronoun, normal sentence order is used in French, as in English; but overgeneralisation from English question forms may still lead to mistakes in reported speech:
   They asked us where were we going.
   I wonder which department does she work for.

4. French uses inversion after *see, hear, let,* and *perhaps*:
   I saw go out a short plump man.
   I heard open the living room door.
   Ms Hadley let play the children a bit longer than usual.
   Perhaps will they be late.

This structure can have a passive meaning in French, leading to English sentences like *I have never seen kill an animal.*

5. In French, expressions of quantity used as direct objects come before the past participle of a two-part verb:
   I have too much eaten.
   She has everything read, but she hasn't found the answer.
   I have them all counted.
   He's a lot done for both the children.

6. Many expressions with infinitives in French are preceded by **de** or **à**, which French speakers sometimes translate as *to*. This has an effect on their realisation of negative infinitives:
   I asked him to not tell his sister.

7. When the question word is the object of a preposition in French, the preposition always comes before the question word. This can sound odd in spoken English:
   From where are you?

8. Problems may arise in 'noun as adjective' and *-s* genitive structures, giving rise to mistakes like:
   a shop shoe
   her blouse's friend

9. Other typical mistakes arising from French word order are:
   a such charming woman
   a lecture rather long
   a request quite reasonable
   ago ten minutes

> **enough sweet*
> **three days, about*
> **the four last days* (for *the last four days*)
> **the three next months*
> **Has been your sister to France?*

Articles

1. In French, the definite article accompanies nouns which are used in a general sense:
     > **I like the Baroque music.*
     > **The whisky is a stronger drink than the sherry.*
2. French uses no article before the names of professions:
     > **Sarah is teacher.*
3. In French, the indefinite article can be omitted after some prepositions:
     > **Did Tom go out without hat?*
     > **I used my spoon as shovel.*
4. Other typical mistakes arising from French use of articles are:
     > **the yours and the mine*
     > **the Mike's book*
     > **What time do you have the dinner?*
     > **The English is a difficult language.*
     > **He's coming the next week.*
     > **the Cambridge University*
     > **the Princess Caroline*
     > **I'm not in the office the Thursday.*
     > **What pretty jacket!*

Gender

1. Nouns are masculine or feminine. Pronouns are used accordingly:
     > **I can't find my book – he was on the table a minute ago.*
     > **This cooker doesn't work as well as she used to.*
2. The possessive adjectives corresponding to *his* and *her* are identical; they agree in gender with the noun they modify:
     > **I had dinner with John and her sister last night.*
     > **Janet lent me his knife to open the parcel.*

Number

1. A number of nouns are countable nouns in French and uncountable (mass) nouns in English. Common mistakes:

> *my hairs   *your luggages
> *informations   *advices
> *The news are good.

2. Some things that are designated by plural nouns in English are designated by singular nouns in French. Possible mistakes:
   > *a jean   *a trouser   *a short   *a pyjama
   > *the middle age (for *the Middle Ages*)
   > *the custom (for *customs*)
   > *The police is on the phone.

3. Quantities of money and measures of liquids, solids, and distances generally take a plural verb and are followed by plural pronouns in French:
   > *I need another five pence, but I haven't got them.
   > *Fifteen litres are more than I can carry.
   > *Six miles aren't far to walk if you're fit.

4. When several people possess the same sort of thing, French often puts the noun referring to the thing in the singular:
   > *We all put our coat on and went out.

5. English 'noun + noun' structures may lead to problems, where one of the nouns has a plural meaning and a singular form:
   > *a teethbrush   *a shoes shop   *a books publisher

Adjectives and adverbs

1. Most attributive adjectives in French are placed after the noun. Some problems in English may occasionally arise from this:
   > *She is the woman the most beautiful that I know.

2. In a series of two or more adjectives, French usually puts et (= *and*) before the last one. This can lead to mistakes with English attributive adjectives:
   > *a short and red dress

3. There are a number of adjectives that can be used as singular nouns in French:
   > *The poor! (meaning *The poor man / woman!*)
   > *The essential is to get the timing right.

Reflexive pronouns

1. Most of the reflexive pronouns in French are identical in form to the ordinary objective pronouns. In addition, French does not have a distinction between the ideas 'oneself' and 'each other':
   > *I hurt me with the hammer.
   > *We just sat there looking at us.

2. Many everyday actions that are expressed with the verb *get* in English are expressed with reflexive verbs in French:
> **I woke me and dressed me early in case she arrived.*

Relative pronouns

1. In French there is one subject relative pronoun (qui, which as an interrogative pronoun means *who*); and one object relative pronoun (que, which as an interrogative pronoun means *what*). This can lead to problems in English:
> **The book who made the biggest impression on me...*
> **The man what I saw yesterday...*
2. The article is not omitted after the French pronoun that corresponds to *whose*:
> **The man whose the car was parked in front of mine...*
3. French uses the word corresponding to *where* as a relative after some time expressions:
> **There was a terrific storm the day where he was born.*

Conjunctions

1. French has the same word for *as* and *like* (referring to similarity):
> **We're from the same family and went to the same school, but he isn't at all as me.*
2. French often does not use ellipsis after *and* and *or*:
> *Have you got a cup and a spoon?*
> *In Germany and in Austria ...*

Clause structure and complementation

1. French often uses a relative clause where English uses an *-ing* form:
> **I love the feel of soft warm rain that falls on my face.*
2. French uses a clause, rather than an infinitive structure, after the equivalent of *want*:
> **She wants that you come right away.*
3. French allows an 'extraposed' subject or object in a sentence:
> **Your sister she came.*
> **The telephone they repaired it?*
4. With comparative adjectives and adverbs in French, the word que, translating as *that* in English, is used:
> **I am taller that two of my brothers.*
> **She doesn't drive as fast that you.*

Prepositions

Most French prepositions have rough English equivalents. Problems arise in cases (too many to list) where an English expression is not constructed with the 'same' preposition as is used in French; or where one of the languages uses a preposition and the other does not. Typical mistakes in this area:

> *responsible of the whole project*
> *made in plastic*
> *married with my sister*
> *listen a record*
> *discuss of a solution*

Other problems (easier to predict) occur when a French preposition has more than one regular English equivalent. Some common difficulties:

1. Depuis can mean *since* or *for*:
   > *I have lived here since ten years.*
2. De can mean *of* or *from*; also used when talking about authorship:
   > *He is of Cannes.*
   > *a novel of Zola*
3. English place prepositions depend on whether one is speaking of movement or position (e.g. *at/in/to*). French place prepositions depend to some extent on the word class of the object of the preposition. A city, for example, will be preceded by à, whether this means *at, in* or *to* in English:
   > *She went at London last year.*
   > *There are hundreds of cinemas at Paris.*
   > *I went in Germany last year.*
4. French uses articles, not prepositions, before the words for days or parts of days:
   > *It's very quiet here the night.*
   > *I usually work in the office the morning and make visits the afternoon.*
   > *I usually see Nick the Tuesday.*

Vocabulary

Very many French and English words are derived from the same roots. The more intellectual or technical a word is, the more this is likely to occur. This facilitates learning on the whole, especially at the intermediate stage and beyond, though there are a number of 'false friends', which have different meanings in the two languages; and – perhaps worse – 'unreliable friends': words that mean almost the same in the two languages, or mean the same in one context and not in another.

False and unreliable friends

An immense number of French words have meanings which are slightly or completely different in use from their English cognates. Here is a very small sample of the words that French speakers may misuse in English:

actual, actually (French actuel = *current, present*; French actuellement = *now*)

advice (French avis = *opinion*)

chance (French chance = *(piece of) luck*)

command (French commander = *order [food, merchandise,* etc.]*)

corpse (French corps = *body*)

cry (French crier = *shout*)

demand (French demander = *ask*)

education (French éducation = *upbringing*)

engaged (French engagé = *committed*)

essence (French essence = *petrol*)

eventual (French éventuel = *potential, possible*)

evident (French évident = *obvious*)

experience (French expérience = *experience* or *experiment*)

fault (French faute = *mistake*)

gentle (French gentil = *kind, nice*)

ignore (French ignorer = *not to know*)

important (French important = *important* or *big, extensive*)

interesting (French intéressant = *interesting* or *lucrative, profitable, financially advantageous*)

large (French large = *wide*)

library (French librairie = *bookshop*)

occasion (French occasion = *opportunity, bargain*)

pass (an exam) (French passer un examen = *take, sit an exam*)

politics (French politique = *politics* or *policy*)

professor (French professeur = *teacher*)

savage (French sauvage = *wild*)

sensible (French sensible = *sensitive*)

sympathetic (French sympathique = *nice, easy to get on with*)

A sample of written French with a word for word translation

Le printemps était venu. Un dimanche, après avoir nettoyé
The spring was come. One Sunday, after to have cleaned

sa boutique à grande eau, Lecouvreur, sentant les chaleurs
his shop at big water, Lecouvreur, feeling the heats

proches, décide de sortir la terrasse : quatre
near, decides to take out the pavement café : four

tables rondes et   huit chaises de jardin, qu'on   aligne sur
tables round   and eight chairs of garden, that one lines up on

le trottoir,   sous un grand store   où   on lit   en lettres
the pavement, under a big   awning where one reads in letters

rouges: HOTEL- VINS-   LIQUEURS.
red: HOTEL-WINES-SPIRITS.

Lecouvreur aime musarder dans le   quartier,   la cigarette
Lecouvreur likes to stroll   in   the neighbourhood, the cigarette

au   coin des   lèvres ... Toujours la même
at-the corner of-the lips ...   Always   the same

promenade, tranquille, apaisante. Il   longe
walk,   quiet,   calming.   He walks along the side of

l'hôpital   Saint-Louis, puis il regagne le quai
the hospital St-Louis,   then he regains   the embankment

de Jemmapes. Des   pêcheurs sont installés sur le   bord du
of Jemmapes.   Some fishermen are   installed on the bank of-the

canal, au   bon endroit. [...] Lecouvreur s'arrête.   Il
canal, at-the good place.   [...] Lecouvreur himself stops. It

fait   beau ...
makes fine ...

Partout   les marronniers   fleurissent,
Everywhere the horse-chestnut-trees blossom,

de   grands arbres qui semblent plantés là
[indefinite number of] big   trees   that seem   planted there

pour saluer les péniches. Des   bateliers
for   to greet the barges.   [Indefinite number of] boatmen

se   démènent ...   Un peu plus haut,
[themselves] work with frantic energy ... A little   more high,

des   montagnes de sable ou de pierre,
[indefinite number of] mountains of sand or of stone,

des   tas de charbon, des
[indefinite number of] piles of coal,   [indefinite number of]

sacs de ciment, encombrent le   quai.
bags of cement, encumber   the embankment.

Des   voitures traversent le pont   tournant.
[Indefinite number of] cars   cross   the bridge turning
                                                  [= the swing-bridge].

(From *Hôtel du Nord* by Eugène Dabit)

Italian speakers

Alison Duguid

Distribution

ITALY, REPUBLIC OF SAN MARINO, VATICAN, SWITZERLAND, Malta, Somalia.

Introduction

Italian is an Indo-European language, directly descended from Latin, and closely related to Spanish, Portuguese, and French. There is a wide variety of regional dialects, many of which are mutually unintelligible, and some of which have a literary tradition of their own.

Most Italians are very conscious of their regional origins, and are quick to point out that they are Neapolitan, or Tuscan, or Sardinian, as well as Italian.

Especially in the industrialised north, most educated Italians use the standard language, which evolved from a variety of Tuscan; but many can adopt the local dialect, and do so when speaking to dialect users, or in particular situations. In rural areas and in the south, dialect may be the first language for many, and this will obviously have an effect on the way English will be learned.

Italian is also the official language of the Vatican and the Republic of San Marino, and is the language of tertiary education in Somalia.

Italian speakers have some assistance in learning English through their awareness of the Latin origins of much English lexis and syntax. The Anglo-Saxon elements in English, however, can cause difficulties, and often the most basic and colloquial English usage causes more trouble than more formal or academic registers.

Phonology

General

Although there are differences between English and Italian in the distribution of the individual sounds, the main difficulties for Italian learners lie in the areas of stress and rhythm, and it is in these areas that learners have most problems in understanding, and in making themselves understood. In addition, the relatively regular match between spelling and pronunciation in Italian sometimes causes learners to become quite indignant about the inconsistency of the English language in this respect.

Vowels

iː	ɪ	e	æ	eɪ	aɪ	ɔɪ
ɑː	ɒ	ɔː	ʊ	aʊ	əʊ	ɪə
uː	ʌ	ɜː	ə	eə	ʊə	aɪə / aʊə

Shaded phonemes have equivalents or near equivalents in Italian, and should therefore be perceived and articulated without great difficulty, although some confusions may still arise. Unshaded phonemes may cause problems. For detailed comments see below.

1. /ɪ/ is frequently realised or perceived as /iː/: *leave* for *live*.
2. /æ/ is frequently realised or perceived as /e/: *met* for *mat*.
3. /ʌ/ is also sometimes pronounced /æ/: *bat* for *but*.
   It should be noted that some loan words from English have adopted Italian pronunciation:
   'flesh' for *flash*
   'krek' for *crack*
3. Diphthongs may not be perceived, giving rise to confusions between /ɒ/ and /əʊ/: *got* and *goat*, both vowels being realised as the Italian /o/.
   A similar confusion may arise between /e/ and /eɪ/: *get* and *gate*, both being realised as the Italian /e/.
4. If diphthongs are pronounced, students may give equal weight to the two elements, rather than stressing the first element. They may even pronounce English off-glides, such as /iː/, as diphthongs through over-compensation.
5. Neutral vowels resulting from English stress-timing cause problems, particularly in the comprehension and production of normal colloquial speech. Vowels are often given their strong pronunciation, and weak forms may not be recognised, even in words the learner is familiar with.

Consonants

Shaded phonemes have equivalents, or near equivalents in Italian, and should therefore be perceived and articulated without great difficulty,

p	b	f	v	θ	ð	t	d
s	z	ʃ	ʒ	tʃ	dʒ	k	g
m	n	ŋ	l	r	j	w	h

although some confusions may still arise. Unshaded phonemes may cause problems. For detailed comments, see below.

1. English alveolar phonemes (/t/, /d/, /n/) have dental equivalents in Italian.
2. /θ/ and /ð/ are often pronounced as /t/ and /d/: *tin* for *thin*, and *udder* for *other*, etc.

   Over-emphasising these sounds can lead to excessive effort on the learner's part, which can be more problematical than the original error.
3. There are various problems related to voicing, particularly with the /s/ and /z/ contrast, which are positional variants in Italian. This gives rise to errors such as '*zmoke*' for *smoke*; and the devoicing of the plural morpheme and the third person singular present tense endings, in cases where English requires voicing.

   Students sometimes have difficulty in perceiving initial voiced consonants in English, because of the late onset of voicing.
4. There is no equivalent in Italian for the phoneme /ʒ/, and a word like *pleasure*, for example, may be pronounced /'plezjʊr/. (This is a result of spelling pronunciation in many cases.)
5. /ŋ/ in Italian is a variant of /n/. The /g/ element is usually pronounced: /siːŋgə/ for /sɪŋə/.
6. There is no equivalent of /h/ in Italian, and students will either fail to pronounce it: '*I 'ope 'e is*', or over-compensate: '*Hai hope he his*'.
7. Italian syllable structure rules are such that final consonants are rare, usually to be found only in foreign loan words, e.g. *bar*, *sport*, etc. One result of this is that final consonants in English are given a following vowel, usually schwa: *I wentə to schoolə onə the busə*.

Consonant clusters

Consonant clusters in general cause problems, especially those containing /θ/ or /ð/, e.g. *sixths*, *clothes*, and although Italian has many of the permissible consonant clusters of English (and some more besides), more than one cluster in any one word proves particularly difficult, for example in *understandable*.

Influence of spelling on pronunciation

Because of the close relationship between spelling and pronunciation in Italian, learners are often dismayed and sometimes quite indignant about the seemingly irregular relationship between the two in English. Many common pronunciation errors typical of Italian learners are a result of grapho-phonemic interference, rather than any particular phonological aspect of Italian. Learners will give Italian values to each letter and expect each letter to be pronounced.

Other notable errors are:

1. The letter *r* is always pronounced in Italian, and this is carried over into English.
2. The letters *c* and *g* vary as to their pronunciation in Italian according to the grapho-phonemic environment: *c* is pronounced /tʃ/ before *i* or *e*, but as /k/ before other vowels; *g* is pronounced /dʒ/ before *i* or *e*, but as /g/ elsewhere; *sc* is pronounced /ʃ/ before *e* or *i*, but as /sk/ elsewhere.

   Where morphological changes demand an alteration between *i* and other vowels, an *h* may be inserted to retain the consonant's sound value, e.g. **bosco** (pron. /bosko/) = *wood* (singular), becomes **boschi** (pron. /boski/) = *woods*.

   Typical errors resulting from this are:
   'kip' for *chip*
   'achent' for *accent*
   'sinjer' for *singer*
3. A /w/ in loan words from English or other languages is often pronounced as /v/: *vat* for *watt*. Students tend to carry this over to all English words with a *w*, even though the sound /w/ exists in Italian in words like **uova** (pron. /wova/).
4. Attempts are sometimes made to pronounce initial silent letters, as in *pneumonia* and *psychology*, since such initial letters are pronounced in Italian.

Rhythm and stress

Italian learners often claim that English people 'eat their words'. The stress-timed patterns of English cause great difficulty to Italian learners, particularly in terms of perception and comprehension. The characteristics of stress-timing need to be pointed out. Special attention needs to be paid to the presentation and production of weak forms, since learners will expect full value to be given to all syllables.

Some factors of assimilation and the change of meaning with word stress have equivalents in Italian, e.g. **un poco** (pron. /umpoko/); and the pairs **an'cora** (*still, yet*) and **'ancora** (*anchor*); or **capi'tano** (*captain*) and

61

'capitano (*they happen*). The same is true of stress changes between parts of speech, which parallel English, e.g. *politics, political*, etc.

However, few students are aware of what happens in their own language, and most consider such phenomena in English to be bizarre.

Finally it should be noted that the word for *stress* in Italian is accento, and this may be confused with *accent*.

Intonation

Many Italians say that they think English sounds 'affected', so some learners may be rather resistent to adopting English intonation patterns. Students have a lot of difficulty in recognising intonation patterns: differences between *yes/no* questions and *wh*-questions cause particular problems. Contrasts in Italian are usually signalled by reordering the components of the sentence, so that the element under focus comes at the end, which coincides with the primary stress:

> Il treno arriva alle nove. (*The train arrives* at nine.)
> Alle nove il treno arriva. (*The train* arrives *at nine.*)

In English, of course, different emphases can be indicated by changes in the primary stress and the intonation pattern, without necessarily changing the order of the various elements. Italian learners need these distinctions to be pointed out.

Students also have problems in recognising affective meaning, which in English is signalled by intonation, and tend to sound arrogant or aggressive when making requests and asking questions.

Orthography and punctuation

Apart from errors resulting from the relationship between spelling and pronunciation, where learners' expectations often lead to phonetic spelling, other problems of accuracy come from the Italian spelling of cognates like psichiatra, psicologia, etc., giving rise to spelling errors such as *psicology*.

Italian conventions in the use of upper and lower case differ slightly from English. Small letters are used initially in the names of the days and months, and in adjectives of nationality and the names of languages.

The use of the comma presents difficulties after initial adverbs, adverb phrases and clauses; with participle constructions; and with non-defining relative clauses.

In informal writing, many Italians pay little attention to punctuation, frequently omitting full stops, or using dashes as all-purpose punctuation marks.

Style

Extended prose causes problems because of different conventions in the use of linguistic resources, and different ideas about what constitutes 'good style'. Students may use long, complex sentences, with more subordination than English would normally prefer, and elaborate periphrasis to avoid repeating the same word. Participle constructions may be overused.

Grammar

General

The main difficulties for Italians learning English lie in the fact that English relies to a great extent on word order and phrase structure to indicate grammatical function, whereas Italian, although it has developed a long way from the free ordering of words of its Latin origins, relies nevertheless much more on morphological inflections. There are exceptions to this: in forming the comparative, English uses inflected forms (*small – smaller*), while Italian does not. Italian speakers will tend to say **more small* in consequence.

The variety of syntactic devices in English, and the relative lack of morphological signals, will often cause students to complain that English has no rules, little grammar, and is unpredictable.

Statements, questions and negatives; auxiliaries

The auxiliary *do* has no equivalent in Italian and causes conceptual difficulties. Interrogatives are formed by putting a heavy functional load on intonation:

> **Where he work?*
> **What you want?*

Negatives are formed by the use of the negative particle non. (There are other negative markers, but all are placed before the verb.):

> **I not smoke.*
> **I no speak English.*

There are also a set of negative particles, which are used with non to express *nothing, never, no-one*, etc. giving rise to the use of double negatives in English:

> **I don't understand nothing.*

Confusion occurs with the negative of infinitives:

> **It is useless to don't speak.*

63

Time, tense and aspect

There is only one word in Italian to express both tense and time: **tempo**. Italian has five tenses, in the sense that there are inflected forms for present, future, conditional, simple past and imperfect. Other tenses are formed by the use of auxiliaries.

The third person singular ending on the present tense is frequently omitted by Italian learners. This is due as much to phonological interference as morphological, and is particularly difficult to cure, although it rarely impedes communication.

> *he go   *she say

Italian forms the present perfect in much the same way as English (using the auxiliary verb *have* and past participles, which may be regular or irregular). But a group of verbs, mostly verbs of motion, and reflexives, form the present perfect with *to be* (**essere**), and this gives rise to errors:

> *He is gone.

The main difficulties, however, lie in the *use* of the tense rather than the form. Italians use the present perfect as a reference to actions in the recent past. There is no firm line drawn to mark the limits of when an action may be considered to be sufficiently in the past to warrant the use of the simple past. Matters are further complicated by the fact that there are differences in use between north and south Italy. The distinction made in English of how the action is viewed with respect to the present has no real meaning for Italian speakers and is often difficult for them to grasp. Use of the present perfect for the simple past is frequent:

> *I have seen her last week.

'Conditional', for Italians, indicates a morphologically signalled verb form rather than a sentence structure, so that references to 'first', 'second' and 'third' conditionals, and to 'conditional sentences' cause a certain amount of perplexity. Italians use the subjunctive in what we would call second and third type conditionals:

> *If you would win a prize, you could share it with me.

A future tense can be used in the Italian equivalent of *if* clauses, and in other subordinate clauses where a present tense would be used in English:

> *When the holidays will be over, I will ...

Progressive verbs exist in Italian, but their use tends to be limited more to strictly ongoing, unfinished actions:

> *What do you read? (for What are you reading?)

There is no equivalent to the *going to* future, or to the use of the present progressive with future meaning; but the simple present does function with future time reference in Italian:

> *What do you do this night? (for What are you doing this evening?)
>
> *I go soon to home.

To talk about how long a state of affairs has been going on, Italians use the simple present tense (often misusing *since* for *for*, or using an *It is* ... construction by analogy with Italian):

>*I live there since ten years.*
>*I am a teacher since 1983.*
>*It is three years that I learn English.*

Modal verbs

There are five modal auxiliaries in Italian, which have all the morphological and syntactic properties of other verbs, unlike their English equivalents. They are followed by a verb in the infinitive:

>*I can to go.*
>*I would to go.*

Would is often treated as a translation of **vorrei** (= *I would like to*):

>*I would very much go.*

The varied shades of meaning in the area of possibility, certainty, obligation, etc., expressed by the English modals, are difficult for Italian students to 'feel'. They tend, for instance, to overuse *must*, since in Italian different tense forms of **dovere** are used to shade meaning, rather than different modals:

>*You must to know.* (for *You should/ought to know.*)

Other distinctions which may cause difficulty are those between *could* and *was able to*; *must* and *have to*; *mustn't*, *needn't* and *don't have to*; *didn't need to* and *needn't have*.

Comprehension problems may be caused by the fact that the weak spoken forms of modals like *can* and *must* may not be perceived by learners.

Non-finite forms

There is no equivalent in Italian of the gerund, or *-ing* form used as a noun. The infinitive tends to be used by learners, even where a verb or adjective is more usually followed by a preposition and gerund:

>*When he had finished to eat* ...
>*I am used to take the bus.*
>*I am afraid to make a mistake.*

Many learners fail to realise that a gerund is needed after a preposition:

>*Before to go home, he* ...
>*I am looking forward to see you.*

The 'object + infinitive' structure causes problems, since Italian tends to use a clause:

>*Does he want that I come, too?*

Italian speakers

The Italian infinitive of purpose structure uses **per** (= *for*):
>*She went out for to buy ... / for buy ... / for buying ...*

The Italian word for *think* is often used with **di** (= *to*) + infinitive:
>*I thought to go shopping early, before the crowds.*

Clause structure: subject and object pronouns

In Italian, use of the subject pronoun is not obligatory in normal colloquial speech:
>*When a man finds a friend, finds also a treasure.*
>*Is difficult to say.*

The order of subject and predicate is freer than in English, and can be used to make distinctions of emphasis, style, etc.:
>*It would be necessary more time.*

Intrusive subject pronouns are common:
>*My family and I we have visited ...*

Object pronouns may be omitted:
>*Yes, I like.*

Reported speech

Difficulty in grasping the English 'one-step' tense shift rules after introductory verbs in past or conditional tenses can often give rise to mistakes:
>*He said that he would have arrived at six o'clock. (for ... that he would arrive ...)*

Word order in reporting *wh*-questions can be a problem:
>*Do you know where is my village?*

Italian has one word only to cover the functions of *say* and *tell*:
>*He said me that he wanted ...*

The passive voice

Italian uses the passive voice much less than English, and students often seem to have been taught the passive in a rather mechanical way:
>(*)*My bicycle has been stolen by somebody.*

Italian cannot make an indirect object the subject of a passive verb, so clauses like *George was given a camera for his birthday* can seem peculiar to learners. And structures like *He was thought to be hiding ...* or *They are alleged to have demanded* do not come easily to Italian students.

Reflexive verbs

Reflexive verbs are more common in Italian than in English:
>*We will meet us after dinner.*

Articles

Although misuse of articles rarely impedes communication, it is none the less one of the greatest problems for Italian learners. Italian has both definite and indefinite articles, which inflect for number and gender, but their use is different from English. The contrast between specific and generic causes problems, since in Italian nouns used in a generic sense take the definite article:

> *The dogs are useful pets.*
> *I think the money is very important.*

Italians do not use the indefinite article when identifying people's professions:

> *I am teacher.*

However, articles are used in Italian in a number of cases where they are dropped in English – for instance, when referring to eating meals:

> *After the breakfast, we went to school.*

Other difficulties include:

> few / little vs a few / a little
> In future vs in the future
> last / next week vs the last / the next week
> (the) church, school, prison, hospital, etc.

Quantifiers

Italians do not usually realise that *much* and *many* are rare in affirmative clauses:

> *She has much money.*

Most is often wrongly used with an article:

> *The most of my friends live in London.*

The use and position of *both* and *all* can cause problems:

> *We all are going to the cinema.*

Instead of *one ... another*, Italians may use *a ... another*:

> *He spent the morning running from a shop to another.*

Possessives

Italian possessive 'adjectives' (determiners) inflect for number and gender. In the third person, there is no three-way distinction between *his*, *her*, and *its*: the choice of word in Italian depends on the gender of what is possessed, not of the possessor:

> *Look – there's Maria and his boyfriend!* (for ... *and her boyfriend!*)
> *He bought some flowers for her wife.* (for ... *for his wife.*)

Other common errors include the use of *your* for *her*; and mistakes like *the my book*, since Italian possessives frequently co-occur with articles.

Confusion of possessive adjectives and pronouns also occurs frequently, as they have the same form in Italian:
> *mine parents

Forms like *a friend of mine* are difficult, and are avoided.

Number and countability

The countable/uncountable distinction is less clear-cut in Italian than in English, and some uncountable English words have countable equivalents in Italian. Examples are: *news, furniture, information, luggage, advice, weather, spaghetti* (and other pasta dishes), *bread*.
> *It's a terrible weather!
> *I need two breads.

Certain Italian phrases use a plural where English does not:
> *A second-hand car in good conditions.

The Italian word for *people* (**gente**) is singular:
> *People is strange.

Italian family names cannot be given a plural inflection:
> *the Smith (for *the Smiths*)

Pronouns

Who may be used as the subject of a main clause:
> *Who finds a purse in the street should take it to the police station.

Italian use of the preposition di (= *of*) gives rise to:
> *something of interesting
> *nothing of important

Adjectives and adverbs

Adjectives in Italian usually follow the noun. They inflect for number, which may lead beginners to make mistakes:
> *an idea stupid
> *the dears children

More advanced learners may make mistakes with expressions like *the poor, the blind*, etc.:
> *We should give money to the poors.

Some expressions in Italian use an adjective where English would use an adverb:
> *speak slow
> *walk quick

In Italian an adverb may separate a verb from its object or complement:
> *I like very much English.
> *I live always in Rome.

Prepositions

The precise meaning of some prepositions is a little elusive in both languages, and English often strikes Italian students as arbitrary. Typical errors caused by Italian transfer include:

> *to discuss about*
> *to read on the newspaper*
> *to go in England*
> *to listen something*

The Italian words for *before* and *after* are also commonly used as adverbs:

> *We went to the National Gallery; after, we went to the British Museum.*

Vocabulary

Previous learning experience usually leads students to rely on word for word translation, and there are the usual problems of false friends. Some of the more frequently encountered of these are:

> *in fact* used to mean *indeed*
> *actually* used to mean *now, at present*
> *sympathetic* used to mean *pleasant, friendly*
> *according to me* used to mean *in my opinion*
> *to know* used to mean *to meet (for the first time)*
> *library* used to mean *bookshop*
> *editor* used to mean *publisher*
> *lecture* used to mean *reading*
> *conference* used to mean *lecture*
> *morbid* used to mean *soft*
> *sensible* used to mean *sensitive*
> *eventual* used to mean *possible*
> *comprehensive* used to mean *understanding*
> *assist* used to mean *attend*
> *control* used to mean *check*

Other common areas of confusion, resulting from different or overlapping coverage in the two languages include:

> *still, yet, again*
> *as, how, like* (all rendered in Italian by come)
> *which, what, who, that* (all rendered in Italian by che)
> *too, too much, too many* (all rendered in Italian by troppo)
> *very, a lot, many, much* (all rendered in Italian by molto)
> *why, because* (both rendered in Italian by perchè)
> *come, go*
> *bring, take*

>*dead, died* (both rendered in Italian by morto)
>*also, even* (both rendered in Italian by anche)

A sample of written Italian with a word for word translation

L'altra   notte ho   fatto un incubo   tremendo.   Mi
The other night [I] have made a   nightmare tremendous. Me

trovavo   nella stazione di una cittadina a   me sconosciuta.
[I] found in-the station   of a   town   to me unknown.

Ero   appena scesa   dal   treno, quando fui
[I] was barely   descended from-the train, when   [I] was

avvicinata da due poliziotti   che mi chiesero i   documenti
approached by two policemen that me asked   the documents

con aria intimidatoria. Presa alla   sprovvista, cominciai
with air   intimidating.   Taken at-the unprepared, [I] began

a cercarli   prima nella borsa, poi nelle tasche ed
to search-them first   in-the bag,   then in-the pockets and

infine nella valigia, da   cui   estraevo   ogni
finally in-the suitcase, from which [I] extracted each

indumento ed   ogni oggetto, uno per uno, prima con calma,
garment   and each object,   one by one, first   with calm,

poi affanosamente anche perchè mi stavo rendendo conto
then breathlessly   also   because me [I] was rendering account

           che quella non era mia valigia. Cominciai
[= realising] that that   not was my suitcase. [I] began

allora a farmi   prendere dal   panico, a guardare in giro
then   to make-me to take   by-the panic, to look   in round

a destra e   a sinistra per cercare   una via di scampo ma
at right   and at left   for to-search a   way of escape   but

la   stazione era circondata da un filo   spinato ed   a poco
the station   was surrounded by a   wire barbed and at little

a poco   mi apparve non più   come una
at little [= little by little] me appeared no   more as   a

stazione ma come un campo di concentramento. Ed   io non ero
station   but as   a   camp of concentration.   And I   not was

più   una viaggiatrice   qualsiasi   ma una deportata
more a   traveller [fem.] of-whatever-kind but a   deported [fem.]

e   quelli non erano poliziotti ma soldati. Presa dall'
and those not were policemen but soldiers. Taken by-the

angoscia e   dal   panico mi svegliai di soprassalto
anxiety   and by-the panic   me [I] awoke of start [= with a

     e   il   cuore mi batteva   così forte che ci
start] and the heart me was beating so   strong that there

vollero alcuni minuti   prima che mi rendessi
wanted some   minutes first   that me [I] render [subjunctive]

conto   che
account [= it took a few minutes until I realised] that

era   tutto un sogno.
[it] was all   a   dream.

(by Anna Ortolani)

Speakers of Spanish and Catalan

Norman Coe*

Distribution

Spanish: SPAIN (including the Canaries); the whole of SOUTH AMERICA except Brazil and the Guianas; CENTRAL AMERICA; MEXICO; CUBA, PUERTO RICO and THE DOMINICAN REPUBLIC; Spanish Morocco, Spanish Guinea and Rio de Oro; some parts of the USA.
Catalan: CATALONIA, ANDORRA, the BALEARIC ISLANDS, parts of Valencia and Alicante, France (eastern Pyrenees). Nowadays there are very few people who speak Catalan exclusively; most Catalan speakers also speak Spanish or French.

Introduction

Spanish and Catalan are Romance languages, closely related to Italian and Portuguese; they belong to the Indo-European family. Variations in Spanish are noticeable within Spain itself, and also between metropolitan Spain and the varieties spoken in the Americas. However, these differences are virtually confined to pronunciation and vocabulary, morphology and syntax being standard everywhere. With a little experience, all varieties are mutually intelligible.

Despite its limited geographical spread, Catalan varies appreciably from one area to another. In central Catalonia, these variations are largely confined to pronunciation and vocabulary. Some Catalan dialects, e.g. Valencian, show grammatical differences. There is a large degree of mutual intelligibility.

Phonology

General

While the Spanish and English consonant systems show many similarities, the vowel systems and sentence stress are very different, and these can cause great difficulty for Spanish-speaking learners of English.

* Additional information on Latin American usage supplied by John Shepherd and Richard Rossner.

72

European Spanish speakers, in particular, probably find English pronunciation harder than speakers of any other European language. Speakers of Catalan, with its broader range of vowels and a stress system more similar to English, in general have less difficulty.

Some common features of the pronunciation typical of Spanish and Catalan speakers of English are:
— Difficulty in recognising and producing English vowels.
— Strong devoicing of final voiced consonants.
— Even sentence rhythm, without the typical prominences of English, making understanding difficult for English listeners.
— Narrower range of pitch (in European speakers), producing a bored effect.

Vowels

Spanish has five pure vowels and five diphthongs; Catalan has eight pure vowels and eight 'falling' diphthongs. In neither language is length a distinctive feature. Consequently, learners find difficulty in differentiating between English vowels, especially where length is a part of the difference. Typically, at least two English vowels share the 'phonetic space' occupied by one Spanish/Catalan vowel, so one-to-one correspondences are practically impossible.

1. /iː/ and /ɪ/ correspond to Spanish/Catalan /i/, so *seat* and *sit*, *sheep* and *ship*, etc. are confused.
2. /ɑː/, /æ/ and /ʌ/ correspond to Spanish/Catalan /a/, so words such as *cart*, *cat* and *cut* are confused in perception, though *cart* as produced by a Spanish/Catalan speaker usually has an intruded flapped /r/, i.e. /kart/. (See also the section 'Influence of spelling on pronunciation' below.)
3. /ɔː/ and /ɒ/ correspond to Spanish/Catalan /o/, so *caught* and *cot*, etc. are confused.
4. /uː/ and /ʊ/ correspond to Spanish/Catalan /u/, so pairs like *pool* and *pull* are confused.
5. English /ɜː/ and /ə/ have no similarity to Spanish vowels. /ə/ is normally replaced by the strong pronunciation of the written vowel, so /abaut/ for *about*, etc. /ɜː/ is replaced by /i/ or /e/ plus flapped /r/, so /birt/ for *bird*; /bert/ for *Bert*, etc. Catalan, on the other hand, does have a neutral vowel, which appears in unstressed syllables containing the letters *a* or *e*; English /ə/ is therefore not such a problem for Catalan speakers.
6. As for diphthongs, there are four that are similar in English and Spanish (except that the second element in Spanish tends to be stronger than in English): /aʊ/, /eɪ/, /aɪ/ and /ɔɪ/. These diphthongs are not difficult for Spanish-speaking learners.

English /əʊ/, however, is often not distinguished from /ɔː/, so *coat* and *caught* (as well as *cot*) are confused, for example.

Catalan has a wider range of diphthong sounds than English; thus, though the exact values do not coincide, Catalan learners have little difficulty in producing acceptable variants.

Consonants

p	b	f	v	θ	ð	t	d
s	z	ʃ	ʒ	tʃ	dʒ	k	g
m	n	ŋ	l	r	j	w	h

Shaded phonemes have equivalents or near equivalents in Spanish and Catalan, and are perceived and articulated without serious difficulty, though even here there are some complications. Unshaded phonemes cause problems.

1. Initial voiceless plosives (/p/, /t/, /k/) are not aspirated as in English, so they often sound like /b/, /d/, /g/ to English ears.
2. Word-final voiced plosives are rare in Spanish and Catalan; learners tend to use /t/ for final /d/, /k/ for final /g/ and /p/ for final /b/.

   Other voiced word-final consonants also tend to be strongly devoiced, so '*rish*' or *rich* for *ridge*; /beiθ/ for *bathe*, etc.
3. Spanish and Catalan have the same three nasal phonemes as English, i.e. /m/, /n/ and /ŋ/, but their assimilation to the surrounding phonetic context differs from English, so for example /aiŋgoiŋ/ is common for *I'm going*.

   In Spanish, /n/ or /ŋ/ tends to replace /m/ in final position, so for example '*drean*' or '*dreang*' for *dream*. Final /n/ in Spanish is not always very distinct, and may be absorbed into a nasalised vowel and/or pronounced more like /ŋ/.

   In Spanish and Catalan, /k/ does not follow /ŋ/ at the end of a word, so *sing* is pronounced for both *sing* and *sink*, etc.
4. Spanish/Catalan speakers tend to give *b*, *d* and *g* their mother-tongue values, which vary according to context. These are quite similar to English initially, but between vowels they are softer continuous sounds, not stops: /b/ is more like /v/, /d/ like /ð/, and /g/ unlike any English sound. This can make learners' pronunciation of words like *robin*, *habit*, *ladder*, *reading*, *bigger*, or *again* very difficult for a native speaker to understand.

5. In Spanish, /z/ does not exist; learners use /s/ for /z/, so *pence* for both *pence* and *pens*, *lacy* for both *lacy* and *lazy*, etc. Moreover, the European Spanish pronunciation of /s/ often approaches /ʃ/, causing confusion between pairs like *see* and *she*.

   Catalan, on the other hand, has a /z/–/s/ distinction similar to that of English, so there is no general problem. However, Catalan /z/ does not appear word-finally, so Catalans will say *face* for both *face* and *phase*, etc.

6. Spanish, and most varieties of Catalan, only have one sound in the area of /b/ and /v/ (generally pronounced as a bilabial continuant); hence confusion between pairs like *bowels* and *vowels*.

7. Of the English phonemes /ʃ/, /tʃ/, /ʒ/ and /dʒ/, European Spanish only has /tʃ/, with obvious consequences for learners. Confusion is common between words such as *sheep*, *cheap* and *jeep*; *pleasure* may be pronounced as '*pletcher*', '*plesher*' or '*plesser*', and so on. In Southern Latin America, /ʒ/ or /dʒ/ occur in words written with *ll*, e.g. **llamar** /dʒamar/.

   Catalan, on the other hand, has four phonemes similar to the English ones, though the voiced ones, /ʒ/ and /dʒ/, do not appear finally, causing problems with words like *bridge*, *beige*.

8. Spanish/Catalan /r/ is flapped and is normally pronounced in all positions; this carries over into English. (See also the section 'Influence of spelling on pronunciation' below.)

9. The nearest Spanish sound to English /h/ is a rougher sound like the *ch* in Scottish *loch* or German **Bach** (but written *j* or *g*). This often replaces English /h/. The sound is somewhat less harsh in American Spanish.

10. Spanish speakers often pronounce English /j/ (as in *yes*) rather like /dʒ/, leading to confusion between pairs such as *you* and *Jew*, *year* and *jeer*, etc.

11. Spanish and Catalan speakers may pronounce /w/ rather like /b/ between vowels, e.g. /ariβalker/ for *Harry Walker*. Before a back vowel, /w/ may be pronounced as /gw/ or /g/: /gwʊd/ or /gʊd/ for *would*.

Consonant clusters

Consonant clusters are in general less frequent in Spanish and Catalan than in English, so that learners have difficulty perceiving and producing English clusters. Typical simplifications:

>   '*espres*' for *express*
>   '*istan*' for *instant*
>   '*brefas*' for *breakfast*
>   '*tes*' for *test* and *text*

> *win* for *win* and *wind*
> '*wen*' for both *when* and *went*
> *can* for both *can* and *can't*
> *cars* for *cars, carts* and *cards*, etc.

Note that /s/ plus another consonant, as in *Spain, sceptic, stop*, never occurs at the beginning of a word in Spanish or Catalan, so '*Espain*', '*esceptic*', '*estop*', etc.

Influence of spelling on pronunciation

1. Spelling and pronunciation are very closely – and simply – related in Spanish, so beginning learners tend to pronounce English words letter by letter. In Catalan, the relationship between pronunciation and spelling is about as complicated as it is in English, so that English orthography seems less of a problem. However, with unknown words Catalan speakers also tend to pronounce letter by letter. Some examples are:

   > *asked* pronounced '*askett*'
   > *break: e* and *a* pronounced separately
   > *answer: w* and *r* pronounced
   > *friend: i* and *e* pronounced separately (but *d* dropped)
   > *chocolate*: second *o* and final *e* pronounced.

2. Flapped /r/ is generally pronounced where written, so it intrudes before consonants (as in *learn, farm*) and for Spanish speakers also at the ends of words (as in *four, bar*). Furthermore, in Spanish and Catalan double *r* is rolled (and in Catalan initial *r* as well), and this habit carries over.

3. /ə/ does not exist in Spanish, so unstressed syllables are pronounced with the written vowel:

   > *teacher* /titʃer/   *interested* /interestet/
   > *photograph* /fotograf/   *photography* /fotografi/

4. In European Spanish and Catalan double *l* is generally pronounced rather like the *-lli-* in million; Latin American pronunciations include /j/, /ʒ/ and /dʒ/. Beginners may carry these pronunciations over into English.

Rhythm and stress

Spanish is a syllable-timed language. In general, all syllables take about the same length of time to pronounce (though extra length may be used for emphasis); to an English ear, there is therefore not a great difference in prominence between stressed and unstressed syllables. In English, on the other hand, stressed syllables tend to be pronounced more slowly and distinctly, while unstressed syllables are reduced and often pronounced with a neutral vowel /ə/ or /ɪ/. Since content words (nouns, verbs, adjectives and adverbs) are stressed in English, they are therefore relatively prominent as compared with the unstressed grammatical words (articles, pronouns, prepositions, auxiliary verbs). So the stress and rhythm of an English sentence give a lot of acoustic clues to structure and meaning. When Spanish speakers pronounce English sentences with even stress and rhythm, these clues are missing, and English listeners find them difficult to understand because they cannot so easily decode the structure. (For example, in *Ann is older than Joe, is* and *than* may be as prominent as *old.*)

Catalan shows a more marked difference between stressed and unstressed syllables, including a neutral vowel like /ə/ in unstressed positions. Catalan is also more stress-timed (with similar time-intervals elapsing between stress and stress, as in English, rather than between syllable and syllable), but these features are still not as marked as in English. Thus, while Catalan learners typically approximate more closely to English sentence rhythm, there is still a remaining margin of difference to be overcome.

Spanish and Catalan learners find variable stress intractable (see also the section 'Intonation' below), and they cannot usually either recognise or produce English alternates like:

> the black bird   the blackbird
> the green house   the greenhouse

Intonation

European Spanish and Catalan tend to use a narrower pitch range than English, and emphatic stress is expressed in extra length rather than in extra pitch variation. Thus some speakers may sound unenthusiastic or bored to English ears.

In English the intonation nucleus can fall on any stressed syllable in the sentence, depending on what is being emphasised. By contrast, in Spanish (and to a large extent in Catalan too) the nucleus falls on the last stressed syllable in the sentence. (If an element is to be stressed, the freer word order allows it to move to the end.) Thus learners can approximate to *'John 'painted the walls* (as an answer to the question *What did John do?*). However, they find great difficulty in producing (and even recognising) the pattern *John 'painted the 'walls* (as an answer to the question *Who painted the walls?*).

Orthography and punctuation

Spelling

Spanish has high sound–spelling correspondence, so obviously the spelling of English does not come easily; in Catalan the correspondence is much more complicated, making the spelling of English less of a shock. For both groups it is common to reduce double letters to single ones:
> *apear   *diferent   *necesary   *forgoten

The problem of spelling is exacerbated because learners do not distinguish English phoneme contrasts, and so they cannot exploit those sound–spelling regularities that do exist. For example:
> *hoping* is confused with *hopping*
> *this* is confused with *these*

Related to this is the difficulty in grasping basic regularities like the English tendency to write either two vowels plus one consonant or one vowel plus two consonants:
> *breack   *crak   *shoutting

Punctuation

Spanish and Catalan punctuation conventions are similar to English, so there are relatively few problems. Commas are often used where English would prefer semi-colons, and semi-colons where English would prefer full stops. Beginners may carry over the Spanish use of an inverted question or exclamation mark at the beginning of a sentence:
> *¿When are you coming to see us?*
> *¡It was fantastic!*

Spanish and Catalan do not use inverted commas for quotations.

Grammar

General

Grammatical similarities between Spanish, Catalan and English include: singular and plural forms of nouns; definite and indefinite articles; regular and irregular verbs; past, present and future tenses; perfect and progressive verb forms; no declension of nouns, adjectives or pronouns. (Similarity of form does not, of course, guarantee similarity of use: see separate points below.)

However, compared with English, both Spanish and Catalan:
– have highly inflected verb systems;
– have freer word order;
– show gender and number in adjectives and nouns;

— have no modal auxiliaries;
— use the passive much less;
— have a subjunctive mood.

At the level of syntax (sentence structure), Spanish and Catalan show very little divergence, so the problems dealt with below are virtually always common to both. At the level of morphology (word endings), the two languages are quite different, but this has little bearing on the learning of English. (Incidentally, it is curious that speakers of languages with scores of verb endings should find the -s of the third person singular of the English simple present tense so recalcitrant. Even advanced learners often make mistakes on this point.)

Word order

This is much freer in Spanish and Catalan than in English.
1. 'Subject–verb' and 'verb–subject' do not regularly correspond to statement and question respectively:
> *Arrived the firemen ten minutes later.*   (statement)
> *The firemen arrived ten minutes later.*   (statement)
> *Maria, when came?*   *When came Maria?*   (questions)
2. The freer word order allows words that are emphasised to be placed last:
> *Yesterday played very well the children.*
> *Played very well the children yesterday.*

as well as:
> Yesterday the children played very well.
> The children played very well yesterday.
3. Frequency adverbs have several possible positions, but not the typical mid-position of English:
> *Often she has helped.*
> *She often has helped.*
4. Adjectives and nouns typically postmodify head nouns:
> *They live in the house white.*
> *Can you lend me a ball of tennis?*

This makes noun phrases like *Cambridge University Bridge Club* paricularly difficult for Spanish and Catalan learners, because for them the elements of the phrase would more naturally be expressed in the reverse order:
> *The Club of Bridge of the University of Cambridge.*

It is interesting that Spanish/Catalan speakers say, for instance, los Rolling for *the Rolling Stones* and un Christmas for *a Christmas card*, i.e. they construe the first word in the noun phrase as the head noun.
5. In Spanish and Catalan, an indirect object must have a preposition (a), and the two objects can go in either order, so:

> *They gave to Sam the book.*
> *They gave the book to Sam.*

The English two-object structure *They gave Sam the book* is difficult for learners, and they try to avoid it.

6. Adverbials and object complements are regularly placed before a direct object:

> *They took to the hospital her mother.*
> *Mrs Smith speaks very well English.*
> *Keep tidy Britain.*

Questions

1. There is no set word order for questions, and auxiliaries play no part:

> *John has bought the books?*
> *Has bought the books John?*
> *Mary came?*
> *When Mary came?*
> *Came Mary?*
> *Mary, when came?*

Naturally, subject and object questions cause difficulty both in recognition and production:

> *Who did kill Oswald?*   *Who Oswald killed?*
> *Who killed to Kennedy?*   *Who Kennedy killed?*

(For this use of *to* with a direct object, see the section 'Prepositions'.)

2. Learners have difficulty with *do/does/did*:

> *Did they went?*
> *Do they went?*
> *Do she goes?*
> *Does she goes?*

Negatives

1. Auxiliaries play no part in forming negative sentences in Spanish or Catalan; the negative word goes before the verb phrase:

> *Peter not found the key.*
> *Peter not has found the key.*

The negative particle is *no*, and beginners may replace *not* by *no* accordingly:

> *I no understand.*

In short answers, the negative goes after the pronoun, adjective, adverb, etc.:

> *Those no.*   *Green no.*   *Here no.*

2. The double negative is standard:

> *I not saw nobody.* or *I didn't see nobody.*
> *Tom not helps her never.* or *Tom doesn't help her never.*

This makes it difficult for learners to appreciate the three English categories of:

assertive:	*some*	*somebody*	*always/once*, etc.
non-assertive:	*any*	*anybody*	*ever*, etc.
negative:	*no/none*	*nobody*	*never*, etc.

In particular, non-assertive forms are construed as negative:

> *I waited but anybody came.*

Verbs

1. Spanish and Catalan have only one category of verbs, and they all show the normal range of tenses (present, past, future, conditional) and composite forms (progressive, perfect). There is thus no separate category of modal auxiliaries as in English, and learners find the concept, the simplicity of their forms, and their uses difficult to grasp. Typical mistakes include:

> *Maria cans cook.*
> *Do you can swim?*
> *May you come tomorrow?*
> *She could find the key.* (meaning ... *managed to* ...)
> *She had to win the match.* (meaning ... *should have won* ...)
> *They will can do it next week.*

2. In many cases where in English there are two different words, or a word is used with two different structures, Spanish and Catalan have verbs with both transitive and intransitive possibilities:

> *She got up at seven o'clock.*
> *She got up the chair.* (meaning ... *lifted* ...)
> *They were waiting.*
> *They were waiting the bus.*

3. Particular problems of verbal structure include the fact that many English phrases consisting of 'be + adjective' are expressed in Spanish and Catalan by 'have + noun':

> *have reason* (= *be right*)
> *have hunger*
> *have heat*, etc.

and in Spanish/Catalan *I like this* is expressed as *This pleases me*, leading to confusions such as:

> *Football likes me.*

Time, tense and aspect

In form, Spanish and Catalan make a simple/progressive distinction:
> Maria visita. (= *Maria visits.*) / Maria está visitando. (= *Maria is visiting.*)

Spanish and Catalan also have a perfective aspect:
> Maria ha visitado.

However, although these forms correspond to English forms, they do not necessarily represent similar distinctions of meaning.

1. The simple present is often used for an action taking place now:
   > *Look! *It rains!*

2. The simple present is often used to refer to future time:
   > **Do I come tomorrow?* (for ... *Shall I ...?*)
   > **I do it next week.*
   > **I see her this evening.* (for *I'm seeing her ...*)

3. The present tenses are used to refer to a period starting in past time and continuing up to the present (where English uses a perfect):
   > **How long are you working in your present job?*
   > **It's a long time that I live here.*

4. In Catalan and European Spanish, the present perfect can be used with time-when adverbials, and it is obligatory when referring to actions and events earlier on the same day:
   > **When has she received the letter?*
   > **Today I've finished work early because I've started at seven o'clock this morning.*

   In Latin America, on the other hand, the simple past is often used where British English requires the present perfect:
   > Yo lo leí = *I have read it.*

5. Spanish and Catalan have more than one form corresponding to the past progressive in English, one of which means the same as *used to (do)*. This causes confusion:
   > **When we were young, we were playing a lot of tennis.*

   In general, this form is more frequent than in English, and is practically standard for the past of stative verbs (the equivalents of *have, know,* etc.):
   > **When I was a teenager, I was having a motorbike.*
   > **She wasn't knowing that he had died.*

6. The imperative often has an expressed subject:
   > **Come you tomorrow!*

7. In Catalan, but not in Spanish, the subordinate clause of a sentence referring to future time can have the future tense:
   > **When Mary will get here, tell her to come in.*

The passive voice

1. Spanish and Catalan have a passive form constructed in the same way as the English passive: with '*be* + past participle'; but in those cases where English uses the passive without an agent phrase, Spanish and Catalan tend to use a form reminiscent of the English reflexive:
   *The house built itself before the war.
2. Spanish and Catalan cannot form passives that parallel:
   They were given bikes for Christmas.
   Polly was owed a lot of money.
   These structures (where the indirect object has become the subject of a passive verb) are difficult for learners.
3. The Spanish/Catalan endings corresponding to -*ing* and -*ed* do not have active and passive meaning respectively, with consequent confusion in English:
   *The lecture was very bored.
   *I'm very interesting in Polish films.

Infinitives

1. Spanish and Catalan often use the infinitive as an abstract noun (corresponding to the English -*ing* form):
   (*)To smoke is bad for you.
   As a consequence, learners may have difficulty in understanding sentences which have -*ing* forms as subjects.
2. Spanish and Catalan have an infinitive marker (a), but its distribution does not square fully with English *to*:
   *It's difficult learn English.
   *Let us to see.
   (See also the section 'Clause structure and complementation' below.)

Articles

Here are some of the main differences in the use of the articles in Spanish and Catalan as compared with English:
1. The definite article goes with mass nouns and plural count nouns that are used with a general meaning:
   *The food is more important than the art.
   *Do you like the big dogs? (meaning ... *big dogs in general?*)
2. Spanish and Catalan use the definite article with possessive pronouns:
   *That is the yours, and this is the mine.
3. In some expressions singular count nouns need no article:
   *Do you have car?
   *Her sister is dentist.

4. Spanish and Catalan make no distinction between the indefinite article and the number *one*:
   > *We used to live in one flat; now we live in one house.*
5. The indefinite article has a plural form (corresponding roughly to *some*). This can cause beginners to make mistakes:
   > *I have ones nice American friends.*

Gender

Spanish and Catalan have grammatical gender: all nouns, as well as accompanying articles and adjectives, are masculine or feminine. Reference is made with the corresponding pronoun:
> *The table is dirty. *Clean her, please.*

Number

1. In Spanish and Catalan the form of the plural is similar to English, (*-s* ending), but the ending is used with articles, adjectives and possessives as well as nouns:
   > *yellows flowers   *hers news shoes*
2. There are several words that can take plural forms in Spanish/Catalan, where English has a mass noun:
   > *furnitures*
   > *informations*
   > *spaghettis*
   > *thunders*
   > *I've got two news for you.*
3. Those 'symmetrical' things that are plural in form in English (*trousers, pyjamas*, etc.) are usually singular in Spanish and Catalan:
   > *a trouser   *a bathing trunk*

   There are no irregular plurals in Spanish or Catalan; learners are liable to construe *people* as singular, and to make mistakes like *a police, *childs, *childrens.*

Adjectives

1. Adjectives can stand without either a noun or a proform *one*:
   > *They showed me two models, and I bought the small.*
2. Comparatives and superlatives are always formed with the equivalents of *more* and *most*:
   > *I am more old than my sister.*
   > *Barcelona is the most large city of Catalonia.*

Personal pronouns

1. Subject personal pronouns are largely unnecessary in Spanish/Catalan because the verb ending indicates person and number:
   > *Rosa isn't French. *Is Spanish.*
   > **Have gone home because wanted to go to bed.*
   > **Was raining.*
   Over-correction may lead students to put in redundant personal pronouns:
   > **That's the man who he lives next door to us.*
2. In Spanish and Catalan most personal pronouns have the same form for subject and object, so:
   > **I saw she.   *They know we.*
3. There is no equivalent for the structure '*it is* + pronoun' as used to identify oneself:
   > *'Who is it?' *'Am I.'* (for '*It's me.*')

Possessives

1. Spanish and Catalan use the definite article, not a possessive, in sentences like:
   > **Mary washed the hair.*
2. Spanish and Catalan have the same word for *your* (formal), *his, her* and *their*, with consequent confusion in English:
   > **Sara and Joe had both got his shoes wet.*
3. Catalan uses the definite article with possessives:
   > **The my cousin is in Portugal.*

Possession

Possession and related concepts that in English are expressed by possessive cases of nouns (e.g. *Jim's bike, Mary's boss*) are expressed in Spanish and Catalan with an *of*-phrase:
> **the book of Rosa   *the gate of the garden*

Learners have problems in distinguishing between *a bottle of wine* and *a wine bottle*, etc.

Relative pronouns and clauses

1. Spanish does not distinguish between personal and non-personal relative pronouns:
   > **the man which came*
   > **the ball who is lost*
2. The relative pronoun can never be deleted in Spanish or Catalan, and

learners have difficulty in understanding English clauses with zero relative pronoun:

The girls we saw looked quite happy.

Did you like the woman we spoke to?

(Examples like the last one, in which a relative clause finishes with a preposition whose object has been deleted, are particularly difficult for students.)

Clause structure and complementation

1. Purpose clauses are expressed with a preposition (**para, per, a**) and the infinitive:

    *They have gone for (to) buy a film.
2. Spanish and Catalan have present and past subjunctives, which allow different structures from English after certain verbs:

    *I want that you stay here.

    *He asked that we went immediately.
3. Spanish and Catalan speakers tend to say, for example, *We are going to paint the house*, regardless of who is actually going to do the painting. So they find problems with such structures as:

    We are going to have the house painted.
4. Although Spanish and Catalan have two non-finite forms (like our infinitive and *-ing* form), their distribution is different:

    *They refused helping their neighbours.

    *I'll never forget to see that accident.

Prepositions

1. Spanish has a 'personal preposition' (**a**), used in transitive sentences when the direct object is human:

    *They took to their mother to the hospital.
2. In Spanish and Catalan, prepositions must always go with their noun phrase, and cannot go at the end of a clause:

    *For what have you come?

    Learners find difficulty in interpreting sentences like:

    I don't know who they're working for.

    Who does Fred sit next to?
3. In Spanish and Catalan, a preposition can be followed by an infinitive:

    *After to see the film, we went for a meal.
4. While in many cases the 'central' meaning of a preposition in one language corresponds to that in another, there are always many exceptions to these simple correspondences. Areas of particular difficulty are:

— *in/on/into*:
  *in Monday   *on July   **lying in the beach*
  **They are into the room.*
— *to/at/in*:
  *go at the beach   **arrive to the station*
  **We stopped in the crossroads.*
— *as/like*:
  **She works like a waitress.*
  **They seem as their mother.*
but there are many other problem areas.

Vocabulary

1. Spanish and Catalan are developments of Latin; their vocabularies therefore correspond to the Latin-derived side of English: estructura = *structure*, derivar = *derive*, dificil = *difficult*, confusió = *confusion*, and so on. While this fact offers the learner access to a large passive vocabulary, it also tends to make his or her language sound formal: he or she uses *enter* rather than *go in*, *arrive at* for *get to*, *extinguish* for *put out*, etc. In particular, learners have difficulty with the forms and multiple meanings of two- and three-part verbs such as *put on*, *put off*, *put out*, *look up*, *look for*, *look forward to*.

2. Spanish and Catalan can refer to both of a male–female pair (or a family group) by using the plural of the male form.

    rey = *king*, reina = *queen*, reyes = *kings* or *sovereigns*
    fill = *son*, filla = *daughter*, fills = *sons* or *children*

   So learners often use *fathers* for *parents*, *brothers* for *brothers and sisters*, *sons* for *children*, etc.

3. Some common 'false friends':

Spanish/Catalan	English translation
actual	*current*
asistir/assistir	*attend*
beneficio/benefici	*profit*
caravana	*traffic jam*
carrera	*race, degree course*
(estar) constipado/constipat	*(have) a cold*
embarazada/embarassada	*pregnant*
en frente/davant (or enfront)	*opposite*
eventual	*possible*
formal	*reliable*
lectura	*reading matter*

⟫→

Spanish/Catalan	English translation
librería/llibreria	*bookshop*
pariente/parent	*relative*
particular	*private*
profesor/professor	*teacher*
propaganda	*advertising*
propio/propi	*own*
sensible	*sensitive*
suburbio/suburbi	*slum*
tiempo/temps	*weather*

A sample of written Spanish with a word for word translation

Sentado en el   suelo se   calzaba
Sat   on the floor himself he-was-shoeing [= putting on]

las ásperas botas de racionamiento de suela clavateada
the rough   boots of rationing   of sole   studded

y   puntera de metal: ellos se   las
and toecap of metal: they [for]themselves them

              miraban   con envidia.
[= the boots] they-were-looking [at] with envy.

¿Un regalito de la   viuda Galán? dijo   Sarnita, y
A present-little of the widow Galan? he-said Sarnita, and

Java se   levantó   y   le   hizo   una seña ...
Java himself raised [= got up] and him he-made a   sign ...

Ven, dijo,   y Sarnita le siguió: bastaba   la
Come, he-said, and Sarnita him he-followed: it-was-enough the

luz que se   filtraba   a través de la   arpillera
light that itself it-was-filtering through .the sacking

para ver   el   escenario de tables, desierto, la   diminuta
for   to-see the stage   of boards, deserted, the tiny

concha del   apuntador, forrada con una tela roja, las
shell   of-the prompter, lined   with a   cloth red, the

candilejas de cinc abollado, y   más allá,   la
footlights of zinc embossed, and more there [= beyond], the

oscura sala con los bancos de missa   en formación,
dark   hall with the benches of mass [= pews] in formation,

sin   pasillo central.
without aisle   central.

(From *Si te dicen que caí* by Juan Marsé)

A sample of written Catalan with a word for word translation

Tenia   prop de divuit   anys quan vaig
I-was-having almost   eighteen years when I-go [past auxiliary]

conèixer   en Raül, a l'estació   de
know [= when I met] the Raul, at the-station of [= in]

Manresa. El   meu pare   havia mort, inesperadament i   encara
Manresa. The my   father had   died, unexpectedly   and still

jove, un parell d'anys abans, i   d'aquells   temps
young, a   couple of-years before, and from-those times

conservo un record   de punyent soledat.   Les meves relacions
I-keep   a   memory of acute   loneliness. The my   relations

amb la   mare   no havien pas   millorat, tot el   contrari,
with the mother not had   at-all improved, all the opposite,

potser fins i tot empitjoraven   a mesura que
perhaps even   they-were-worsening at step   that

              em feia   gran.
[= in proportion as] me I-was-making grown-up

              No existia,   no existí   mai
[= I was growing up]. Not it-was-existing, not existed never

entre   nosaltres, una comunitat d'interessos, d'afeccions.
between us,   a   community of-interests, of-affections.

Cal   creure   que cercava ...   una persona
It-is-necessary to-believe that I-was-seeking ... a   person

en qui   centrar   la   meva vida afectiva.
in whom to-centre the my   life   affective.

(From *Un amor fora ciutat* by Manuel de Pedrolo)

Portuguese speakers

David Shepherd

Distribution

BRAZIL, PORTUGAL, ANGOLA, MOZAMBIQUE, GUINEA, CAPE VERDE ISLANDS, GOA, MACAO.

Introduction

Portuguese is a romance language closely related to Spanish. Educated speakers of European (or Continental) Portuguese (henceforth EP) have little trouble understanding each other, both within Portugal itself, and with people from the former empire. However, the differences between European and Brazilian Portuguese (henceforth BP) are very much greater than those between British, American, or Australian varieties of English, as there is relatively little cultural, linguistic or commercial interchange. The prestige dialect in Portugal is that of Lisbon, which also serves as the model for the *lingua franca* of the recently independent former colonies. It has many more Arabic words than that of BP, which has borrowed an increasingly large number of words from American English. Portuguese is the native language of approximately 97 per cent of Brazilians. Despite its size, Brazil's regional varieties of Portuguese show few variations, when compared with most European countries. The prestige variety of BP is that of Rio de Janeiro.

Phonology

General

The English and Brazilian Portuguese phonological systems are quite different. While English has twelve vowels and ten diphthongs, Portuguese has only eight and six respectively.

Among the features of Portuguese which give rise to a 'Portuguese accent' in English are:
- Pronunciation of most unstressed syllables, influenced by the syllable-stressed Portuguese.

- Strong articulation of pure vowels, with nasalisation in some contexts, e.g. *-en, -on, -un, -ing, -em*.
- The insertion of intrusive vowels between consonants: '*closis*' for *clothes*; before initial consonant clusters: '*esteam*' for *steam*; and after some final consonants. Few consonants can occur finally in Portuguese, and so a vowel is often added: '*parkie*' for *park*; '*cabbie*' for *cab*.
- Unstressed vowels, especially at the ends of words, may become almost inaudible: '*sit*' for *city*; '*cough*' for *coffee*; '*offs*' for *office*.

Vowels

iː	ɪ	e	æ	eɪ	aɪ	ɔɪ
ɑː	ɒ	ɔː	ʊ	aʊ	əʊ	ɪə
uː	ʌ	ɜː	ə	eə	ʊə	aɪə / aʊə

Shaded phonemes have equivalents or near equivalents in Portuguese, and should therefore be perceived and articulated without great difficulty, although some confusions may still arise. Unshaded phonemes may cause problems. For detailed comments, see below.

1. /iː/ has a slightly shorter duration and is confused with /ɪ/: *rich* for *reach*; *hit* for *heat*.
2. /e/ is confused with /æ/: *head* and *had*.
3. /ɑː/ is shortened and confused with /æ/: *ant* and *aunt*; *cant* and *can't*.
4. /ɒ/ is confused with /ɔː/: *caught* for *cot*, or *spot* for *sport*, or even with /ʌ/: *hut* for *hot*.
5. /ʊ/ is confused with /uː/: *fool* for *full*.
6. /ʌ/ may be pronounced as /æ/: *lack* for *luck*, or even, because of orthographic interference, as /uː/: *mood* for *mud*.
7. Unstressed vowels are often given their full value: '*Ann*' for *an*; *thee* for *the*.

Diphthongs

There are fewer diphthongs in Portuguese than in English. The greatest problems arise with /ɪə/ and /eə/: *hear* and *hair*.

Consonants

p	b	f	v	θ	ð	t	d
s	z	ʃ	ʒ	tʃ	dʒ	k	g
m	n	ŋ	l	r	j	w	h

Shaded phonemes have equivalents or near equivalents in Portuguese and should therefore be perceived and articulated without great difficulty, although some confusions may still arise. Unshaded phonemes may cause problems. For detailed comments, see below.

1. The 'dark' /l/ in final position or before a consonant is often pronounced as a vowel similar to /ʊ/: '*bottue*' for *bottle*, and '*heeoo*' for *heel*.
2. /p/, /k/, and /t/ are unaspirated initially in Portuguese, and are confused with /b/, /g/, and /d/: *peg* and *beg*; *Kate* and *gate*; *tin* and *din*.
3. Initial and medial /t/ and /d/ are both pronounced quite forcefully and may be confused: *tale* and *dale*; *latter* and *ladder*. But when followed by /iː/, /ɪ/, or /e/, they are often pronounced as affricates, /tʃ/ and /dʒ/: '*cheam*' for *team*; '*jean*' for *dean*.
4. There is also confusion between the /t/ (a short flap) and the /r/ (a short trill): *better* and *bearer*; *heating* and *hearing*.
5. Vowels before final /m/, /n/, and /ŋ/ are nasalised, often to the point where the final consonant is inaudible.
6. An initial /r/ is an unvoiced trill or fricative and is often confused with a strong initial /h/: *red* and *head*; *right* and *height*.
7. In BP, final /s/ and /z/ are pronounced /s/: *rice* for *rise*. In EP final /s/ and /z/ are pronounced as /s/ or /ʃ/: *peace* for *peas*; *hash* for *has*.
8. /θ/ and /ð/ are realised either as /s/ and /z/, or as /t/ and /d/, confusing *thinker* and *sinker* or *tinker*; and *breathes* with *breeds* or *breezes*.
9. /tʃ/ and /dʒ/ are pronounced /ʃ/ and /ʒ/, confusing *chair* and *share*; *pledger* and *pleasure*.
10. Initial /h/ has no equivalent in Portuguese and is either omitted, confusing *ear* for *hear*, or inserted unnecessarily because of overcompensation: '*High ham is holdest friend*' for *I am his oldest friend*.

Consonant clusters

The range of consonant clusters is much wider in English than in Portuguese, causing the insertion of extra vowels by Portuguese speakers to 'assist' pronunciation of English, particularly in clusters with an initial *s*.

Initial clusters not occurring in Portuguese include *str*, *skr*, *spl*, *spr*.

Influence of spelling on pronunciation

Spelling and pronunciation are very closely related in Portuguese. Mistakes will be made at all levels of competence. The phoneme /ʒ/ exists in Portuguese, but is represented either by *j* (as in caju) or *g* (as in gelo). The /ʒ/ phoneme is frequently misused in English for these letters, e.g. in *jury*, *jockey*, etc.

Rhythm and stress

EP is a stress-timed language, like English, but BP is syllable-timed, like Spanish, and this leads to difficulties of the following kind:
— Giving appropriate stress in compound nouns, e.g. *a telephone 'box, a tea 'cup.*
— Giving appropriate syllable stress in long words, e.g. *polit'ical demonstra'tors.*
— Giving appropriate stress, or lack of stress, to auxiliary verbs, articles, conjunctions, prepositions, etc. The stressing of such words often suggests an unintended emphasis or aggressiveness:

I saw them yesterday.
They were happy.
It was his book, not his bag I wanted.

The fact that these normally unstressed syllables in English are pronounced more clearly by BP speakers also creates difficulties at all levels in perceiving meaning. Speakers of EP do have a strong/weak differentiation, unlike Brazilians, and can perceive and produce stresses.

Intonation

Declarative sentences are given a marked low fall, often making the last word inaudible.

All question tags tend to be pronounced with a rising tune, irrespective of meaning.

Juncture

There is a tendency, where there are doubled consonants, to pronounce both, and add an intrusive vowel, for example in *this stop, at that time.*

Orthography and punctuation

Portuguese speakers have considerable difficulty with English spelling. At all levels there is a tendency to represent English sounds (learned orally) with their standard Portuguese spelling forms. The following areas of error are typical:

1. All words ending in consonants (except *l*, *m*, *s*, *z*, and *r*) tend to be given a final vowel sound. This vowel is often included when writing English:
    > *She is a cookie.*

2. Where the phonemes /ɪ/ or /iː/ occur:
    > *'Inglish' for English*
    > *'clined' for cleaned*
    > *I have bin.*

3. With the diphthong /aɪ/:
    > *'traying' for trying*
    > *'laying' for lying*
    > *She is dating a nayce gay.*

4. With the phoneme /ʃ/:
    > *'finiched' for finished*
    > *'choes' for shoes*

5. Where words are similar in both languages, beginners will tend to use the Portuguese spelling (see the section 'False friends' below).

Grammar

General

The Portuguese grammatical system has much in common with English and many other western European languages. There are similar 'parts of speech'; Portuguese adds an *s* to plural nouns, has regular and irregular verbs, auxiliary and modal verbs, active and passive forms, and past, present, and future tenses. There are perfect verb forms, although the present perfect has a much more limited application in Portuguese, and informal BP does not have perfect progressive tenses. Portuguese is inflected in much the same way as French, Italian and Spanish, which means that word order can be somewhat freer than in English.

Questions and negatives; auxiliaries

In Portuguese, question forms are marked by intonation, and not by changes of word order, in all tenses:
> *You know John?*
> *He is married?*

The negative form in Portuguese is marked by placing the word não before the main or auxiliary verb, independent of tense:

He no would like it.

The double negative is used in Portuguese:

He doesn't know nothing.
He doesn't know if it isn't the right place.

There is no equivalent of the auxiliary *do*. Short answers to questions, for example, are formed by repeating the verb of the question:

'*Do you like dancing?*'   *'*Yes, I like.*'

Time, tense, and aspect

A. PAST TIME

Portuguese has simple past, present perfect, and past perfect tense forms.

The present perfect, in particular, covers many semantic areas quite different to its English equivalent.

1. As in English, Portuguese uses the present perfect for recent actions and events:

   The weather has been terrible (lately).
   I haven't seen him.

2. But where *already* can be added, the verb *to be* is used with a participle:

   I am (already) finished the exercise.

3. Where *ever* can be added, the simple past is used:

   Did you (ever) go to London? (for *Have you (ever) been to London?*)

4. To express the idea of duration, the simple present is used with Ha (= *It is*):

   It is years since I don't see him.

5. The presence of an adverbial referring to an unfinished time-span has no relevance in Portuguese:

   I didn't visit my mother this week.

6. There is no present perfect progressive in spoken Portuguese. The present simple or present progressive are used in most equivalent situations:

   She is living in Manchester since 1981.
   I am here since five o'clock.

B. PRESENT TIME

BP has two forms commonly used, which are syntactically equivalent to the present simple and present progressive in English. Ele percebe (= *he understands*), and ele está trabalhando (= *he is working*), the latter being formed with the verb **estar** and the present participle. Problems arise, however, with verbs which take this construction in Portuguese, but not in English, e.g. **ela não esta entendendo** (**she is not understanding*).

EP forms its present tense with **estar a** and the infinitive with stative and active verbs, e.g. **está a cortar a relva** (= *he is cutting the grass*) and **está a perceber** (= *he understands*). Thus the structural differentiation in English is new and causes many problems.

Modal verbs

Where English would use *can*, Portuguese uses only the verb:
> **He swims.* (for *He can swim.*)

In Portuguese the infinitive form is used after all modals:
> **He must to do it now.*

The passive voice

There are few problems in using the passive, which functions in a very similar way in Portuguese and English.

The causative uses of *have*, *get*, and *make* are expressed using simpler, active verbs:
> *He told someone to paint his house.* (for *He had/got his house painted.*)

Non-finite forms

There is no equivalent in Portuguese for the substantival use of the *-ing* form (gerund):
> **She stopped to look in the shop window* (for *She stopped looking . . .*) *and continued hurry home.*

The passive infinitive is often used where English would use a gerund:
> **I object to be called mean.*

Word order

1. The verb follows the question word in indirect speech in Portuguese:
> **I wonder where is your office.*
> **I asked who was her friend.*

There are also problems with the use of auxiliary verbs in indirect speech:
> **Please tell me what did he say.*
> **She couldn't explain where he does work.*

2. Adverbs usually separate a verb from its object:
> *I like very much Samba.*
> *He wanted a lot to go to England.*
3. Adverbial phrases of time or place can be placed between the verb and its object:
> *I visited on Sunday afternoon her in her house.*
4. The declarative word order is used in exclamations with como (= *how*):
> *How he is clever!*
5. Personal pronouns may be placed before, after, or between elements of the verb:
> *He me explained the theory.*
> *I asked what to do to him.* (for *I asked him what to do.*)
6. There is no equivalent in Portuguese for the 'cleft sentence' (*It was John who gave me the present.*). A relative pronoun is used:
> *Who gave me the present was John.*

Articles

In Portuguese, nouns must be accompanied by an article, and the definite article is used with the following.
— Nouns used in a general sense:
> *The bees produce the honey.*
> *The life is difficult.*
— Proper nouns:
> *The Paulo is a friend of the Maria's parents.*
— Names of meals:
> *He didn't eat at the breakfast, the lunch, or at the dinner.*
— The adverbs of time *next* and *last*:
> *I hope to meet her the next Sunday.*
> *I saw him the last weekend.*
— Words for 'institutions' used in the general sense, where English prefers a possessive pronoun or no article:
> *He went to the church, then to the club to have the lunch; later he went to the hospital and finally to the bed.*

Some nouns in Portuguese take an indefinite article and the plural *s*, while their English equivalents do not:
> *I asked him for an advice and he gave me many informations about furnitures.*

Adjectives and adverbs

Adjectives normally follow the noun in Portuguese:
> *That is a book very exciting.*
> *What a city marvellous!*

Pronouns

1. Both BP and EP regularly suppress the direct object pronoun (*him, her, them*, etc.):

   *I've seen (for *I've seen him, her* or *them*, according to context)
2. Speakers of EP extend the use of the double object:

   *Explain me why.

   *Repeat me the words of the song.
3. In Portuguese there is a single possessive pronoun for *his* and *her*, which agrees in gender with the thing possessed. When carried over into English, this can cause problems:

   *He is very fond of her wife and his brother.
4. In Portuguese the second and third persons have the same form (**seu, sua, seus, suas**) (= *your*):

   *She likes your brother very much. (for *She likes her brother very much.*)
5. BP, however, unlike EP, does have an alternative form **dele** (= *his*) and **dela** (= *her*), e.g. **a casa dele** (= *his house*).
6. *One*, used as a pronoun, has no equivalent in Portuguese. It is normally expressed by **a gente** (lit. *the people*), meaning *we* or *you* in English:

   *The people have to admit ... (for *One has to admit ...*)

Prepositions and particles

There are a far greater number of prepositions in English, which is therefore more precise in its definitions of time, location and movement. Problems occur when a Portuguese preposition has more than one English equivalent.

1. **Até** is used for both time (= *until*) and distance (= *as far as*):

   *He walked until the station.
2. **Durante** can mean *during, throughout*, or *for*:

   *I lived in London during three years.
3. **Para** means *for, to*, and *at*:

   *She bought a present to her sister.

   *He is travelling for Edinburgh next week.

   *They gave a lot of importance for their possessions.

   *He was looking for the pretty girl. (for *looking at*)
4. **Para** is also used with an infinitive meaning *in order to*:

   *John travelled for to spend his holidays at the coast.
5. **Em** means *in* (for time), and also *at* and *on*:

   *She always comes home in Christmas.

   *It's nice to go to the beach in a hot day.

6. No(a), the preposition of place (= *in* or *on*), also means *at*:
   *He's in the beach.
   *I'll meet you in the cinema. (for *at*)
   *They're sitting on the table. (for *at*)
7. There is no equivalent for the preposition *into*, as with verbs such as *go, transform, change*, etc.
8. Many verbs in Portuguese take the preposition de (= *of*):
   *They like of the food here.

Subordinate clauses

CONJUNCTIONS

Portuguese has the same word for *why* and *because*:
   *He didn't come why he felt tired.
Portuguese has the same word for *as* and *like*:
   *He looks as he is tired.

CONDITIONALS

Although in formal Portuguese grammar the three subjunctive tenses are structurally equivalent to the tenses used in the three types of conditional sentence in English, because of the influence of modern spoken BP, the present and simple past are used with the first and second types of condition:
   *If I see him, I tell him.
   *If I went to London, I visited the British Museum.
   *If I were you, I went there at once.

Other problem areas

1. *There + to be*: The verbs há and tem (the grammatical and colloquial equivalents in BP of *to have*) are used to express *there is/are*, etc. (EP speakers use only há here, which has different tense forms, but does not differentiate number.)
   *There are/were a man from Scotland next door.
   *Had lots of people at yesterday's match.
   *Has wonderful beaches in Rio.
2. The impersonal subject *it* does not exist in Portuguese:
   *In Brazil, when is the summer, is sunny.
3. There are no equivalents for *any* or the *an* in *another*:
   *That does not make difference.
   *We visited him in other town.
4. In Portuguese, *all* is used for singular and plural nouns, and there is no equivalent for *each* or *every*, even in compounds, such as *everything*:

> **We went to see him all day. (for *every day*)*
> **He is successful in all that he does.*

5. There is only one question tag in Portuguese, namely **não é?** (= *isn't it?*), which is used indiscriminately in English:
> **They want to go at seven o'clock, isn't it?*

6. The verbs *come* and *go* have a slightly different semantic relationship in Portuguese. *Go* may be used to refer to direction from speaker to listener:
> *'Are you coming here, or not?' *'Of course I'm going, right now.'*

Similar errors are made with *bring, fetch, give,* and *take*:
> **Bring this book to John. He's next door.*

7. The verb **ficar** is very widely used in Portuguese. It can mean *to stay,* but can also refer to a change of state of a person, e.g. *to become, to turn, to grow, to remain*:
> **He stayed furious as he waited so long for them. (for *he became furious* ...)*

8. The verb *to tell* in Portuguese is used with the equivalent of the preposition *to,* and need not be followed by a pronoun:
> **They told to us what happened.*

Vocabulary

Because Portuguese is a European language, EP and BP speakers find reading academic or scientific prose much less hazardous than understanding colloquial spoken English. However, these similarities can often lead to misinterpretations of compound noun word order: *administrative activities* can be understood as **administration of activities*; *few moving parts* can be understood as **little movement of the parts.*

In comparing EP and BP, one finds that phrasal and prepositional verbs are much rarer in EP. Typically EP has **esperar** and BP **esperar por** for the English *to wait for*. About half the lexicon in current use in EP is not in current use in BP. Any picture dictionary that gave both English and Portuguese words would have to be brought out in separate editions for EP and BP, when dealing with the everyday words of the spoken language.

False friends

A very small selection:

discuss	(**discutir** = *to argue,* or *debate*)
disgust	(**desgaste** = *worn-out*)
distracted	(**distraido** = *absent-minded*)

educated	(educado = *well-mannered*)
expect	(esperar = also *to hope* and *to wait*)
expert	(esperto = *intelligent, sly*)
familiar	(familiar = *decent, respectable*)
intend	(entender = *to understand*)
library	(livraria = *bookshop*)
licence	(licença = *leave of absence*)
local	(local = *place*)
lunch	(lanche = *snack*)
parents	(parentes = *relatives*)
presently	(presentemente = *at the moment*)
pretend	(pretender = *to intend, to plan*)
private	(privada = *toilet, privy*)
real	(real = *royal; sure; that exists*)
use	(usar = *to wear*)

Areas of particular lexical confusion

1. Where there is one Portuguese word for two or more words in English:

rob – steal	*lend – borrow*
hear – listen	*see – look*
speak – talk	*across – through*
amuse – enjoy	*say – tell*
still – yet	*like – as*
as well – too	*after – afterwards – then*
then – therefore	

2. Where two words with the same form can have different meanings, e.g. *like*:
   > *He like his father. (for *He's like his father.*)

3. *Be careful* and *take care* use the same verb stem and the equivalent of the prepositions *with* or *of* in Portuguese:
   > *Take care of him. or *Be careful with him.* (for *Beware of him.*)

4. The Portuguese word obrigado (= *thank you*, or *much obliged*) is used to express polite refusal. When the words *thank you* in English are given the same stress and intonation pattern, (i.e. the *you* is stressed, as the penultimate syllable is stressed in obrigado) it gives an impression of impoliteness and sarcasm.

5. There are no equivalents for *just* and *ever* when used as intensifiers, e.g. *Have you ever ... ?*; *He lives just nearby.*

6. The following words should be avoided as they are similar to vulgar words in Portuguese: *fodder, put a ... , deer.*

Miscellaneous

Forms of address

In Brazil, people are usually addressed and referred to by their first names together with a title:

Miss Jane; *Mr John*; *Dr Henry*, etc.

Paralinguistic elements

Brazilians tend to speak at a lower pitch than the British, but at a higher volume. The strong syllable stress and lack of markers for question forms (polite requests are made in the imperative) often create the (erroneous) impression that the Brazilian is rude, irritated or angry.

Non-verbal communication

Normally accepted non-emotional eye contact is lengthier among Brazilians than with most Europeans. Proximity between participants in neutral face-to-face interaction is closer, and physical touch is more widely acceptable. These conventions can be misinterpreted.

A sample of written Portuguese with a word for word translation

Ao acordar   disse para a   mulher:
On to wake-up said to   the woman [wife]:

Escuta, minha filha: hoje é dia de pagar a
Listen, my   girl: today is day of to pay the

prestação da televisão, vem aí o   sujeito com a
instalment of television, comes here the subject with the

conta, na certa.   Mas acontece que ontem   eu não
bill,   on certain. But happened that yesterday I no

trouxe dinheiro da   cidade, estou a nenhum.
brought money from the city, am   on none [slang].

– Explique isso ao   homem – respondeu a   mulher.
– Explain this to the man   – answered   the woman.

– Não gosto dessas   coisas. Dá um ar de vigarice,
– No like   of these [plural] things. Gives an air of swindling,

gosto de cumprir rigorosamente as minhas   obrigações.
like of to fulfil rigorously   the my [plural] obligations.

(*O Homen Nu* by Fernando Sabino)

Acknowledgement

The author would like to thank Tanya Shepherd who helped at all stages of the preparation of this chapter, and Barbara Skolimowski and Chester Graham who provided suggestions for the European Portuguese examples.

Greek speakers

Sophia C. Papaefthymiou-Lytra

Distribution

GREECE, CYPRUS.

Introduction

Greek is an Indo-European language, but is not very closely related to any other languages in this family. Greek and English phonology, syntax and vocabulary are very different in nature, and English is therefore not an easy language for Greeks.

Phonology

General

The Greek and English phonological systems are broadly dissimilar. Greek speakers have serious difficulty in perceiving and/or pronouncing correctly many English sounds. The English vowel system, which makes far more distinctions than the Greek system, causes particular problems. Stress and intonation patterns are also very different.

Among the features of Greek which give rise to a 'Greek accent' in English are:
- Less energetic articulation than English, with lax vowels, less lip-rounding and less spreading.
- Lack of contrast between weak and strong forms in natural speech as compared with English.
- Lack of elisions and assimilations; this makes Greeks' L2 speech sound slow, drawling and rather formal.
- Tendency to speak at a higher volume and on a more uniform pitch level than most English people do.
- Different stress and intonation patterns.

Vowels

Shaded phonemes have equivalents or near equivalents in Greek and should therefore be perceived without serious difficulty. Greek learners

iː	ɪ	e	æ	eɪ	aɪ	ɔɪ
ɑː	ɒ	ɔː	ʊ	aʊ	əʊ	ɪə
uː	ʌ	ɜː	ə	eə	ʊə	aɪə / aʊə

do, however, have difficulty in articulating these sounds correctly. Diphthongs tend to be articulated as two separate vowels pronounced in two syllables.

Unshaded vowels may cause more problems:

1. /ɪ/ is usually replaced by /iː/, causing pairs like *sit* and *seat* to sound similar.
2. /æ/ is usually replaced by /e/ or the Greek sound /a/. So for example *bad* may be pronounced /bad/ instead of /bæd/.
3. /ʌ/ is usually replaced by the Greek sound /a/. So for example *hut* may be pronounced /hat/. And pairs like *hat* and *hut*, *lack* and *luck* may be confused.
4. /ɜː/ and /ə/ are usually replaced by /e/. So for example *bird* may be pronounced /berd/ instead of /bɜːd/.
5. Long vowels /ɑː/, /ɔː/ and /uː/ are usually shortened and replaced by their nearest Greek equivalents /a/, /o/ and /u/ respectively.
6. /ɒ/ and /əʊ/, like /ɔː/, are usually replaced by the Greek vowel /o/. So for example *off* is pronounced /of/ instead of /ɒf/; *home* is pronounced /hom/ instead of /həʊm/. There is serious confusion between English words which are distinguished by these vowels, such as *nought/not/note*, *cord/cod/code*, *walk/woke*, *hop/hope*, *want/won't*.
7. /ə/ in diphthongs such as /eə/, /ɪə/, /ʊə/ is usually replaced by the nearest Greek sound /a/. So for example *sure* is pronounced /ʃuar/ instead of /ʃuə/.

Consonants

p	b	f	v	θ	ð	t	d
s	z	ʃ	ʒ	tʃ	dʒ	k	g
m	n	ŋ	l	r	j	w	h

Most of the shaded phonemes approximate only roughly to English sounds; although learners will perceive them easily, accurate articulation may prove difficult.

Unshaded phonemes, as well as some shaded phonemes in certain environments, may cause problems.

1. /ʃ/ is often pronounced as /s/. So for example *shirt* may be pronounced 'cert'.
2. /ʒ/ is often replaced by /z/. *Garage*, for example, may be pronounced 'garaz'.
3. /s/ before /m/ becomes /z/. *Small*, for example, may be pronounced 'zmall'.
4. /b/ is usually preceded by /m/, and /d/ by /n/. So *able* may be pronounced /eɪmbl/, and *idle* /aɪndl/.
5. /ŋ/ is usually pronounced as /ŋg/. For instance, *sing* is pronounced /sɪŋg/ instead of /sɪŋ/.
6. /h/ is non-existent in Greek. It is often replaced by the rougher Greek sound /x/ (like *ch* in *loch*). For instance, *him* may be pronounced /xim/.
7. /r/ is pronounced wherever it is written, leading to mistakes in British English where *r* follows a consonant or comes at the end of a word (as in *card, hair*).
8. /tʃ/ and /dʒ/ may be pronounced like /ʃ/ and /ʒ/ respectively, leading to confusion, for instance, between *choose* and *shoes*, or *ledger* and *leisure*.

Influence of spelling on pronunciation

Greek spelling is phonetic: there is almost a one-to-one correspondence between sound and graphic symbol, with few ambiguities. As a result Greek learners, especially beginners, have a tendency to pronounce all the letters that are written, often giving them their Greek values:

/kʊld/ for *could*
/me/ for *me*

Stress

There are some similarities in patterns of word and sentence stress in Greek and English. Note, however, that there is usually one stress – primary stress – in Greek words, as against English where syllables may carry primary, secondary or weak stress. As a result, Greek learners tend to put only primary stress on English words:

substitution pronounced /sʌbstɪ'tju:ʃn/ instead of /ˌsʌbstɪ'tju:ʃn/

Rhythm

1. Greek has syllable-timed rhythm. Each syllable has approximately the same duration, regardless of the number or position of stresses in an utterance. In English, however, the stressed syllables in an utterance are evenly spaced regardless of the number of unstressed syllables that intervene. Greek learners tend to transfer their syllable-timed rhythm into English.
2. Beginners may also have difficulty in perceiving and articulating secondary and weak stresses in sentence patterns. Very often they unnecessarily stress 'weak forms' such as *but, were, than*, etc., pronouncing them as they are spelt; and they may find it difficult to hear such words when they are pronounced at natural speed.

Intonation

Intonation patterns differ in Greek and English. Some features of Greek intonation carried over into English (such as the use of a high fall where English would use a low rise) may make speakers sound abrupt and impolite. Special practice is needed in the intonation of polite requests, suggestions, commands, offers, question tags and interruptions, and in the use of stereotyped responses such as *Mm, Yes, I see, That's right* with appropriate intonation patterns.

Orthography and punctuation

Spelling

1. Most Greek alphabetic symbols are different from the English letters, and beginners need practice in handwriting.
2. Beginners may tend to use one letter consistently for each sound, as in Greek, leading to mistakes like:
     *sistem   *Inglish   *kut   *taim (for *time*)
     *trein
3. Students may leave out silent letters:
     *bot (for *bought*)   *tok (for *talk*)

Punctuation

Punctuation conventions are roughly the same in Greek and English. The main differences are:
— Semicolons, question marks and quotation marks are written differently in Greek, which can cause problems for beginners:
     Greek semicolon

> Greek question mark ;
> Greek quotation marks « »

Grammar

General

The Greek and English grammatical systems are similar in many ways. There are the same 'part of speech' categories, and Greek has, for instance, singular and plural noun forms, definite and indefinite articles, regular and irregular verbs, active and passive verb forms and past, present and future tenses. There are perfect verb forms but the present perfect, for instance, is not used in Greek in the same way as in English. Greek has no equivalent of the English present progressive or present perfect progressive forms (though the meanings expressed by these forms can be expressed in Greek in other ways). There is however a rough equivalent of the past progressive form.

Greek is a highly inflected language – articles, adjectives, nouns and pronouns have four cases, for example. Word order is consequently freer in Greek than in English, where the grammatical function of a word is mostly indicated by its position in the sentence. Greek learners have difficulty with word order in English.

Greek has grammatical gender – nouns and pronouns are masculine, feminine or neuter – but there is no systematic relationship between gender and meaning. Adjectives always conform to the gender of the noun to which they refer. The lack of any systematic inflectional system in English leads Greek learners to feel that English has 'no grammar'. However, word order and the choice and structure of verb forms present them with serious problems.

Questions and negatives; auxiliaries

1. Perfect tenses are formed with εχω (= *have*) + past participle, as in English, but the auxiliary *do* has no equivalent in Greek. Inversion is not used to make questions in Greek, and spoken interrogatives differ from affirmatives by intonation only:
    * *You come back from school early?*
    * *What she doing?*
    * *How many brothers she has?*
2. Negatives are formed by putting δεν (= *not*) before the verb:
    * *They not come to see us.*
    * *What he not did yesterday?*
    * *He did not agreed with me.*

Time, tense and aspect

A. PAST TIME

1. Greek has past perfect, past, present perfect and imperfective tenses. There are no progressive forms, though in many cases the imperfective tense functions like the past progressive in English.
2. The present and past perfect are not much used in Greek; the past tense is commonly used instead:
   He did not yet return the money he borrowed.
   *I am sorry I am late. *Did you wait long?*
   I just finished reading that book when he telephoned me.
3. To say how long a present state has been going on, Greek may use a present tense:
   I know them since I was a kid.
   He works at that office for many years.
4. Overgeneralisation of the English present perfect may lead to mistakes like:
   She has married long ago.
5. In reported speech, Greek tends to use the present tense where English uses a past tense after a past reporting verb:
   He did not say if she is at home.

B. PRESENT TIME

1. The third person singular ending is often omitted:
   He go to school every day.
2. The lack of a Greek present progressive causes mistakes:
   'Where's Tom?' *'He waters the flowers.'
   Look! Those two boys fight!
   I am eating breakfast after I get dressed.
3. In the present progressive the verb *to be* is often omitted:
   They running fast.
   whereas it is sometimes unnecessarily added in the simple present:
   We are walk to school every day.
   She is speaks English.

C. FUTURE TIME

1. Greek and English future tenses are constructed quite differently, and Greek has no equivalent of the *going to* future. Mistakes are common:
   I will to see them tomorrow.
   They will fighting each other soon.
2. Greek learners may use a simple present tense instead of a future:
   I go to school tomorrow.

3. On the other hand, problems are caused by the English use of present tenses in subordinate clauses referring to the future:
    > *I shall meet him before the train will go.*

Conditionals and 'unreal' forms

1. Greek conditional sentences may have the same verbal structure in both clauses. This is transferred into beginners' English:
    > *If you will come early I will meet you at the station.*
    > *If she would have money she would buy you a present.*
2. Past conditionals are difficult:
    > *If you had fixed the car we had went for a ride.*
3. Learners have difficulty with structures after *I wish* and *If only*:
    > *Mary is gone. If only she is here.*

The passive voice

The use of the passive is roughly equivalent in Greek and English. A common mistake is to omit *-ed* from the past participle:
> *The sky is cover with clouds.*
> *The girl was punish.*

Modal verbs

The English modals *can, may, must, have to, ought to*, etc. do not have one-to-one equivalents in Greek. Inevitably there are differences which lead to mistakes. Some common problems:
1. Beginners tend to use '*to* + infinitive' after modals:
    > *I cannot to come to see you.*
2. Past modal structures cause problems. Instead of making the modal verb past, students may use a present modal with a past main verb:
    > *I can saw it.*
    > *We must made it.*
3. The differences between *can* and *may, must* and *have to*, etc. take time to master.

Non-finite forms

In Greek there is no equivalent of the substantival use of the *-ing* form (gerund), which creates problems for beginners:
> *Before to reach home she ate all the sweets.*
> *I must stop to smoke. It's bad for my health.*
> *Please excuse me to be so late.*
> *She is busy to write a book.*

Infinitive of purpose

1. In English, a negative infinitive of purpose is generally introduced by *in order* or *so as*. This may be dropped:
   > *He crossed the road not to see me.*
2. Learners may replace the infinitive after *to* by a past tense form (a transfer from Greek):
   > *I called George to told him the good news.*

Complementation

1. Greek learners often use the *to* infinitive in cases where English uses the infinitive without *to*:
   > *She saw them to come down the stairs.*
   > *I made her to eat her food.*
2. An infinitive complement may be replaced by a main clause:
   > *I want the book I read it.*

The causative structure

This does not exist in Greek. Learners tend to replace it with the equivalent Greek form which, in English, results in confusion about who does what for whom:
> *She had cut her hair at the hairdresser's.*

Word order

Word order is free in Greek, which causes learners to make frequent mistakes.
1. A sentence may begin with the direct or indirect object or complement:
   > *The book to Mary I gave on Sunday.*
   > *Wonderful is the house you bought.*
2. An adverb may separate a verb inappropriately from its subject, object or complement:
   > *I last night did my homework.*
   > *The teacher speaks always English in class.*
   > *The girls will be tomorrow very happy.*
3. Adverbs of place may precede adverbs of time in cases where English would use the reverse order:
   > *They will be tomorrow here.*
4. *Ago* may precede an expression of time:
   > *I sent the letter ago three days.*

Articles

1. In Greek, the definite article may accompany nouns which are used in a general sense. This leads students to make mistakes with uncountable and plural nouns in English:
      The gold is very expensive.
      The honesty is a great virtue.
      We must buy the bread for two days.
      The dogs are faithful animals.
2. Definite articles are used with proper names in Greek:
      She speaks the French very well.
      The Peter is my friend.
3. In Greek, a definite article is not used before a subject complement:
      She is doctor.
      He is porter.
      Alex is good footballer.

Gender

Nouns in Greek are masculine, feminine or neuter. Pronouns are used accordingly. Beginners often write or say such things as:
      My bag is in my room. *Can you bring her here?*
      The river is long. *He runs all the way to the sea.*

Number

1. Some uncountable English nouns have countable Greek equivalents:
      Can you give any informations?
      I left all my luggages at the station.
      I have many works to do.
2. Irregular plurals are also a problem:
      There are a lot of sheeps in the meadow.

Adjectives and adverbs

1. In Greek, adjectives are inflected. They conform to the number (as well as the gender and case) of the noun to which they refer. This is a potential source of mistakes for beginners:
      There are four greens chairs in the room.
2. In modern Greek, adverbs of manner often resemble adjective forms:
      All cars must move slow on this part of the road.
3. Very often, adjectives such as *friendly, lovely* are treated as adverbs:
      She looked at him friendly.

Pronouns and determiners

1. Greek learners tend to use *who* in relative clauses which modify nouns that are masculine or feminine in Greek, and *which* in relative clauses which modify nouns that are neuter in Greek, regardless of meaning:
      The river who runs across the valley is shallow.
2. Personal pronouns are often omitted:
      Is very hot today.
      When he saw his father, sat down.
      He saw him play football and we admired.
      I want to tell me the truth.
3. On the other hand, noun subjects or fronted objects may be picked up by redundant pronouns:
      My brother he came to see me.
      Mary who sits next to me she is sixteen years old.
      The car I bought it yesterday.
4. In relative clauses and after infinitive complements, object pronouns may be inserted unnecessarily:
      That is the man whom I saw him.
      That is not fit to drink it.
5. Other pronouns and determiners easily confused by learners are:
      some – any
      anything – nothing
      my – mine
      mine – myself
      this – that
      other – another
      much – many
      little – few
      few – a few

Conjunctions

That tends to replace *what* in indirect questions:
      I do not remember that you said to me.

Comparisons

1. Beginners often transfer Greek forms of comparison into English:
      Mary is taller from Jane.
      Mary is more tall than Jane.
2. The same Greek word may correspond to both *as* and *like* in certain contexts. This is a potential source of confusion:
      She looks as her mother.

Prepositions

1. Greek learners have considerable difficulty with English prepositions. Most Greek prepositions have rough English equivalents, but problems arise in cases (too many to list) where an English expression does not require the 'same' preposition as is used in Greek:
    > *She was dressed with a white suit.*
    > *He walked in the bridge.*
    > *Dinner was prepared from my mother.*
2. Problems also occur when a preposition in Greek has more than one English equivalent, depending on the context. Some examples are:
    - μεχρι = *to* or *till*:
        > *We walked till the river and back.*
        > *They shall stay with us to next month.*
    - σε = *in* or *into*:
        > *He was into the room all day.*
        > *She came in the room and took a book.*
    - σε = *on*, *at* or *in* to refer to time:
        > *We have a meeting at Saturday.*
        > *I usually get up on five o'clock.*
    - απο = *from*, *of*, *in* or *since*:
        > *She has been here from Sunday.*
        > *He is deprived from his fortune.*
3. Prepositions may be incorrectly omitted after certain verbs, a transfer from Greek:
    > *He came and asked my pencil.*
    > *He explained me the matter.*
    > *They knocked the door and then left.*
4. In other cases, inappropriate prepositions are added after verbs, again under the influence of Greek:
    > *They left to England last Friday.*
    > *He entered in the room noiselessly.*
    > *I returned to home at four.*

Phrasal verbs

In Greek there are no lexical items equivalent to English phrasal verbs. Greek learners have difficulty with them and tend to avoid using them, preferring to use one-word verbs, which can make a rather formal and bookish impression:

> *He returned on Sunday.* (for *He came back on Sunday.*)
> *I telephoned him.* (for *I rang him up.*)
> *They visited us last weekend.* (for *They called on us last weekend.*)
> *We had no petrol.* (for *We ran out of petrol.*)

Vocabulary

1. Some English words are loans from Greek (e.g. *telephone, television, crisis, phenomenon, catastrophe*). Others have been borrowed into Greek (e.g. *jeans, pullover, bowling, goal, picnic*). This facilitates learning in certain cases, but there are also some 'false friends' which may lead to confusion. For example, Greeks may misuse:

   agenda to mean *notebook*
   agnostic to mean *foreign, stranger*
   air to mean *wind*
   antenna to mean *aerial*
   barracks to mean *small shop*
   cabaret to mean *bar*
   ephemera to mean *newspaper*
   fortune to mean *storm*
   idiotic to mean *private*
   pneumatic to mean *witty, intellectual*
   sympathise to mean *like*
   trapeze to mean *table*

2. Learners may have difficulty in cases where one Greek word has several English equivalents, or where a related pair of English words does not have an exact counterpart in Greek. Examples:

   beat/hit/strike/knock
   woman/wife
   house/home
   finger/toe
   office/desk/study
   made of / made from
   know/learn/study
   interesting/interested
   remember/remind
   make/do
   room/space
   Excuse me / Sorry
   very/much
   too/very
   say/tell
   annoy/bother

3. Phonetically motivated confusions are also a possible source of mistakes:

   man/men
   woman/women
   prize/price

A sample of written Greek with a transliteration and a word for word translation

Ητανε τόσο δυνατό το χτύπημα, που δε βρήκε   το κουράγιο να
Itane toso dinato to htipima, pou de vrike   to kourajio na
Was so   hard   the blow,   that not found-he the courage to

διαμαρτυρηθεί. Τι   νόημα   θα είχε μια οποιαδήποτε διαμαρτυρία;
diamartirithi. Ti   noima   tha ihe mia opiadipote diamartiria;
protest.   What meaning will had a   whatever   protest?

Ο   άλλος,   τη δουλειά του: έκοβε συνέχεια   το κρέας.
O   allos,   ti doulia tou: ekove sinehia   to kreas.
The other, [continued] the work   his: cut-he continuously the meat.

Και το μαχαίρι, αυτό το κατακαίνουριο, το αστραφτερό μαχαίρι,
Ke to maheri, afto to katakenourjio, to astraftero maheri,
And the knife, that the all-new,   the shiny   knife,

είχε γίνει   αγνώριστο.   Παγωμένο λίπος είχε κολλήσει στην
ihe jini   agnoristo.   Pagomeno lipos ihe kolisi   stin
had become unrecognisable. Cold   fat   had stuck   on the

λεπίδα του και στην   λαβή,   μικρά κομμάτια κρέας.
lepida tou ke stin   lavi,   mikra komatia kreas.
blade its and on the handle, small pieces [of] meat [genitive].

Δεν μπορούσε να δει καλά, το φως   λιγοστό, η καρδιά
Den borouse na di kala, to fos   ligosto, i kardia
Not could-he to see well, the light [was] little, the heart

του   αναστατωμένη. Πώς να το πιάσει στα χέρια του το
tou   anastatomeni. Pos na to pjiasi sta herjia tou to
his [was] upset.   How to it take-he in hands his the

εξαθλιωμένο μαχαίρι, πώς να το καρφώσει στο στήθος   της...
exathliomeno maheri, pos na to karfosi sto stithos tis...
miserable   knife,   how to it nail-he in the breast her...

(From *The Passport* by A. Samarakis)

Russian speakers

Bruce Monk and Alexander Burak

Distribution

THE UNION OF SOVIET SOCIALIST REPUBLICS.

Introduction

Russian belongs to the Slavonic branch of the Indo-European family of languages. It is very closely related to Byelorussian and Ukrainian; other related Slav languages are Polish, Czech, Slovak, Bulgarian and Serbo-Croatian. At the present time about 280 million people in the USSR speak Russian. This includes about 140 million people living in the Russian Federation proper, who speak it as their first language; the majority of the rest of the people in the Soviet Union use Russian (which they learn at school) alongside their native language. At a conservative estimate, 20 million people in other countries are learning Russian.

Phonology

General

The two major features which distinguish the Russian sound system from English are the absence of the short–long vowel differentiation and the absence of diphthongs. English rhythm and stress patterns are also hard for Russian speakers to master.

Vowels

iː	ɪ	e	æ	eɪ	aɪ	ɔɪ
ɑː	ɒ	ɔː	ʊ	aʊ	əʊ	ɪə
uː	ʌ	ɜː	ə	eə	ʊə	aɪə / aʊə

Shaded phonemes have equivalents or near equivalents in Russian, in the form either of individual sounds or of combinations of sounds, and are perceived and articulated without serious difficulty, although some confusions may still arise. Unshaded phonemes may cause problems. For detailed comments, see below.

1. The sound/ɜ:/, which is not found in Russian, causes Russian learners of English the greatest difficulty. They often substitute the Russian sounds /ə/ or /o/. Particularly troublesome are words beginning with *w*, such as *work, worm, worth, worse*.
2. /ɑ:/ tends to be replaced by the more frontal Russian /a/.
3. /æ/ tends to be replaced by a more close sound resembling /e/, leading to confusion between pairs such as *sat* and *set*.
4. The second parts of diphthongs, and the second and third parts of triphthongs, tend to be 'overpronounced'.
5. The sound /ɔ:/ is often replaced by the more frontal Russian /o/ or diphthongised into /oʊ/.
6. In general, long vowels are pronounced insufficiently 'tense', which makes them sound similar to short vowels. *Field* may be pronounced like *filled*, for example, or *seat* like *sit*.
7. The difference in length of long vowels depending on the final consonant (compare *pea, peal* and *peat*) is also difficult to master.
8. /ɒ/ is often pronounced as a 'glide', almost like /wɒ/.

Consonants

p	b	f	v	θ	ð	t	d
s	z	ʃ	ʒ	tʃ	dʒ	k	g
m	n	ŋ	l	r	j	w	h

Shaded phonemes have equivalents or near equivalents in Russian, and are perceived and articulated without serious difficulty, although some confusions may still arise. Unshaded phonemes may cause problems. For detailed comments, see below.

Of the 24 English consonants, the sounds /θ/, /ð/, /ŋ/ and /w/, which are not found in Russian, prove very difficult.
1. /θ/ and /ð/ present major difficulties and are often replaced by /s/ and /z/. Typical mistakes: *sin* for *thin*; *useful* for *youthful*; *zen* for *then*.

2. /ŋ/ is usually replaced by the Russian /g/ or dental /n/. So for example *wing* might be pronounced *wig* or *win*.
3. The difference between /w/ and /v/ is often not clearly felt, leading to confusion between, for instance, *while* and *vile*, or *west* and *vest*.
4. The sounds /t/, d/, /l/, /n/ are often made with the tongue touching the top teeth, which gives them a foreign sound.
5. Final voiced consonants such as /b/, /d/, /g/ are devoiced in Russian, causing learners to pronounce such words as *lab*, *said* and *pig*, for instance, as *lap*, *set* and *pick*.
6. The sounds /p/, /k/ and /t/ are not aspirated in Russian, which causes learners to mispronounce them at the beginnings of words in English. So for example *pit* may sound rather like *bit*, *come* like *gum*, or *tart* like *dart*.
7. Learners may replace /h/ (which does not occur in Russian) by a rougher sound (like *ch* in Scottish *loch*).
8. Russian learners tend to 'soften' (palatalise) many consonants before front vowels such as /iː/, /ɪ/, /e/, /eɪ/, /ɪə/.
9. 'Dark' /l/ (as in *full* or *hill*) often replaces 'clear' /l/ (as in *light* or *fly*).

Consonant clusters

1. The combinations /θ/ + /s/, /ð/ + /z/ or /s/ + /θ/ (as in *months*, *clothes*, *sixth*) are generally a major challenge even for quite good learners, who often tend to substitute /ts/ and /z/.
2. Problems also arise in pronouncing /t/, /d/, /s/, /z/ followed by /j/, as in *situation*, *education*, *Did you see the film?*.
3. In combinations of two plosive consonants (such as /p/, /b/, /t/, /d/, /k/, /g/), the first plosive is usually exploded in Russian. This is carried over into the pronunciation of such words as *picked* and *begged*.
4. Russians tend to insert the neutral sound /ə/ in the combinations /tl/, /dl/, /tn/, /dn/, leading to pronunciations such as *little* /lɪtəl/, *button* /bʌtən/, *modern* /mɒdən/.
5. The initial clusters /tw/, /tr/, /pr/, /dr/, /br/ are also difficult, leading to problems with words like *twice*, *tree*, *price*, *dry*, *bright*.

Rhythm and stress

Russian stress patterns are as variable as English ones. However, Russian speakers tend to lose secondary stresses in long English words:

competition /kəmpɪˈtɪʃn/
intelligibility /ɪntələdʒəˈbɪlɪtɪ/
compatibility /kəmpətəˈbɪlɪtɪ/
imperturbability /ɪmpətəbəˈbɪlɪtɪ/

Sentence rhythm presents problems. For instance, learners often pronounce the slower 'strong' forms of words like *as, than, can, must* or *have*, instead of the faster 'weak' forms.

Intonation

1. Russians tend to finish their *yes/no* questions with a fall, which can make them sound impolite:
   > *Did you tell her?*
2. Tag questions may also cause confusion:
   > *It's a nice day, isn't it?*
3. Alternative questions are often ended with a rise:
   > *Do you want coffee or tea?*

Juncture

1. Junctures involving two plosives cause trouble (see above); the two consonants tend to be pronounced separately: *used to, brought to mind, caused delay.*
2. Some other assimilations are difficult for Russian learners to make – for instance, between /s/, /z/ or /t/ and /j/: *as-you know, in case-you, look at-you.*

Influence of spelling on pronunciation

Great difficulties often arise for Russians, as for other learners, from the lack of correspondence between what is written and the way that it is pronounced. Typical mistakes:
> *knife* /knaɪf/
> *comb* /kɒmb/
> *break* /briːk/
> *risen* /raɪzn/
> *singing* /sɪŋgɪŋg/
> *mind* /mɪnd/
> *through* /θraʊ/

Writing and punctuation

Writing

Although Russians use the Cyrillic alphabet, many English letters are similar in form to Russian letters: *a, o, e, n, m, p, c, k, g, x, y, M, T, H* (certain of them are pronounced differently). Russians may experience difficulties in writing *s, r, i, h, l, f, b, t, j, I, G, Q, N,* which do not occur in Cyrillic.

Punctuation

Russian punctuation marks and the rules for their use are basically similar to English. The main difference is in the use of commas to mark off nearly all subordinate clauses in Russian. This leads by transference to the following typical mistakes:

> *I think, that you're right.*
> *I don't know, which book to choose.*

Inverted commas are usually written like this: „ "

Grammar

General

The grammatical systems of Russian and English are fundamentally different. English is an analytic language, in which grammatical meaning is largely expressed through the use of additional words and by changes in word order. Russian, on the other hand, is a synthetic language, in which the majority of grammatical forms are created through changes in the structure of words, by means of a developed system of prefixes, suffixes and endings. Russian therefore has fairly complicated systems of noun and adjective declension and verb conjugation, but the Russian sentence has no real fixed word order.

The Russian and English verb systems express rather different kinds of meaning. Russian has only three tenses: past, present and future. The verb system is mainly built on the notion of aspect. This is the contrast between actions which are uncompleted (imperfective aspect) and those which are completed (perfective aspect). These contrasts are indicated through affixation. Perfect and progressive forms of verbs, as understood in English, do not exist. But for a few exceptions there are no auxiliary verbs like *do*, *have* or *will*.

'Phrasal' verbs do not exist in Russian, and the use of prepositions in general is far more limited than in English.

Nouns have grammatical gender.

There are no articles in Russian.

With such basic differences between the grammatical systems of the two languages, it is inevitable that there will be certain major difficulties for a Russian learning English.

Questions and negatives; auxiliaries

1. The auxiliaries *do*, *have*, *will* and *be* have no equivalent in Russian. Typical mistakes in statements, questions and responses are:
    > *I no like it.*

> **When you went there?*
> **How you like it?*
> *'Do you like football?' *'Yes, I like.'*

2. *Do* is often confused with *does*, and vice versa:
   > **She don't go there now.*
3. Negative question forms may be wrongly used:
   > **Don't you know when he's coming?* (for *Do you know ... ?*)
4. Not having auxiliary verbs, Russian lacks question tags. Russians have great difficulty in forming these, and thus tend to employ them far less frequently than native speakers:
   > **You like her, doesn't it?*
   > **Is many people in room, isn't it?*
5. Russians have difficulty with the use of *Let* in imperatives:
   > **Let they to do it.*
   > **Let's no do it.*

Time, tense and aspect

A. PAST TIME

Russian has no perfect or past progressive tenses. One simple past form is used to refer to actions and events denoted by perfect and progressive tenses in English. Typical mistakes are:

> **I read when he came.*
> **He said he already finished work.*
> **I still didn't read the book.*

B. PRESENT TIME

1. In Russian there are no present perfect or present progressive forms. There is only one simple present tense. This leads to mistakes like:
   > **Where you go now?*
   > **Your article is typed now. Please wait.*
   > **How long you be/are here?* (for *... have you been here?*)
2. In reported speech Russian speakers often do not observe the sequence of tenses rule:
   > **He said he live here long.*
   > **I knew she (is) in town.*
3. In the third person singular Russians often omit the suffix *-(e)s*:
   > **He very like her.* (for *He likes her very much.*)

C. FUTURE TIME

1. A simple present tense may be used to refer to the future:
   > **I promise I come tomorrow.*

2. There are no future perfect or future progressive tenses:
> *She will work here ten years by Thursday.*
> *This time tomorrow I will lie on beach.*
3. In subordinate clauses of time the future tense is used in Russian where a present tense would be used in English:
> *When she will ring you, tell her I called.*
4. Mistakes are made with sequence of tenses:
> *He said he will come.*
> *They said they will do the work by five.*

The passive voice

The passive voice in general causes considerable difficulties for Russian speakers, in particular the progressive and perfect forms:
> *The house is (was) building.*
> *The book has finished.*

Conditionals

1. In subordinate clauses of condition the future tense is used in Russian where the present tense would be used in English:
> *If she will come, I will tell her.*
2. More problems inevitably arise in complex conditional forms:
> *If he would (to) helped me I had did it.*

Modal verbs

1. The system of modal verbs in Russian is simpler than in English, and interference may therefore cause mistakes such as the following. The constructions *to be able to* and *to have to* need particular care:
> *I can to do it.*
> *You must to work hard.*
> *Yesterday he must go home early.*
> *I shall must phone him.*
> *She will can do it.*
2. Answers to questions with *may* and *must* cause difficulty:
> 'May I come in?' *'No, you may not/can't.' (meaning 'Please don't.')
> 'Must I do it now?' * 'No, you must not.' (meaning 'No, you needn't.')

Be

1. The link verb *to be* is not used as a rule in the present tense in Russian:
> *He good boy.*
> *They no nice.*

2. In all tenses Russians experience difficulties in the use of the *there is* construction:
>*Is table in room?*
>*Many tables are in room, yes?*
>*No people are here.*

3. When the *there is* construction has been learnt, Russians may still confuse it with the use of *it* as a dummy subject:
>*There is hot here, is it?*
>*It is very good stereo in room.*

Non-finite forms

1. The more complex *-ing* forms and infinitives (progressive, perfect and passive) cause difficulty:
>*I heard of his appointing headmaster.* (for *I heard that he had been appointed headmaster.*)
>*I like inviting by my friends.* (for *I like being invited by my friends.*)
>*She is said to live here long.*
>*She is believed to write a new book now.*

2. The 'infinitive of purpose' is difficult to master:
>*I came for to help you.*
>*I came that to help you.*

Verbal complements

1. 'Object + infinitive' structures cause problems for Russian learners:
>*I could see that he goes across the street.*
>*I could see him to go across the street.*
>*They made me to do it.*

2. Causative structures are also difficult:
>*I've just made it.* (for *I've just had it made.*)
>*I must go to cut my hair.* (for *I've got to have my hair cut.*)

Word order

1. Since Russian expresses basic grammatical relations through inflections, word order in the Russian sentence is rather more free than in English. Moreover, it is common for Russian sentences to begin with adverbial phrases of time and place. This leads to certain typical mistakes:
>*Yesterday on table lied my book.*

2. Clause-final prepositions cause problems of style:
>*At what are you looking?*
>*With whom were you talking when I saw you?*

Articles

1. There are no articles in Russian. One of the initial problems for Russian learners is learning how to use articles in general:
    New house is building near cinema that is near us.
    Have you mother?
2. Then there is the problem of choice between the definite and indefinite articles:
    Have you the mother?
    Is she a woman you told us about?

Gender

Nouns in Russian are masculine, feminine or neuter. This leads learners to make mistakes with personal pronouns:
    'Where's book?' *'She is on the table.'*
    'Where's my umbrella?' *'He is here.'*

Number

1. The category of number exists in Russian. However, the countable/ uncountable distinction causes problems, since some English uncountable nouns have countable Russian equivalents:
    Her hairs are nice.
    I have one news.
    I'll give you a good advice.
    'Where are money?' 'They on table.'
2. Special care is also needed with *this/these, that/those*:
    I don't like this songs.

Adjectives and adverbs

1. The greatest difficulties arise for Russians in the formation of the degrees of comparison of the adjectives *bad, good* and *far*:
    He is more bad than I think.
    They are badder.
    It is farer.
2. Adjectives can also be confused with adverbs, for instance, *bad/badly, good/well*:
    He speak English very good.
    She play piano bad.

Relative pronouns

1. Usually *who* is confused with *which*:
    The people which came I no like.

and *that* with *what*:
> *I know what he work here.*
2. Mistakes occur in the use of *who, which* and *whose*:
> *Who of you knows English?*
> *Who book is this?*

Prepositions and adverb particles

1. The use of prepositions often results in errors:
> *I listen music very much.*
> *I want to explain you this.*
> *I can do it for three o'clock.* (for ... by three o'clock.)
> *He work on factory.*
2. Russian has no equivalent of English adverb particles; nor does postposition exist. Phrasal verbs therefore cause difficulties, especially when the particle follows the object, as in *I'll look it up.*

Vocabulary

False friends

There are quite a few words that sound similar in English and Russian, but that have different meanings or shades of meaning. Examples are:
> aktual'niy (= *current*, not *actual*)
> simpatichniy (= *nice, friendly*, not *sympathetic*)
> biskvit (= *sponge cake*, not *biscuit*)
> manifestatsiya (= *demonstration*, not *manifestation*)
> salyut (= *firework display*, not *salute*)

A more complete list of Russian–English false friends is to be found in the dictionary edited by V. V. Akulenko (*Lozhnykh druzey perevodchika*, Moscow, 1969).

Other confusions

A number of widely-used words have different rules of usage from their closest Russian equivalents.
1. *yet/already*:
> *Have you seen her already?* (meaning *Have you seen her yet?*)
2. *so/such*:
> *He is so clever man.*
> *It is such difficult.*

So is often wrongly used to start sentences:
> *Well, so, let's begin our lesson.*

3. *say/tell*:
> * *He said me that you are ill.*
> * *The story says about the war.*

4. *Please*:
> '*Here's a book for you.*' '*Thank you.*' * '*Please.*'

or:
> '*Give me the book, please.*' * '*Please.*' (instead of *Here you are.*)

5. Rather over-used are *to my mind, you see, you know, well*:
> '*What time does the film start?*' * '*To my mind at seven.*'
> * *Well, you see, I often go to the Crimea, you know.*

6. Failure to use 'conversational fillers' in other situations may make Russians sound impolite when, in fact, they do not mean to be so:
> '*Would you like to go there?*' * '*No, I wouldn't.*' (for '*Well, I'm afraid I can't because ...*')
> * *Tell me please how to go to the station.* (for *Excuse me, could you tell me the way to the station, please?*)

7. The expression *of course* tends to be inadvertently misused:
> '*Can you speak French?*' * '*Yes, of course.*' (for '*Yes, I can.*')

Attitudes to language learning

All children in Soviet secondary schools learn a foreign language. The majority of pupils learn English (British English being taken as the norm), although French, German, Spanish and a number of other languages are also taught. Communicative methods are widely used, with an emphasis on oral skills. Soviet citizens are therefore reasonably experienced language learners, and they are generally enthusiastic about language lessons, no doubt because they live in a multicultural and multilingual society.

Samples of written Russian with transliterations and word for word translations

Знаете	ли	вы,	что ...
Znayete	li	vi,	shto ...
Know	[interrogative]	you,	that ...

взяв	обыкновенный	русский	алфавит	и	расположив
vzyav	obiknovenniy	russkiy	alfavit	i	raspolozhiv
taking	ordinary	Russian	alphabet	and	disposing

буквы	определённым	образом,	можно	получить	не
bukvi	opredelyonnim	obrazom,	mozhno	poluchit'	ne
letters	definite	way,	can	receive	not

127

только кандидатскую, но и   докторскую диссертацию.
tol'ko kandidatskuyu, no i   doktorskuyu dissertatsiyu.
only   candidate,   but and doctor   dissertation.

(From *Literaturnaya Gazeta*, 7 November 1984)

После десятимесячного   отсутствия вернулся к жене и
Posle desyatimesyachnovo*   otsutstviya vernulsa k zhene i
After ten month   absence   returned to wife and

детям   участник прошлогодних соревнований по
detyam uchastnik proshlogodnikh sorevnovaniy po
children participant last year   competitions on

спортивному ориентированию Ф. Уклоняев. Сразу же
sportivnomu orientirovaniyu F. Uklonyaev. Srazu zhe
sport   orienteering   F. Uklonyaev. At once

после возвращения   спортсмен начал усиленную
posle vozvrashcheniya sportsmen nachal usilennuyu
after return   sportsman began strengthened

подготовку к новым весенним стартам.
podgotovku k   novim vesennim startam.
preparation for new   spring   starts.

*this ending is written -ogo but pronounced -ovo.

(From *Literaturnaya Gazeta*, 12 June 1985)

Farsi speakers

Lili and Martin Wilson

Distribution

IRAN, Afghanistan, Pakistan, Southern Russia, India.

Introduction

Farsi is an Indo-European language, which has been greatly influenced by Arabic. The alphabet of modern Farsi consists of 32 characters written in Arabic script, from right to left. Before the conquest of Persia by desert Arabs in the seventh century, the Farsi alphabet contained 24 characters, written in Pahlavi script. Pahlavi was the language of the Sassanians, who were conquered by the invading Arabs. After the conquest, a great deal of Arabic vocabulary entered Farsi, and Arabic script was adopted, bringing in eight extra characters, to produce the modern alphabet of 32 letters.

Although Farsi is an Indo-European language, Farsi speakers have great difficulty with reading and writing English, especially during the early stages of learning, because they are not familiar with the Latin script.

Phonology

General

The Farsi and English phonological systems differ in their range of sounds, as well as in their stress and intonation patterns. Farsi has only eleven vowels and diphthongs to 32 consonants, while English has 22 vowels and diphthongs to 24 consonants. Farsi speakers, therefore, have great difficulty in perceiving and articulating the full range of English vowels and diphthongs. In addition, there are five English consonant phonemes that do not have near equivalents in Farsi.

Vowels

Shaded phonemes have equivalents or near equivalents in Farsi, and should therefore be perceived and articulated without great difficulty,

i:	I	e	æ	eɪ	aɪ	ɔɪ
ɑ:	ɒ	ɔ:	ʊ	aʊ	əʊ	ɪə
u:	ʌ	ɜ:	ə	eə	ʊə	aɪə / aʊə

although some confusions may still arise. Unshaded phonemes may cause problems. For detailed comments, see below.

The most common pure vowel errors are likely to be:
1. /ɪ/ is often pronounced as /i:/: *sheep* for *ship*.
2. /ʌ/ is often pronounced as /ɑ:/: *cart* for *cut*.
3. /æ/ is often pronounced rather like /e/: *bed* for *bad*.
4. /ʊ/ is often pronounced as /u:/: *fool* for *full*.
5. /ə/ is often pronounced as a stressed vowel related to its orthographic form.
6. /ɔ:/ is often pronounced rather like /ɒ/: *cot* for *caught*.
7. /ɜ:/ often becomes /e/ + /r/.

With diphthongs the problems are accentuated and in particular the following are likely to cause special difficulty:
8. /aʊ/ is often pronounced as a sound approaching /ɑ:/.
9. /eə/ is often pronounced as /e/ + /r/.
10. /əʊ/ is often pronounced closer to /ɒ/.
11. /ʊə/ is often pronounced as /u:/.

Consonants

p	b	f	v	θ	ð	t	d
s	z	ʃ	ʒ	tʃ	dʒ	k	g
m	n	ŋ	l	r	j	w	h

Shaded phonemes have equivalents or near equivalents in Farsi, and should therefore be perceived and articulated without great difficulty, although some confusions may still arise. Unshaded phonemes may cause problems. For detailed comments, see below.

1. /ð/ and /θ/ tend to be confused or pronounced as /t/: *ten* for *then*; *tinker* for *thinker*.

2. /ŋ/ may be pronounced as two separate phonemes, /n/ and /g/, because of its orthographic form.
3. /w/ and /v/. Although /v/ has a near equivalent in Farsi, the two phonemes tend to be confused.
4. /r/ has a weak roll or tap in Farsi and many learners have great difficulty in producing the English /r/.
5. /l/ exists in Farsi as the 'clear' /l/, (as in *leaf*), but there is no equivalent of the 'dark' /l/, (as in *feel*) and learners are likely to have problems with this.

Consonant clusters

Consonant clusters do not occur within single syllables in Farsi, and Farsi speakers therefore tend to add a short vowel, either before or in the middle of the various English clusters. Examples of initial two-segment clusters that cause difficulty are *bl, fl, pr, pl, gr, gl, thr, thw, sp, st*. These produce pronunciations such as:

> '*perice*' for *price*
> '*pelace*' for *place*
> '*geround*' for *ground*
> '*gelue*' for *glue*

The intrusive vowel in initial position usually approximates to the phoneme /e/, so *start* becomes '*estart*'.

With initial three-segment clusters the problem becomes greater. Clusters such as:

> *spl, spr, str, skr*

in initial positions produce pronunciations such as:

> '*esperay*' for *spray*
> '*esteraight*' for *straight*
> '*escceam*' for *scream*

The intrusive /e/ is particularly common before clusters beginning with /s/.

Final consonant clusters are also likely to cause problems, with learners again inserting an /e/:

> '*promptes*' for *prompts*
> '*warmeth*' for *warmth*

Influence of spelling on pronunciation

As there are no direct links between Farsi and English spelling (apart from a few transliterations, such as *stainless steel*), the Farsi speaker has no previously known orthographic patterns which are likely to interfere with his or her pronunciation. However, spelling in Farsi is more or less phonetic, except for the omission of short vowels, and, as a result, Farsi speakers tend to associate particular letters with particular sounds. This can cause problems with reading aloud and when words are initially encountered only in their written form. In particular Farsi speakers are likely to have difficulty with phonemes which have a wide variety of orthographic representations. For example, the phoneme /iː/, which has a single orthographic form in Farsi, can have any of the following forms in English: *ee, e, ea, ie, ei, ey, i* or *ay* (as in *quay*).

It is particularly hard for Farsi speakers to recognise that the post-vocalic *r* is not a consonant, but usually indicates a lengthening of the vowel sound.

Stress

In Farsi stress generally falls on the final syllable of a word. This is true for nouns, compound nouns, adjectives, pronouns, most adverbials and prepositions. The only exceptions to this are some adverbials and most conjunctions, where the stress falls on the initial syllable.

Verbs are only slightly more complex. For affirmative forms the stress falls on the final syllable, but with non-verbal parts of compounds and certain prefixes, including the negative na, it falls on the initial syllable.

Word stress is thus highly predictable in Farsi, and learners have great difficulty in mastering the unpredictable stress patterns of English. Particular problems occur when stress alters meaning, as in 'content and con'tent. Weak forms also cause considerable problems. There is no equivalent to a weak form in Farsi, and vowels in unstressed syllables lose neither quantity nor quality. So learners are likely to retain the full value of, say, the *a* in *can*, even in an unstressed position. It follows that they will also have problems in perceiving weak forms in speech.

Intonation

Farsi sentences are divided into a series of tone groups, with each tone group containing one prominent stressed syllable, which makes a change of tone direction. Intonation groups can be divided into 'suspensive' (with more to follow), and 'final'. The basic final patterns are similar to those used in English, with a fall typical for a completed statement, a rise for a yes/no question, and a fall when an interrogative word is used. For the suspensive tone groups there is a rise to high tone on the stressed syllable, which is maintained to the end of the tone group. When carried over into English, some of these intonation patterns can produce an unusual high-pitched 'whining' effect, which is disconcerting.

In general, Farsi-speaking students do not have major difficulties with the main intonation patterns, although some of the more unusual patterns which imply distinctive attitudes and meanings present difficulties. Some students will tend to adopt a chanting tone when reading aloud, with a lack of clearly indicated stress, and little or no tonal variation.

Juncture

Farsi speakers often have similar problems with English juncture to those they have with consonant clusters. Therefore, with a word boundary such as in *next street*, they will often insert an extra /e/ in several places, and produce something like '*neksetestreet*'.

In Farsi, words are spoken without assimilation (phonetic change) in juncture, so whenever this occurs in English, such as in *Would you* ... /wʊdʒə/ it is likely to cause difficulties.

Orthography and punctuation

As stated above, Farsi is written in Arabic script, and this is completely different from the Latin script of English. It is written from right to left with the letters joining each other according to very definite rules. Farsi speakers usually have to learn a completely new alphabet, and new way of writing. There are no capital letters in Farsi and their use in English is difficult for them to master. Farsi numbers, although Arabic, are different from those used in English. They are, however, written from left to right, and normally cause relatively few problems. Beginners are also likely to have problems in the following areas:
1. Letters with mirror images, e.g. *b* and *d*, *p* and *q*.
2. Combinations of letters that could be confused if read from right to left, e.g. *tow* and *two*; *pot* and *top*; *form* and *from*.

Spelling is invariably phonetic in Farsi, and students' written English tends to be the same. Owing to the American influence in Iran in the past, American spellings such as *color* are often used.

Punctuation

Until the late nineteenth century punctuation was little used in Farsi, but during the last hundred years a system similar to that used in English has been adopted. There is, however, a greater degree of freedom in the use of commas and question marks. The question mark is reversed, ؟, and the comma is inverted, ' . Full stops are used approximately as in English, but quotation marks are rarely used, and then not in a set way.

Generally there is less punctuation in Farsi, and Farsi writers have a tendency to join sentences together more with conjunctions, such as *and* and *but*.

Paragraphing is a recent introduction, and indentation or separation usually only occurs in newspapers.

Grammar

General

As Farsi is an Indo-European language, it is similar in many ways to English. There are, however, some areas that are very different from English, and these can cause considerable interference for the Farsi speaker learning English.

Word order in Farsi is fundamentally different from English and will cause difficulties in the early stages. Adjectives always follow their nouns; verbs are usually placed at the end of a sentence:

> *Yesterday girl beautiful (I) saw.

Questions and negatives; auxiliaries

The auxiliary *do* does not occur in Farsi, and questions are either signalled by a special question word, **aya**, or by use of a rising tone. Farsi speakers tend to overuse questions marked only by intonation and, more seriously, omit to use the auxiliary when it is obligatory:

> *When you came to England?

In Farsi it is possible to make a statement negative merely by prefixing the verb with **na**. *Not* may well be treated in the same way:

> *She not eat supper. (for *She didn't eat supper.*)

In Farsi the auxiliary *to be* is sometimes added to nouns as a suffix instead of being used in its full form. Therefore Farsi speakers will sometimes omit it:

> *She (a) teacher. (for *She is a teacher.*)

Although *to have* exists as an auxiliary verb in Farsi, it is used only with a tense equivalent to the English present progressive. Its use with the English present and past perfect tenses in statements, questions, and negatives, may cause some difficulties.

Special confusion – Chera (= *Why not?*)

Farsi has a special positive response to a negative question. This can loosely be translated as *Why not?*. When this is used in English, as it often is by Farsi speakers, it sounds unintentionally aggressive:

> 'Aren't you going out tonight?' 'Why not?'

It is necessary to explain that this is not an acceptable reply in English.

Question tags

Farsi does not possess a wide range of question tags. **Chera** (= *Why not?*) has to serve in nearly all situations. Students, therefore, find all question tags extremely complex:

*He said he was coming. Why not? (for *He said he was coming, didn't he?*)
*You said you would pay me back. Did you? (for *You said you would pay me back, didn't you?*)

Time, tense, and aspect

A. PAST TIME

1. *Simple past and present perfect*
In Farsi, both the past tense and the present perfect are formed with the auxiliary *to be*, but the distinction in their use and meaning is not as clear as in English. In the everyday spoken language, they are interchangeable. Farsi speakers will, therefore, find it extremely difficult to use these tenses appropriately:
*I saw 'Star Wars'. (for *I have seen 'Star Wars'.*)
*I lost my purse. Did you see it?

2. *Past progressive*
The past progressive tense in Farsi is formed with the auxiliary *to have*, and this leads Farsi speakers to produce:
*When I arrived, he had eating his dinner. (for *When I arrived, he was eating his dinner.*)

3. *Reported speech*
In Farsi, reported speech is usually reported directly in the form in which it was spoken. Punctuation marks are usually omitted, and the conventions of inverted comma use are not strictly observed. For the learner, the rigid conventions governing the reporting of speech in English seem complex and unnecessary:
*He said I am feeling ill.

B. PRESENT AND FUTURE TENSES

The present tense in Farsi is used for a variety of functions:
1. It is used in the same way as the English present progressive for an action taking place in the present, as in English: *He is reading a book.*
2. It is used for an action beginning in the past and still continuing, as in English: *I have lived here for two years.*
3. It is used for the future, as in English: *He will come / He is coming next week.*
This leads students writing in English to confuse the uses of the present progressive, present perfect, and to some extent future tenses.

There is also a present progressive tense formed with the auxiliary *to have*, which has a meaning similar to the English present progressive; and a general present, which is similar to the English simple present, used to describe general truths.

Farsi speakers

There is a future tense in Farsi, formed with the auxiliary *to want*, but it is very formal. It is never used in speech, and only rarely in modern writing.

Modal verbs

Modal verbs do not work in the same way in Farsi as in English. Both the modal and the main verb can be inflected, and this may be carried over into English:

*I can I go.

But it is in the use of modals that the real difficulty arises. Farsi does not have the range of meanings expressed through modals in English, and most of them will cause problems.

Non-finite forms

There is no gerund form in Farsi, and the infinitive form is normally used in its place. Where distinctions are required in English, Farsi speakers find difficulties:

*Instead to fight, they danced.

Articles

There are no articles in Farsi, but suffixes are added to nouns to indicate whether they are definite or indefinite. The system is quite different from English, and Farsi speakers have considerable difficulty with all areas of article use:

*His father is milkman.
*Most of the people think ... (for Most people think ...)
*I go to the school every day. (for I go to school every day.)

Adjectives and adverbs

Adjectives and adverbs are usually used in similar ways in Farsi, and there is no set pattern for forming adverbs from adjectives. For example, there is no equivalent word for *dangerously*, and it is necessary to use a phrase, *in a dangerous manner*. Therefore Farsi speakers are likely to confuse adjectives and adverbs in both form and meaning, and to use rather awkward adverbial phrases.

Comparatives and superlatives are always formed by the addition of a suffix, so the two different methods used in English are very confusing to the Farsi speaker.

Gender and number

In Farsi there is no *he/she* gender distinction, a single pronoun being used for both. This is likely to lead to regular errors, even at quite advanced levels:

> *My mother is a dentist. He works in London.*

Plurals in general do not cause Farsi speakers major difficulties. However, nouns in Farsi do not take plural forms when used with numerical determiners, and this is likely to carry over into English:

> *I saw two man.*
> *Ten ship sailed by.*

Prepositions and particles

In Farsi, prepositions are frequently used after verbs, but often they are different from the ones used in English. Farsi speakers tend to translate these prepositions directly into English:

> *He climbed from the hill.* (for *He climbed up the hill.*)
> *She threw it out from the window.*
> *I travelled there with car.*

Phrasal verbs

Phrasal verbs do not exist in Farsi, and learners find them very confusing. Two difficulties arise:

1. The difficulty of accepting that the addition of a particle can totally change the meaning of a verb, as in *to **run up** a skirt* (i.e. to make one quickly).
2. The fact that the verb can be separated from the particle by its object. One error that frequently results is the omission of the particle:

> *He cannot do his buttons.*
> *I put my coat.*

Subordinate clauses

A. RELATIVE

There is only one relative pronoun in Farsi and this is used for humans, animals, and inanimate objects. It is also used when the pronoun is the subject or the object of the verb, or when a possessive is required. The selection of the correct relative pronoun in English, therefore, causes serious problems:

> *The man which was here ...*

137

The object pronoun in a relative clause, which is omitted in English, is included in Farsi:
> *The book, which I gave it to you ...*
> *The man, which I saw him ...*

B. CONDITIONAL

Conditional sentences of the probable or improbable types are formed essentially in the same way in Farsi and English. The expression of the impossible (or Type 3) conditional is different. In Farsi the past tense is used in the main clause, giving rise to:
> *If I had finished my work, I went to the party.* (for *If I had finished my work, I would have gone to the party.*)

C. CONCESSION

In Farsi the equivalents of *although* and *but* can be used in the same sentence. This use is frequently carried over into English:
> *Although he had no money, but he travelled to America.*

Conjunctions

In Farsi, conjunctions are used much more frequently than in English, particularly at the beginning of sentences. As the most commonly used conjunction in Farsi is *and*, Farsi speakers have a tendency to join many clauses together, usually with a string of *and*s.

Vocabulary

Although Farsi is an Indo-European language, there are few similarities between English and Farsi vocabulary, with only a few non-technical words such as *mother* and *brother* showing their Indo-European origins. On the other hand, Farsi contains many vocabulary items with Arabic roots. The rest nearly all have old Persian or Pahlavi roots.

The advent of modern technology has brought in a number of scientific and technical words of European origin, such as *radio, television* and *helicopter*, many of which are used internationally; but their pronunciation has been adapted to Farsi patterns, and they produce their own kind of interference problems, e.g. *radio* pronounced '*rahdioo*'. In the 1970s there was an attempt by the government to 'Persianise' all foreign technical words, but this met with only limited success.

Acquiring English vocabulary is therefore much more difficult for a Farsi speaker than, for example, a European student, and teachers must not expect the same rate of progress from them. It cannot be assumed either that a large amount of vocabulary will be absorbed naturally through reading and everyday conversation. In particular, Farsi speakers tend to learn large quantities of vocabulary by heart through lists of synonyms, but find it very hard to understand or use more than a fraction of this language accurately.

Compound nouns in Farsi are frequently translated directly into English, giving rise to strange errors:

> *a work house* (kar khane – lit. *house of work*) = *a factory*
> *a book house* (ketab khane – lit. *house of books*) = *a library*

False friends

As there are few similarities between Farsi and English vocabulary, there are relatively few false friends. Most problems arise from words which have been borrowed by Farsi and now have different meanings. When such words are encountered in English, they are assumed to have the same meaning as in Farsi:

> lastiki = *tyre*, not *elastic*
> machin = *car*, not *machine*
> nylon = *plastic string bag*, not *nylon*
> chips = *crisps*, (as in US English), not *chips*

Culture

Almost all Farsi-speaking learners of English will be Iranian. The Iranian education system is extremely formal, and lays great emphasis on the value of formal literary language and rote learning. As a result, it is often difficult to persuade Iranian students to accept the importance of mastering colloquial spoken forms, and writing in a simple, clear style.

Most Iranians expect the teacher to be an authoritarian figure, and they expect to be tested or 'quizzed' regularly. Examinations are taken very seriously, and the grades and marked scripts are scrutinised with great care. Iranians, however, are natural communicators, as Iranian society places great importance on the art of conversation. Introduced with care, communicative methodology will lead to a rapid development of oral/aural skills, particularly with young learners. Nevertheless, it is prudent to take advantage of Iranian students' willingness to accept formal methods, such as choral drilling, rote learning, and regular testing, rather than to insist on a totally communicative approach. An exclusively communicative methodology may cause students to feel that a course is not really 'serious'.

Study in Britain may involve a cultural as well as an educational shock. For many Iranians familiar with pre-revolutionary middle-class Tehran, the British social scene will probably offer relatively few surprises. However, students from less affluent backgrounds, and those from the 'provinces' may well find the changes very difficult to accept. Most students adapt well to life in Britain, but some develop an anti-Western attitude, often with a strong vein of Islamic Fundamentalism. Those reacting against Western mores may show a degree of hostility to much of the recently-produced EFL materials, with their emphasis on boy/girl relationships, fashion, and the consumption of alcoholic beverages. Hostility to women teachers is unlikely, though the changing nature of today's Iranian society may well cause it to increase in the future.

A sample of written Farsi

صدها سال است که مردم فارسی زبان همواره دیوان حافظ را میخوانند
وازآن لذت میبرند واین یادگار گرانبهای لسان الغیب را عزیز و
گرامی میشمارند .

"حافظ" دارای این خصلت دوگانه است که در عین جالب
بودن برای محققین و نویسندگان و ادبا و دانشمندان سخت
مورد علاقه و دلبستگی همگان هم هست .

A direct transliteration

Sadhaa saal ast ke mardome Farsizabaan hamvare divane Haafez raa mikhaanand va az aan lezzat mibarand va in iaadegaare geraanbagh-aaie lesanalgheib raa aziz va geraami mishemaarand.

"Haafez" daaraaie in kheslate dogaaneh ast ke dar eine g'daaleb boudan baraaie mohagheghin va nevisandegaan va odabaa va daaneshmandaan, sakht morede alaagheh va delbastegie hamegaan ham hast.

A word for word translation

Hundreds year is that people Farsi language always anthology Hafez read and from that enjoy and this heritage precious fortune teller love and respect.

"Hafez" has this virtue dual is that at the same time interesting being for students of literature and writers and literary critics and scientists, hard liked and loved general public also.

An idiomatic translation

For hundreds of years Farsi speakers have enjoyed reading Hafez's anthology, respecting and loving the precious heritage of this 'fortune teller' ...
Hafez has the dual virtue that at the same time as he is interesting to students of literature, writers, literary critics and scientists, he is popular with and loved by the general public.
(From *Hafez's Anthology* by A. Bagheri)

Handwriting difficulties: a sample written by a Farsi-speaking student

The English language is the most important language in the world, and every one who want to find a better job must learning English. I want to learning English because I want to stady in English language University. Now I cant speak and understand English but when I wand to go to university I must know the meaning of the English word that I must use in university

Arabic speakers

Bernard Smith

Distribution

ALGERIA, EGYPT, IRAQ, JORDAN, KUWAIT, LEBANON, LIBYA
MOROCCO, NORTH YEMEN, OMAN, QATAR, SAUDI ARABIA,
SOUTH YEMEN, SUDAN, SYRIA, TUNISIA, UNITED ARAB
EMIRATES.
Many native speakers also in Chad, Mauretania and
some other African countries not listed here, and in Israel.

In addition, Arabic being the language of the Koran, the holy word of
Islam, all Muslims of whatever nationality are to some extent familiar
with Arabic, can recite extensively in it, and are therefore influenced by it
in their ideas of how language works. Islam has a significant following in
Senegal, Mali, Niger, Chad, Nigeria, Guinea, Somali Republic, Kenya,
Iran, Afghanistan, Pakistan, Malaysia, Indonesia, Brunei, the Philip-
pines, southern Soviet Union, northern China, Mongolia and Turkey:
approximately 400,000,000 people in all.

Introduction

Arabic is a Semitic language, having a grammatical system similar to
Assyrian, Aramaic, Hebrew and Ethiopian. There is a universal 'pan-
Arabic' language, which is taught in schools, used by the mass media in
all Arab countries, and for all communications of an official nature.
Within each country, often in quite small areas, a wide variety of
colloquial dialects have developed, differing one from another not only in
pronunciation, but also in common lexical items and, to some extent, in
structure. The differences from country to country are more marked
than, say, differences between UK, US and Australian English.

Because the Arabic writing system is also totally different from that of
Indo-European languages, Arabic speakers have far greater difficulties in
learning English than most Europeans.

Phonology

General

The Arabic and English phonological systems are very different, not only
in the range of sounds used, but in the emphasis placed on vowels and

consonants in expressing meaning. While English has 22 vowels and diphthongs to 24 consonants, Arabic has only eight vowels and diphthongs to 32 consonants.

Short vowels in Arabic have very little significance: they are almost allophonic. They are not even written in the script. It is the consonants and long vowels which give meaning. Arabic speakers tend, therefore, to gloss over and confuse short vowel sounds, while unduly emphasising consonants, avoiding elisions and shortened forms.

Among the features of Arabic which give rise to an 'Arabic accent' in English are:
- More energetic articulation than English, with more stressed syllables, but fewer clearly articulated vowels, giving a dull, staccato 'jabber' effect.
- The use of glottal stops before initial vowels, a common feature of Arabic, thus breaking up the natural catenations of English.
- A general reluctance to omit consonants, once the written form is known, e.g. /kleɪmbɪd/ for *climbed*.

Vowels

iː	ɪ	e	æ	eɪ	aɪ	ɔɪ
ɑː	ɒ	ɔː	ʊ	aʊ	əʊ	ɪə
uː	ʌ	ɜː	ə	eə	ʊə	aɪə
						aʊə

Shaded phonemes have equivalents or near equivalents in Arabic and should therefore be perceived and articulated without great difficulty, although some confusions may still arise. Unshaded phonemes may cause problems. For detailed comments, see below.

While virtually all vowels may cause problems, the following are the most common confusions:
1. /ɪ/ and /e/ are often confused: *bit* for *bet*.
2. /ɒ/ and /ɔː/ are often confused: *cot* for *caught*.
3. Diphthongs /eɪ/ and /əʊ/ are usually pronounced rather short, and are confused with /e/ and /ɒ/: *raid* for *red*; *hope* for *hop*.

Consonants

Shaded phonemes have equivalents or near equivalents in Arabic and should therefore be perceived and articulated without great difficulty,

p	b	f	v	θ	ð	t	d
s	z	ʃ	3	tʃ	dʒ	k	g
m	n	ŋ	l	r	j	w	h

although some confusions may still arise. Unshaded phonemes may cause problems. For detailed comments, see below.

1. The glottal stop is a phoneme in Arabic.
2. Arabic has only one letter in the /g/ – /dʒ/ area, which is pronounced as /g/ in some regions, notably Egypt, and as /dʒ/ in others. Arabic speakers tend, therefore, to pronounce an English *g*, and sometimes even a *j*, in all positions according to their local dialects.
3. /tʃ/ as a phoneme is found only in a few dialects, but the sound occurs naturally in all dialects in junctures of /t/ and /ʃ/.
4. There are two approximations to the English *h* in Arabic. The commoner of them is an unvoiced, harsh aspiration; Arabic speakers tend to pronounce an English *h* rather harshly.
5. /r/ is a voiced flap, very unlike the RP /r/. Arabic speakers commonly overpronounce the post-vocalic *r*, as in *car park*.
6. /p/ and /b/ are allophonic and tend to be used rather randomly:
   *I baid ten bence for a bicture of Pig Pen.
7. /v/ and /f/ are allophonic, and are usually both pronounced as /f/.
8. /g/ and /k/ are often confused, especially by those Arabs whose dialects do not include the phoneme /g/.
9. Although /θ/ and /ð/ occur in literary Arabic, most dialects pronounce them as /t/ and /d/ respectively. The same tends to happen in English.
10. The phoneme /ŋ/ is usually pronounced as /n/ or /ng/, or even /nk/.

Consonant clusters

The range of consonant clusters occurring in English is much wider than in Arabic. Initial two-segment clusters not occurring in Arabic include: *pr, pl, gr, gl, thr, thw, sp*. Initial three-segment clusters do not occur in Arabic at all, e.g.: *spr, skr, str, spl*. In all the above cases there is a tendency among Arabic speakers to insert short vowels to 'assist' pronunciation:
   '*perice*' or '*pirice*' for *price*
   '*ispring*' or '*sipring*' for *spring*
The range of final clusters is also much smaller in Arabic. Of the 78

three-segment clusters and fourteen four-segment clusters occurring finally in English, *none* occur in Arabic. Arabic speakers tend again to insert short vowels:

> '*arrangid*' for *arranged*
> '*monthiz*' for *months*
> '*neckist*' for *next*

Teachers will meet innumerable examples of such pronunciations, which also carry over into the spelling of such words in Arab students' written English.

Note: For a detailed comparative analysis of English and Arabic consonant clusters (and much other useful information) see *The Teaching of English to Arab Students* by Raja T. Nasr (Longman, 1963).

Influence of English spelling on pronunciation

While there are no similarities between the Arabic and English writing systems, Arabic spelling within its own system is simple and virtually phonetic. Arabic speakers tend, therefore, to attempt to pronounce English words phonetically. Add to this the reverence for consonants, and you get severe pronunciation problems caused by the influence of the written form:

> '*istobbid*' for *stopped*
> '*forigen*' for *foreign*

Rhythm and stress

Arabic is a stress-timed language, and word stress in particular is predictable and regular. Arabic speakers, therefore, have problems grasping the unpredictable nature of English word stress. The idea that stress can alter meaning, as in *a toy 'factory* and *a 'toy factory*, or *con'vict* (verb) and *'convict* (noun) is completely strange.

Phrase and sentence rhythms are similar in the two languages, and should cause few problems. Primary stresses occur more frequently in Arabic, and unstressed syllables are pronounced more clearly, with neutral vowels, but not 'swallowed' as in English. Arabs reading English aloud will often avoid contracted forms and elisions, and read with a rather heavy staccato rhythm.

Intonation

Intonation patterns in Arabic are similar to those of English in contour and meaning. Questions, suggestions and offers are marked much more frequently by a rising tune than by any structural markers, and this is carried over into English.

When reading aloud, however, as opposed to conversing, the Arabic speaker tends to intone or chant, reducing intonation to a low fall at the ends of phrases and sentences. Speech making, news reading and religious recitation are all quite different in rhythm and intonation from normal informal speech, and Arabic speakers called on to read aloud in front of a group may produce a very unnatural recitation for this reason.

Juncture

As the glottal stop is a common phoneme in Arabic, and few words begin with a vowel, there is a resistance in speaking English to linking a final consonant with a following initial vowel.

Junctures producing consonant clusters will cause problems, as described above under the section 'Consonant clusters'. A juncture such as *next spring* produces a number of extra vowels.

The many instances of phonetic change in English through the juncture of certain phonemes, e.g. /t/ + /j/ as in *what you need* /wɒtʃuː niːd/, or /d/ and /j/ as in *Did you see him?* /dɪdʒə siː hɪm/ are resisted strongly by Arabic speakers, who see any loss or change in consonant pronunciation as a serious threat to communication.

Orthography and punctuation

Arabic orthography is a cursive system, running from right to left. Only consonants and long vowels are written. There is no upper and lower case distinction, nor can the isolated forms of letters normally be juxtaposed to form words.

Arabic speakers must, therefore, learn an entirely new alphabet for English, including a capital letter system; and then master its rather unconventional spelling patterns. All aspects of writing in English cause major problems for Arabic speakers, and they should not be expected to cope with reading or writing at the same level or pace as European students who are at a similar level of proficiency in oral English.

Typical problems are:
- Misreading letters with 'mirror' shapes, e.g. *p* and *q*; *d* and *b*.
- Misreading letters within words by making right to left eye movements, e.g. *form* for *from*; *twon* for *town*. These errors occur in the writing of Arab students, too, of course.
- Malformation of individual letters, owing to insufficient early training, or the development of an idiosyncratic writing system. This is most usually seen with capital letters (often omitted), with the letters *o*, *a*, *t*, *d*, *g*, and the cursive linking of almost any letters. Many adult Arabs continue to print in English rather than attempt cursive script.

The numerals used in Arab countries are different from the 'Arabic' numerals used in Europe, but they *are* written from left to right. Reading and pronouncing numbers is a major problem.

Punctuation

Arabic punctuation is now similar to western style punctuation, though some of the symbols are inverted or reversed, e.g. ؟ for ?, and ، for ، .

The use of full stops and commas is much freer than in English, and it is common to begin each new sentence with *And* or *So*. Connected writing in English tends therefore to contain long, loose sentences, linked by commas and *and*s.

Grammar

General

As Arabic is a Semitic language, its grammatical structure is very different from that of Indo-European languages. There are, therefore, far fewer areas of facilitation, and far greater areas of interference. This must be borne in mind when Arabic speakers are mixed with, say, European students.

The basis of the Arabic language is the three-consonant root. A notion such as *writing*, *cooking*, or *eating* is represented by three consonants in a particular order. All verb forms, nouns, adjectives, participles, etc. are then formed by putting these three-root consonants into fixed vowel patterns, modified sometimes by simple prefixes and suffixes.

Root	/k/ /t/ /b/	(= *writing*)
A person who does this for a living	kattaab	(= *a writer*)
Passive participle	maktoob	(= *written* or *a letter*)
Present tense	yaktubuh	(=*he writes it*)
Root	/g/ /r/ /h/	(= *wounding* or *cutting*)
A person who does this for a living	garraah	(= *a surgeon*)
Passive participle	magrooh	(= *wounded* or *a battle casualty*)
Present tense	yagruhuh	(= *he wounds him*)

There are over 50 patterns, and by no means all forms are found for each root, but this is the structural basis of the language.

It follows that Arabic speakers have great difficulty in grasping the confusing range of patterns for all words in English; that nouns, verbs, and adjectives follow no regular patterns to distinguish one from another, and may, indeed, have the same orthographic form. Such regularities of morphology as English has, particularly in the area of affixes, will be readily grasped by Arabic speakers, e.g. *-ing, -able, un-*, etc.

Word order

In principle the Arabic sentence places the verb first, followed by the subject. This convention is followed more in writing than in speech, especially the better style of writing, and may carry over into English writing:

> *Decided the minister yesterday to visit the school.

Questions and negatives; auxiliaries

The auxiliary *do* has no equivalent in Arabic. Where no specific question word is used, a question is marked only by its rising intonation:

> *When you went to London?
> *You like coffee?

Note that the Arabic for *where?* is **wayn?**, which is inevitably confused with *when?*

Negatives are formed by putting a particle (**laa** or **maa**) before the verb:

> *He not play football.

Be

There is no verb *to be* in Arabic in the present tense. The copula (*am, is, are*) is not expressed. It is, therefore, commonly omitted in English by Arabic speakers, particularly in present progressive verb forms:

> *He teacher.
> *The boy tall.
> *He going to school.

Pronouns

Arabic verb forms incorporate the personal pronouns, subject and object, as prefixes and suffixes. It is common to have them repeated in English as part of the verb:

> *John he works there.

Time, tense, and aspect

A. PAST TIME

1. Arabic has a past, or perfect tense, which signifies an action completed at the time of speaking. There is, therefore, in colloquial Arabic, no distinction drawn between what in English would be a simple past or a present perfect verb:
   > *I lost my camera. Did you see it?*
2. There is a past perfect tense, used approximately as in English, formed by the past tense of the verb *to be*, followed by the past tense verb (*he was he ate = he had eaten*):
   > *He was eat his dinner when I came. (for He had eaten his dinner when I came.)*
3. There is a past progressive tense formed by the past tense of the verb *to be* followed by the present tense verb (*he was he eats = he was eating*):
   > *He was eat his dinner when I came. (for He was eating his dinner when I came.)*
4. In reported speech Arabic tends to use the tense of the original speech, not the past tense conventions of English:
   > *He said he (is) going to London.*

B. PRESENT TIME

1. Arabic has a simple present tense form, which signifies an action unfinished at the time of speaking. It covers the areas of the English simple and progressive present tenses, including their use to refer to future time. The lack of a present tense of the verb *to be*, coupled with this single present tense, causes a wide range of error in present tenses in English:
   > *He go with me now / every day.*
   > *He going with me now / every day.*
   > *He is go with me now / every day.*
   > *What you do?*
   > *When you come / coming back?*
2. This present tense also refers to duration of time up to the time of speaking, expressed in English by the present perfect:
   > *I learn / I learning English two years now.*
3. This present tense is also used as a subjunctive after *that* for subordinate clauses, a very common pattern in Arabic, which only occasionally overlaps with English usage:
   > *He wants that he go with me.*
   > *It was necessary that he goes to the office.*
   > It is impossible that he stay here.

4. With a few verbs of movement, a present participle pattern (literally *going, walking*, etc.) is used (without a copula) to express movement happening at the time of speaking or in the near future. This approximates in a limited way to a present progressive tense, and Arabic speakers use it easily, though omitting the copula:
> *Where you going tomorrow?*
> *I going to London.*

C. FUTURE TIME

1. There is no future tense form in Arabic. As often happens in English, a present tense form is used to refer to the future.
2. Various future-indicating particles are used in colloquial and pan-Arabic to indicate a reference to the future. They are placed before the present tense verb and, thus, approximate to the English use of *will* and *shall*.

Modal verbs

There are no modal verbs in Arabic. Their function is performed by normal verbs, often impersonal, or prepositions followed by the subjunctive (present) tense:

I can go:	*I can that I go.*
	From the possible that I go.
I must go:	*From the necessary that I go.*
	On me that I go.
I may go:	*From the possible that I go.*

Arabic speakers, therefore, have problems in understanding the form and use of anomalous finites, and will add regular verb endings to them, use auxiliaries with them, and overuse *that* clauses with them:
> *Does he can do that?*
> *It possible that I come with you?*

Non-finite forms

There are no gerund or infinitive forms in Arabic; their functions are filled by verbal nouns of various patterns, or finite verbs:
> *I prefer I work to I play.*

The active and passive voices

There are active and passive forms for all tenses in Arabic, but they are virtually identical, differing only in the (unwritten) short vowelling. A passive verb in a text is therefore only recognisable as such from its context. The passive voice is used far less frequently in Arabic writing than in English, and hardly at all in everyday speech. Thus while the concepts of active and passive will readily be understood, the uses and forms of the passive cause problems.

Articles

There is no indefinite article in Arabic, and the definite article has a range of use different from English. The indefinite article causes the most obvious problems as it is commonly omitted with singular and plural countables:

> *This is book. or even *This book. (for *This is a book.*)
> *He was soldier.

When the English indefinite article has been presented, it tends to be used wherever the definite article is not used:

> *These are a books.
> *I want a rice.

There is a definite article form in Arabic, though it takes the form of a prefix (al-). It is used, as in English, to refer back to indefinite nouns previously mentioned, and also for unique reference (*the sun, on the floor,* etc.).

The most common problem with the definite article arises from interference from the Arabic genitive construction:

English	Arabic
John's book. (or *The book of John.*)	*Book John.*
A man's work. (or *The work of a man.*)	*Work man.*
The teacher's car. (or *The car of the teacher.*)	*Car the teacher.*

Most errors of word order and use of articles in genitive constructions are interference of this kind:

> *This is book the teacher.
> *This is the key door.

It follows that Arabic speakers have great difficulties with the Saxon genitive construction.

The special cases in which English omits the article, e.g. *in bed, at dawn, on Thursday, for breakfast,* etc. usually take the definite article in Arabic:

> *At the sunset we made camp.
> *What would you like for the breakfast?

All days of the week, some months in the Muslim calendar, and many names of towns, cities and countries include the definite article in Arabic, which is often translated, appropriately or not:

> *We lived in the India.
> *We had a flat in the Khartoum.

151

> **On the Monday we went to Cardiff.*
> BUT: *We lived in the Sudan / the Yemen.*

Adjectives and adverbs

Adjectives follow their nouns in Arabic and agree in gender and number. This may cause beginners to make mistakes:
> **He is man tall.* (for *He is a tall man.*)

Adverbs are used less commonly in Arabic than in English and, except for adverbs of time, do not have a fixed pattern. Adverbs of manner are often expressed in a phrase: *quickly* is expressed as *with speed*, and *dangerously* as *in a dangerous way*. There is frequent confusion between the adjective and adverb forms in English, and the adjective form is usually overused:
> **He drives very dangerous.*

Gender and number

Arabic has two genders, masculine and feminine, which are usually evident from word ending or word meaning. Plurals of nouns not referring to human beings are considered feminine singular:
> *Where are the books? *She is on the table. *I gave her to the teacher.*

Plurals of nouns in Arabic are very often formed by internal vowel changes, (as with *mouse – mice* in English). The addition of an -s suffix for the plural seems almost too easy for Arabic speakers, and it is often omitted:
> **I have many book.*

For nouns following numbers above ten, it is the rule in Arabic to use a *singular* form, and this is often transferred:
> **I have ten brothers and sixteen uncle.*

Prepositions and particles

Arabic has a wealth of fixed prepositions and particles, with both verbs and adjectives. Many of these do not coincide with their direct English translations:

*to arrive to	**afraid from*	**angry on*
*a picture from (for *of*)	**near from*	**to look to* (for *at*)
*to be short to	**in spite from*	**an expert by*
*responsible from		

Some prepositions have verbal force.
– *On* expresses obligation:
> **It is on me that I pay him.*

— *To* and *for* express possession:
> **This book is to me / for me.* (for *This book is mine.*)
— *With* expresses present possession:
> **With me my camera.* (for *I have my camera with me.*)
— *For* expresses purpose:
> **I went home for (I) get my book.* (for *I went home to get my book.*)

There are no phrasal verbs in Arabic and this whole area is one of great difficulty for Arabic speakers.

Subordinate clauses

A. PURPOSE

Clauses introduced by *in order that* are introduced in Arabic by a conjunction loosely translated as *for*, and followed by the subjunctive (present) tense:
> **I went to the shop for (I) buy some shoes.*

B. RELATIVE

The relative pronoun (*which, who, that*) makes a distinction in Arabic according to gender, but not human and non-human. There is, therefore, confusion in the choice of *who* or *which*.

In Arabic it is *necessary* to include the object of a verb in a relative clause, which in English must be omitted:
> **This is the book which I bought it yesterday.*
> **The hotel, which I stayed in it last year, was very good.*

C. CONDITIONAL

Arabic has two words for *if*, which indicate the degree of likelihood of the condition. In conditional sentences which in English use conditional verb forms, Arabic uses the simple past in both main and conditional clauses:
> **If he went to Spain, he learned Spanish.* (for *If he went to Spain, he would learn Spanish.* and *If he had gone to Spain, he would have learned Spanish.*)

Vocabulary

The acquisition of vocabulary is particularly difficult for Arab learners. They have virtually no positive transfer: only a minimal number of words in English are borrowed from Arabic. A small range of mainly technical words, such as *radar*, *helicopter*, and *television*, have been taken into

Arabic, but these are common to most languages. Arabic speakers have very few aids to reading and listening comprehension by virtue of their first language, and they should not be expected to acquire English at anything like the same pace as European learners.

The following English words sound similar to vulgar words in Arabic, and sensitive teachers should avoid them if possible: *zip, zipper, air, tease, kiss, cuss, nick, unique.*

Culture

Literacy is highly regarded in the Arab world and the teacher is a very respected figure. But it is the written language which is revered, and the teacher's superior knowledge. There is among most Arab learners a dislike of 'colloquial' language. Their own educational system attempts to impose the educated pan-Arabic forms on the local dialects, just as in many country schools in Britain the teacher imposes RP and more literary style on local speech patterns.

There is, therefore, among mature Arab learners particularly, opposition to learning 'everyday colloquial English', which is considered slang, or worse. Teachers emphasising shortened forms and colloquialisms may meet strong resistance.

Add to this the difficulties which adult Arab learners have in coping with an informal teaching approach, which may be totally different from their grammar-based school English lessons, (though TEFL methodology in schools in most Arab countries is being up-dated rapidly) and you have a situation in which lesson content, methodology, and teacher may be rejected as useless. If in doubt, err on the side of formality.

Most Arab learners no longer look on all female teachers under 30 as automatically incompetent, but female teachers should always dress carefully and keep legs and arms reasonably covered. They should remember that in many Arab countries men are not allowed to see or speak to any women outside their own immediate family circle, and the casual mixing of the sexes in a language school can produce emotional turmoil. Above all, teachers should maintain a firmly professional relationship with learners. Once a teacher has reached an age which bestows on her the mature 'mother' image, rather than the 'sister' image, she will have fewer problems.

Written samples of Arabic

Type-written Arabic

في, قلب لندن تقع, ساحة واسعة تسمى ترافلغار سكوير أو ، إذا أردنا أن نستعمل

لها إسمها العربي الأصلي, ، ساحة الطرف الأغر. هذه الساحة المقصود منها إحياء ذكرى

تلك المعركة التي إنتصر فيها اللورد نلسون, على, نابليون غربي شبه جزيرة أيبريا . ويتوسط

هذه الساحة عمود مرتفع يعتليه تمثال اللورد نلسون. وبجانب هذه الساحة المعرض الوطني,

للصور الزيتية المشهورة وكنيسة القديس مارتن .

A direct transliteration

fee qalbi lundun taqa' saaHa waasi'a tusummee traafulghaar skweer
aw, idha aradnaa an nasta'mil lahaa ismhaa al-'arabee al-aSlee,
saaHat aT-Taraf al-agharr. haadhi-s-saaHa al-maqSood minhaa iHyaa'
dhikra tilka l-ma'raka intaSar feehaa al-loord nilsoon 'ala naabulyoon
gharbee shibh gazeerat eebeeryaa. wa-yatawassaT haadhi-s-saaHa
'amood murtafi' ya'taleeh timthaal il-loord nilsoon. wa-bigaanib
haadhi-s-saaHa al-ma'raD al-waTanee li-S-Suwar az-zeeteeya
al-mashhoora wa-kaneesat il-qadees maartin.

A word for word translation

in heart London she-stands square broad she-is-called Trafalgar Square
or, if we-wanted that we-use to-her name-her the-Arabic the-original,
square the-headland the-beautiful. this the-square the-intended from-her
commemoration memory that the-battle which he-was-victorious in-her
the-lord Nelson on Napoleon westwards resemblance island Iberia.
and-he-centres this the-square column high he-surmounts-it statue
the-lord Nelson. and-beside this the-square the-gallery the-national
for-the-pictures the-oiled the-famous and church the-saint Martin.

An idiomatic translation

In the heart of London there is a broad square called Trafalgar Square
or, if we want to use its original Arabic name, the Square of Taraf
Al-Agharr (the Beautiful Headland). This square was designed to per-
petuate the memory of that battle in which Lord Nelson won a victory

over Napoleon, west of the Iberian Peninsula. Standing in the centre of this square is a tall column on top of which is a statue of Lord Nelson. Beside the square is the National Gallery of famous oil paintings and St Martin's Church.

Printed Arabic

(This extract is from the catalogue of the Qatar National Museum. The English translation from the same source is beside it.)

قطر في العهد الاسلامي

كان سكان شبه جزيرة قطر من اول الاقوام التي اعتنقت الدين الاسلامي . وتاريخ المنطقة منذ ذلك الحين يشمل نمو وازدهار تجارة اللؤلؤ التي لعبت قطر فيها دورا على غاية من الأهمية . ويصف هذا القسم من المتحف ايضا ظهور اسرة ال ثاني في القرن التاسع عشر لتتبوء زعامة الدولة ورجالها الافذاذ الذين خدموا البلاد كحكام للدولة .

Qatar in the Islamic Era
The people of the Qatar peninsula were amongst the first in Eastern Arabia to embrace Islam. The history of the region since then includes the growth of the pearl trade, in which Qatar played a particularly important role.

This section of the Museum also describes the emergence, during the 19th century, of the al-Thani family's leadership of the State and the remarkable men who have served the State as Rulers.

A direct transliteration

qatar fee-l-'ahd il-islaamee
kaan sukkaan shibh gazeerat qatar min awwal il-aqwaam allatee a'tanaqat ad-deen al-islaamee. wa-taareekh il-minTaqa mundhu dhaalik al-Heen yashmal numoow w-izdihaar tigaarat il-lu'lu' allatee la'ibat qatar feehaa dawran 'ala ghaaya min al-ahamiyya. wa-yaSif haadha al-qism min al-matHaf aiDan DHuhoor usrat AL THAANEE fee-l-qarn at-taasi' 'ashar li-tatabbu' ad-dawla wa-rigaalhaa al-afdhaadh alladheen khadamoo al-bilaad ka-Hukkaam li-d-dawla.

A word for word translation

it-was inhabitants resemblance island qatar from first the-peoples which she-embraced the-religion the-islamic. and-history the-area since that the-time he-includes growth and-flourishing trade the-pearl which she-played qatar in-her role on extreme the-importance. and-he-describes this the-part from-the-museum also appearance family Al Thani in the-century the-ninth ten for-she-occupies leadership the-state and-men-her the-unique who they-served the-country as-rulers for-the-state.

Handwriting difficulties: samples written by two Arab-speaking beginners

Fon holiday I am going to Lomdan Icee
Fon Fear and Zoo. I go to Haid Bark
aw and haer the pipole spaiekeng
of tej lebatity amd come back with undur-
graw-nd ito ma rbolarch steation. And
go to restrant .al am aeting. and go to

My country is , Sauide Arabie ,
and everyone know that S.A is a big a coun try
its about one mellone K/M square. Almost
of it is a desiartes ,, so everboday in S.A like
the desiante. You can amagen how it is beautful
in the naught, wateching the stares in the sky
lying on the rand and lecitning to the
anmails sound. In the spring the desiarte

Turkish speakers

Ian Thompson

Distribution

TURKEY, NORTH CYPRUS, Eastern Bulgaria. The Azeri language of
northwestern Iran is largely co-intelligible with Turkish.

Introduction

The Turkic languages are scattered over a wide area from Turkey itself
through northern Iran and the southwestern republics of the USSR, on
through northern Afghanistan and northwestern China and into Siberia,
yet there is great homogeneity within the family, which is related neither
to the Indo-European tongues nor to the Semitic. Turkish is therefore
fundamentally different from both Persian and Arabic, though it has in
the past borrowed heavily from both, as well as from French. Since 1928,
Turkish has been written in a modified version of the Roman script.

Turkish is often taken as a copybook example of the agglutinative type
of language, where numerous endings are tacked on to simple roots. For
example, küçümsenmemeliydiler (= *they shouldn't have been belittled*)
can be analysed as follows:

    küçük = *small* (final *k* disappears here)
    -mse- = *regard something as* ...
    -n- = passive/reflexive
    -me- = negative
    -meli- = *should*
    -ydi- = past
    -ler = *they*

Turkish shares with Korean and Japanese a word order based on two
principles: (a) modifier stands before modified, i.e. adjective before noun,
adverb before verb, and (b) the finite verb stands at the end of the
sentence. Here is an example from a popular science magazine:

    Yeraltı   suyundan   düşük dereceli ısı
    Ground-under-its water-its-from low   degree-d heat

    çıkartan   ısı   pompalarından banliyölerdeki
    get-out-ing heat pump-s-its-from suburb-s-in-being

bahçelerde kârlı   bir biçimde
garden-s-in profitable one form-in

yararlanılabilir.
benefit-passive-passive-can.

or more freely:

> *Heat pumps that extract low-grade heat from underground water can profitably be made use of in suburban gardens.*

In popular speech, however, word order varies widely for rhythm, emphasis and good discourse flow; the case and possession suffixes anyway make it clear who does what to whom, regardless of word order. Turkish speakers therefore find English word order less alien than a glance at the passage might suggest, but it is nevertheless a major stumbling block in long, complex sentences.

Phonology

Vowels

1. /iː/ as in *key* is often pronounced like the diphthong /ɪə/, or in a closed syllable as /ɪ/ – the Italian error in reverse: /kɪə/ for *key*; *kip* for *keep*. The Turkish word **giy** contains a good approximation to English /iː/.
2. /e/ as in *bed* is often far too open before *n*, approaching /æ/: *man* for *men*.
3. /æ/ as in *back* plagues Turkish learners, lying as it does between their /c/ and /a/. They often substitute /e/: *set* for *sat*.
4. /ɔː/ is often pronounced as /oʊ/, leading to confusion between pairs such as *law* and *low*. Turks can pronounce /ɔː/ successfully if they lengthen Turkish /o/.
5. /uː/ tends to become /ʊə/ when final and /ʊ/ in closed syllables: /dʊə/ for *do*; '*pullink*' for both *pooling* and *pulling*. Turks are able to pronounce the sound successfully after /j/, as in *few*.
6. /ə/ finds a nearish equivalent in Turkish ı, which is however higher and tenser. Under the influence of spelling, Turks often give unstressed vowels their stressed value: '/ɪnkonwɪnient/ for *inconvenient*; /eddɪʃonal/ for *additional*.
7. When the diphthongs /eɪ/, /aɪ/ and /ɔɪ/ occur in final position, /ɪ/ may be devoiced and pronounced with friction (rather like German *ch* in ich, or the sound at the end of French oui, or the *h* in *human*): /bɔɪç/ for *boy*; /deɪç/ for *day*.
8. /eə/ as in *care* usually becomes /eɪ/. Ask students to imagine *care* spelt in Turkish as **keğır**.
9. /əʊ/ is often heard as /oʊ/, with a fully back first element. This is

generally more acceptable to native English speakers than the 'posh' /eʊ/ or /œʊ/ at which some Turks aim.

10. Between *s* and a consonant, /ɪ/ and /ə/ may become devoiced or disappear altogether: /stɪə/ for *city*; *sport* for *support*.

Consonants

1. /θ/ and /ð/ do not occur in Turkish, and they give a great deal of difficulty. Turks often replace them by over-aspirated /t/ and /d/, so that, for example, *through* becomes /tʰruə/ instead of /θruː/.
2. Turkish /b/, /d/ and /dʒ/ lose voice when final, and /g/ does not occur finally: *bet* for *bed*; '*britch*' for *bridge*.
3. Turkish /v/ is much more lightly articulated than the English equivalent, and with back vowels is close to English /w/. Except as a variant of /v/, /w/ does not occur in Turkish: '*surwiwe*' for *survive*; '*vait*' for *wait*.
4. /ŋ/ only occurs before *g* and *k* in Turkish: '*singgingk*' for *singing*.
5. Speakers from Istanbul and Thrace tend to drop *h*.
6. Standard Turkish has three varieties of *r*, none of them very like standard British *r*. *R* is pronounced whenever written.
7. Turks have both 'clear' /l/ (as in *let*) and 'dark' /ɫ/ (as in *tell*). However, their distribution is not the same as in English, and mistakes can be expected before vowels ('dark' /ɫ/ instead of 'clear' /l/ in some cases) and before consonants ('clear' /l/ instead of 'dark' /ɫ/ in some cases).
8. When /p/, /b/, /m/, /f/ and /v/ are followed by /æ/ or /ɑ/, a glide (like a *w*) is inserted. /bwaɪ/ for *buy*; /fwɑn/ for *fun*.
9. Final /m/, /n/ and /l/ tend to be pronounced very short and devoiced. This makes them difficult to perceive, and may lead to intelligibility problems.

Consonant clusters

The Turkish consonant system does not allow initial clusters in native words, and clusters of more than three consonants in any position are unusual. Although some loan words have an initial easing vowel (e.g. istasyon = *station*), the tendency when speaking English is to insert the vowel after the first consonant: '*siprink*' for *spring*; '*filute*' for *flute*.

Rhythm, stress and intonation

The rhythmic pattern of English, with its stretched-out stressed syllables and hurried unstressed syllables with their reduced vowels, is alien to and difficult for the Turks. Sentences like *There was considerable confusion over them*, where only *-sid-* and *-fu-* are fully stressed, need much practice.

Word stress exists in Turkish. Most words are stressed on the final syllable, but many verb-forms – particularly negative ones – have an earlier stress. Adverbs and proper names also tend not to be finally stressed. Sets like '*photograph/pho'tographer/photo'graphic*, are, quite predictably, troublesome.

Remarkably often English and Turkish agree on which word is to carry the main stress in a sentence, but *wh*-question words (such as kim = *who*, ne = *what*, niçin = *why*) are usually stressed in Turkish, whereas they are only stressed in English for special emphasis or when standing alone. Turks therefore tend to say '*WHERE are you going?* for *Where are you 'GOING?*

In declaratives and orders, stress is expressed as a fall in pitch on the stressed syllable, together with slight lengthening and an increase in loudness – much as in English. But an English characteristic not found in Turkish is the rising pitch on repeated, afterthought or otherwise secondary material *after* the main stress, as in:

> *There's a badger in the garden.*
> *Oooh – I've never seen a badger.*
> *Ssh! He'll run away if we make too much noise.*

Also unfamiliar is the fall–rise with its connotations of warning, incompleteness and partial congruence of information:

> *Can you lend me a pen?*
> *Well, I can lend you a red one.*
> *That'll do fine. Don't let me run off with it.*

Many Turks – particularly men – find this pattern embarrassing. Falling–rising patterns do occur in Turkish, but mainly to give shape to strings of clauses, the final clause taking a fall. This pattern is often carried over into English. Note the lack of conjunctions, too:

> *I went to bus-station, I searched my brother, I couldn't see, I went to home.*

Punctuation

Turkish makes use of most of the punctuation marks available to Latin-script languages, but in its own way:

1. A comma is usually written after the topic of a sentence, which often happens to be the subject:
    > ** My father, works in a factory.*
2. Subordinate clauses are usually not marked off with commas:
    > *When you get home please remember to telephone me.*

Sentences opening with the equivalent of *He said, I imagine, It's*

161

obvious and similar expressions use a comma *after* the particle ki (=
that), which gives rise to:
 He told that, his passport at Home Office.
3. A comma often separates two co-ordinate clauses:
 She has a good voice, she enjoys singing.
4. Sentences opening with Çünkü (= *because*, explaining what has gone
 before) normally stand after a full stop:
 *She was tired. *Because worked very hard.*
 Otherwise the use of the full stop and paragraphing conventions are
 much as in English.
5. Colons are used as in English, but are usually followed by capital
 letters. Semi-colons are little used.
6. Quoted speech is found between English-style inverted commas,
 between « and », or unmarked. Often a quoted single word or phrase
 is enclosed in parentheses ( ); parenthetic material may be found
 between « and », and emphasis – where English might underline or use
 bold type – is shown by capital letters or even inverted commas.

Grammar

Word order

Turkish is a 'subject–object–verb' language, where qualifier precedes
qualified, topic precedes comment and subordinate precedes main, but
departures from this ideal are common in speech and lively writing. All
adjectivals, however long, precede their substantive. What correspond to
English prepositions follow the noun, and what correspond to subordinating conjunctions follow their clauses. Modal verbs follow lexical
verbs. The following example illustrates Turkish word order:

> Genç kalmak için enerji tasarrufu yapmak
> *Young stay-(infinitive) for energy economy-its make-(infinitive)*
>
> kadar iyi bir yol yoktur.
> *extent good one road nonexistent-is.*
> (*There's no better way to stay young than to save your energy.*)

Students quickly learn the fundamentals of English word order as it
applies to simple sentences, but continue to have difficulty in more
complex structures.

Verbs: general

The Turkish verb shows person, number, tense, aspect, voice, mood,
modality and polarity, and students will therefore be prepared for these
concepts to be expressed through changes in verb forms, though the

English forms themselves cause great difficulty. The object is not expressed within the verb; nor is gender.

Be

There is no independent verb *be* in Turkish. The simple copula use usually goes unexpressed:

> *My uncle farmer.*

The Turkish equivalent of *there is* can be used (unlike the English structure) with definite subjects:

> *There was not the driver in the bus. (for The driver wasn't in the bus.)*
>
> *Yesterday I looked you from telephone, but there wasn't you. (for Yesterday I tried to phone you, but you weren't at home.)*

Time, tense and aspect

Differences in the coverage of Turkish and English verb-forms result in the following difficulties:

1. Students may use the present progressive inappropriately with stative verbs such as *know* and for habitual actions:

   > *I am knowing her. I am seeing every day.*

2. The simple present may be used instead of the *will* future, especially in requests, offers and promises, and when referring to conditions and inevitable outcomes:

   > 'Will you bring one?' *'Yes, I do.'*
   >
   > *Don't drop it – it breaks!*
   >
   > *Ask Gülay; she tells you.*

3. The past progressive and the *used to* construction may be confused:

   > *I was often going to the mountains when I was younger.*

4. Learners tend to overuse the past perfect, substituting it for the simple past in cases where a past event is seen as being separated from the present by a long time lapse, a delay, or intervening events:

   > *This castle had been built 600 years ago.*
   >
   > *I had written to you last month, but I couldn't receive any reply till now.*

Modal verbs

Turkish has a comprehensive set of modal verbs which express similar meanings to the English modals, including separate forms corresponding to structures such as *I was able to go / I could have gone*, or *We had to do it / We should have done it*. Students are therefore broadly familiar with the meanings expressed by the English modals (though the differences between *should, must, have to* and *have got to* cause difficulty). The sheer mechanics of the English forms, however, with their contractions and neutralised vowels, cause a good deal of trouble.

Conditionals

All the above is true of conditionals, with the added complication that Turkish uses the *past* unreal form even for present unreals if they really are unfulfillable:

> *If I had been English I would have missed the sun.* (for *If I were English I'd miss the sun.*)

The passive voice

Passives present no conceptual difficulties, but structurally the English passive strikes Turks as clumsy, and the triple role of *be* as tense-auxiliary, passive former and modal is a source of difficulty, leading students to confuse such structures as *was taking, was taken, was to take, was to be taken.*

Turkish is often more specific than English as to passive and active:

> *This tea is too hot to be drunk.*
> *It's easy to be written.*

Overlapping the active–passive opposition is that of transitivity. English says *I broke the window* and *The window broke*; *She burnt the wood* and *The wood burnt*; *I couldn't start the engine* and *The engine wouldn't start.* In each case Turkish distinguishes between transitive and intransitive; students may therefore find it confusing to use the same verb in both cases. A common mistake:

> *When will school be opened?*

Participles and subordinate clauses

English participle and clause structures are organised very differently from their Turkish equivalents, and present a serious learning problem. Each of the following expressions corresponds to a single complex participial verb-form in Turkish:

> *write and . . .*
> *who writes/wrote*
> *when someone writes/wrote*
> *unless it is/was written*
> *while they are/were writing*
> *as if it had been written*
> *without writing*

> *by not writing*
> *because we couldn't write*
> *of the things you write/wrote*

Since the Turkish forms do not show tense, students may have difficulty getting the right tense in English subordinate clauses (e.g. in indirect speech constructions).

Relative clauses

Since relative clauses are adjectival, they go in Turkish before the noun they modify:

Çalıştığımız günler ...	*The days on which we work ...*
Çalıştığımız mesele ...	*The problems we're working on ...*
Çalıştığımız yer ...	*The place we work in ...*

English relative structures are therefore difficult for Turkish learners.

Nominalised clauses

English has a variety of ways of nominalising clauses, so as to use them as subjects, objects or complements. Turkish students find the use of structures such as the following difficult and unpredictable; they tend to overuse the possessive structure in such cases:

> I *advised her* **to go.**
> I *suggested* **she went.**
> **Her going** *was a good thing.*
> *It was a good thing* **she went.**
> **The fact that she went** *was a good thing.*
> *It was a good thing* **for her to go.**
> I *approved of* **her going.**

Nouns

Turkish nouns are genderless, but they show number, possession and case. The plural is less used than in English – particularly when a noun is indefinite or generic, and after number-words. Mistakes resulting from this take a long time to eradicate:

> **In the Turkey, tomato too cheap.*
> **I spend the evenings writing letter.*
> **We saw a few animal.*
> **three week ago*

Formation of nouns from other parts of speech is highly regular, and Turks have predictable trouble with English word-formation.

Pronouns

Personal pronouns are much less used than in English: the subject pronoun is expressed only for emphasis, contrast or to introduce the subject as a topic, which are uses normally distinguished in English by changes in stress and intonation. Object pronouns are used even less. Possessives are also normally unnecessary, since the 'possessed' form of the noun makes the relationship clear:

> *When my father had finished breakfast, went out.
> *Tramp asked some money, for this reason I gave.
> *John is having trouble with car.

Articles

Turkish has an indefinite article, which is sandwiched between adjective and noun. As in many European languages, it is not used for professions or in negative existentials:

> *I am student.
> *There wasn't bus.

The choice between *a/an* and *some* is difficult for Turks, since the line between countable and uncountable is less sharply drawn than in English. Turkish students tend to overuse *some*:

> *I asked some policeman, he told you will see some bridge.

Turkish has no definite article, but direct objects are different in form according to whether or not they are definite in meaning. This encourages Turks to put *the* with all definite direct objects, leading to mistakes such as:

> *Librarian controlled the my ticket.
> *I like the Cambridge.

Adjectives

Comparatives are not always marked in Turkish:

> *We eat few butter than you.

Quantifiers

The pessimistic/optimistic distinction in *few / a few* and *little / a little* is observed in Turkish, whereas the uncountable/countable distinction in *few/little* is not (see previous example).

The differences between *much*, *many* and *a lot*; *long* and *a long time*; and *far*, *a long way* and *distant* are difficult for Turks as for other learners.

Adverbs

Adverbs that modify verbs are usually identical in form to adjectives in Turkish:
> *He generally works slow.*

Here and *there* can be nouns in Turkish:
> *Here is boring place.*
> *Do you like there?*

Intensifiers are a problem area: çok soğuk represents, according to context, *very cold*, *colder* or *too cold*, causing students to confuse the English forms.

Conjunctions

Among the conjunctions that cause special difficulty for Turkish leaders are *even if*, *however* and *whether ... or*. Often the same Turkish word corresponds both to a conjunction and to a preposition in English, leading to confusion between, for instance, *although* and *despite*; *as far as*, *until* and *by*; *before*, *ago* and *earlier*; *after*, *next*, *afterwards*, *in ...'s time* and *later*.

Other groups of words which may have single Turkish equivalents (causing confusion in certain contexts in English) are: *and* and *whether*; *and*, *also*, *either* and *even*; *called*, *saying*; *because* and *in order to*.

Co-ordinate clauses are often juxtaposed without a conjunction in spoken Turkish, leading learners to drop obligatory *and*, *so* or *but*:
> *We looked, they had gone.*
> *I ran, I caught the ferry.*

Prepositions

Prepositions that cause confusion include *at/in/on*; *than/from*; *with/by*; *to/for*; *until / as far as / as much as / up to / by*; *with/near / up to*. Students sometimes leave out the preposition altogether, even at an otherwise good intermediate level.

> *in Saturday*   *for learn English*   *by pencil*
> *until the bank*
> *I must get back until Monday.*
> *He came near me and asked me my name.*
> *I am living near my landlady.*
> *He went Newcastle.*

Vocabulary

The only lexical common ground between Turkish and English is a body
of modern borrowings from French, such as **enflasyon** (= *inflation*),
kalite (= *quality*), **debriyaj** (= *to declutch*). Available dictionaries range
from abominable to very good, but an excellent idiomatic Turkish–
English dictionary has yet to appear. Turkish lacks equivalents for many
English abstract nouns, and groups of not-quite-synonymous English
words, such as *shorten, abbreviate, abridge* often have one Turkish
counterpart. Some especially common confusions:

> *mind/idea/opinion/thought*
> *tell/say*
> *definitely/exactly/completely*
> *cut/kill*
> *turn/return*
> *finish/leave / graduate from* (university, etc.)
> *food/meal*
> *nearly/about*
> *pass / go on*
> *already/before*
> *still/yet*
> *now / no longer*
> *always / every time*

In Turkish you *pull* trouble, telegrams and photographs; you *give*
decisions; you *stay* (fail) in an exam; you *throw* a swindle and your victim
eats it; you *see* education, work and duty; it *comes* (seems) to me that . . .;
you *become* an illness, injection or operation.

The language classroom

Society and its institutions have traditionally been fairly authoritarian in
Turkey. What the textbook and the teacher say are expected to be right,
and to be prescriptive rather than descriptive. Turks are by no means
meek, passive students, though. They have a strong awareness of
language, are not particularly shy and are resourceful in expressing a lot
even with little language. They tend to voice their opinions openly and
attach little importance to compromise. Occasionally they may criticise
aspects of their homeland and its politics, but the teacher should not join
in the criticism, for the Turks have enormous national pride and are
highly sensitive to the world's opinion of them. They warm immediately
to anyone who shows an interest in the nation and its language.

Language learning opportunities within Turkey and North Cyprus
vary greatly. Many village youngsters will leave school with no foreign

language at all – unless they have lived for a spell in, say, France or Germany as the children of guestworkers. At the other end of the scale are those who have had six years at kolej, private high schools where much of the teaching is through the medium of English.

Given the great differences between the two languages, most learners learn to speak English, and to understand spoken English, remarkably well. Reading material with much abstract vocabulary presents difficulty. Written composition is often dreaded, since here one must use complex constructions that can be deftly sidestepped in speech, and because composition may not have been 'studied' at home.

Speakers of Indian languages

Christopher Shackle

Distribution

INDIA, PAKISTAN, BANGLADESH, NEPAL, SRI LANKA, Arabian Peninsula, East Africa, Mauritius.

Introduction

Some sixteen major languages are spoken in the countries of the Indian subcontinent. The four languages of south India (Tamil, Malayalam, Kannada, Telegu) are members of the independent Dravidian family. The others are all Indo-Aryan languages, members of that branch of the Indo-European family which derives from Sanskrit. They include the national languages of India (Hindi), Pakistan (Urdu), Bangladesh (Bengali), Nepal (Nepali), and Sri Lanka (Sinhalese), besides many important regional languages (Panjabi, Gujarati, Marathi, Oriya, Assamese, Kashmiri, Sindhi). Several of these languages have been spread by emigration to other parts of the world, and the United Kingdom now has large communities of speakers of Bengali, Gujarati, and Panjabi.

As a result of the long period of British rule, English has become very firmly established in the subcontinent. Even those with no direct command of English will have been exposed to its indirect influence through the very numerous loanwords which have entered all Indian languages. At the other end of the spectrum, English continues to be used as a natural medium of expression by those with the highest level of education, for whom the most prestigious variety of the language remains British RP. In between these two groups lie those who have varying degrees of command over 'Indian English'. This is the local variety of English, which is current with a surprising degree of uniformity (though inevitably with some regional variation, especially of accent) throughout the subcontinent, and which is chiefly distinguished by the presence of features drawn from Indian languages. This genuine Indian English is to be distinguished from the often misleading caricatures of it presented by the late Peter Sellers and his imitators in the British entertainment industry.

Many of the distinctively Indian features of Indian English are

170

common to most or all of the Indo-Aryan languages, and several are also found in Dravidian. They are most conveniently described by referring to the typical example of Hindi, which is here taken to include the colloquial Hindustani that is the most widely used *lingua franca* of the subcontinent, besides its officially fostered literary varieties, the High Hindi of India and the Urdu of Pakistan.

The less significant features which may cause problems in learning English for speakers of only one particular Indian language cannot properly be dealt with in a chapter of this limited size.

Given the long-established position of English in the schools of the subcontinent, the problems encountered by learners are generally likely to be determined by their educational rather than their particular language background. Apart from Urdu, which is written in a variant of the Arabic script, almost every Indian language has its own script, written from left to right, to record both consonants and vowels. The English writing system poses no general problems for most Indian learners.

For the sake of brevity the term Indian is used here in its widest sense to refer to all the countries of the Indian subcontinent.

Phonology

General

The phonological systems of Indian languages and of English differ in important respects, notably in the very different prominence given to distinctions between vowels and distinctions between consonants. While English has 22 vowels and diphthongs and 24 consonants, the Nagari script used for writing Hindi has signs for only ten vowels, but distinguishes 40 different consonants. Sets of aspirated and unaspirated consonants are carefully distinguished, and in place of the English alveolar series /t/, /d/, there is both a series of dentals produced with the blade of the tongue behind the teeth, /t/, /tʰ/, /d/, /dʰ/, and the typically Indian retroflex series produced with the tip of the tongue curled back behind the alveolar ridge, /ʈ/, /ʈʰ/, /ɖ/, /ɖʰ/.

Among the features of Indian languages which give rise to an 'Indian accent' in English are:
- Tenser articulation than English, with vowels produced further forward, leading to the loss of some distinctions between different vowels.
- The pronunciation of the voiceless consonants /p/, /t/, /tʃ/, /k/ without aspiration in all positions.
- The pronunciation of the English alveolar consonants /t/ and /d/ as the heavier retroflex consonants /ʈ/ and /ɖ/.
- A different intonation system from English (see below).

Vowels

iː	ɪ	e	æ	eɪ	aɪ	ɔɪ
ɑː	ɒ	ɔː	ʊ	aʊ	əʊ	ɪə
uː	ʌ	ɜː	ə	eə	ʊə	aɪə / aʊə

Shaded phonemes have equivalents or near equivalents in most Indian languages, and should therefore be perceived and articulated without serious difficulty, although some confusions may still arise. Unshaded phonemes may cause problems. For detailed comments, see below.

1. /e/ and /æ/ are often confused: *said* and *sad*.
2. /ɒ/ and /ɔː/ are generally confused with /ɑː/, and the same vowel /ɑː/ is typically heard in pronunciations of such sets of words as *lorry, law, laugh*.
3. The diphthong /eɪ/ is usually pronounced as the close monophthong /eː/; /meːd/ for *made*. The diphthongs /aɪ/ and /ɔɪ/ are both liable to be realised as /aːɪ/: *tie* for *toy*.
4. The diphthong /əʊ/ is usually pronounced as the close monophthong /oː/: /koːʈ/ for *coat*.

Consonants

p	b	f	v	θ	ð	t	d
s	z	ʃ	ʒ	tʃ	dʒ	k	g
m	n	ŋ	l	r	j	w	h

Shaded phonemes have equivalents or near equivalents in most Indian languages, and should therefore be perceived and articulated without serious difficulty, although some confusions may still arise. Unshaded phonemes may cause problems. For detailed comments, see below.

1. The voiceless consonants /p/, /t/, /tʃ/, /k/ are pronounced without aspiration in all positions; the /p/ in *pit* having the same value as that in *spit*.
2. The fricative consonants /θ/ and /ð/ are replaced by the aspirated dental /tʰ/ and the unaspirated /d/ respectively: /dem/ for *them*.

/f/ is often replaced by the aspirated /pʰ/: thus /pʰɪt/ for *fit*, as opposed to /pɪt/ for *pit*.

3. The alveolar consonants /t/ and /d/ are regularly replaced by the retroflex consonants /ʈ/ and /ɖ/: thus /ɖen/ for *den*, as opposed to /dem/ for *them* (see above).

4. There is only one Indian phoneme in the area of /v/ and /w/, and the distinction between these two sounds is a major difficulty for Indian learners: *vet* and *wet*.

5. In many Indian languages /z/ is an allophone of /dʒ/, and words like *bridges* may be tongue-twisters for some learners.

6. Most Indian languages lack the phoneme /ʒ/, which may be variously realised as /z/, /ʃ/, /dʒ/, or even /j/, in such words as *pleasure*.

7. The 'dark' /l/ as in *fill* is generally replaced by the 'clear' /l/ as in *light*.

8. /r/ is pronounced as a tap or fricative in all positions where it is written (see below), without affecting the quality of the preceding vowel.

9. Some Indian languages have only one phoneme in the area of /s/ and /ʃ/, and many speakers of, for example, Bengali or Gujarati, find it difficult to distinguish between these two sounds, e.g. *self* and *shelf*.

Influence of spelling on pronunciation

Indian scripts are for the most part phonetic, so that spelling is largely an accurate guide to pronunciation. Indian pronunciation of English words is consequently often over-faithful to the written forms:

1. /r/ is pronounced wherever *r* is written, including positions where it follows a vowel, as in *market*, *officer*, *order*, etc. The quality of the preceding vowel is not neutralised as in RP, and some common false rhymes are created, notably /diːər/ for *there*, rhyming with *here*.

2. A written *h* may be interpreted as indicating one of the Indian voiced aspirate consonants and pronounced as such in words like *ghost*, *which*.

3. The written *-ed* of the regular past tense is often pronounced as it is written, even after stems ending in a voiceless consonant, as in /ɖeveləpeɖ/ for *developed*, or /aːskeɖ/ for *asked*.

4. The written *-s* of the plural may be pronounced as /s/, even after a voiced consonant, as in *walls*, or a long vowel, as in *fees*, where it should be pronounced /z/.

Consonant clusters

The range of consonant clusters occurring at the beginning and end of English words is much wider than in Indian languages. Many such clusters are simplified:

1. Initial two-segment clusters beginning with *s* may be prefixed by /ɪ/:
     '*istation*' for *station*
     '*istreet*' for *street*, etc.
2. Initial clusters of most types are liable to be broken by inserting the short vowel /ə/ to assist the pronunciation:
     '*faree*' for *free*
     '*salow*' for *slow*, etc.
3. Final clusters may be similarly broken, or simplified by the omission of a consonant:
     '*filam*' for *film*
     '*toas*' for *toast*, etc.

Words with a final *l* or *n* in English, like *little, button,* etc., are pronounced as two-syllable words with a clear vowel /ə/ in the second syllable.

Rhythm and stress

As distinct from English, which is a stress-timed language, in which word stress is both heavily marked and not always predictable, Indian languages are syllable-timed, and stress is secondary to the rhythm, which is based primarily upon the arrangement of long and short syllables. Word stress in them accordingly tends to be weakly realised, and is always predictable.

The appropriate stressing of syllables in English words and compounds is therefore an area of great difficulty for speakers of Indian languages.

1. The variation in stress in sets of related words may not be properly realised, producing, for example *ne'cessary*, following *necessity*. Incorrect stressing of the initial syllable is particularly common, as in '*development*, '*event*.
2. The grammatical contrast between nouns with stress on the first syllable and verbs with second syllable stress is lost in favour of a weak stress on the second syllable for both nouns and verbs, as in *re'cord*, *trans'port*.

     There is a similar confusion between compounds and free combinations of noun with noun, so that a '*toy factory* is not distinguished from a *toy 'factory*.
3. Full vowels tend to be retained, even in unstressed syllables, so that both the *e* of *cricket* and the second *o* of *Oxford* retain their value. Many common words normally pronounced as reduced '*weak forms*' in English, like *and, but, than, as, is, has, was, will, would,* similarly keep their full '*strong form*' values in all positions, and receive a relatively strong stress.

Intonation

This naturally varies greatly in detail over the vast speech areas covered by the Indian languages. The most notable difference from English lies in the use of raised pitch rather than heavier articulation to indicate emphasis. This prominent contrast with the normal English pattern contributes further to the 'sing-song' impression of Indian English that derives primarily from the syllable-timed character of Indian languages.

The typical rising intonation of questions in English is reserved for expressions of surprise in most Indian languages. Their characteristic interrogative pattern, in which the end of a question is marked by a rise that is followed by a fall in the intonation, is quite unlike the English norm, and can easily cause misunderstanding. Particularly in polite requests, an unfortunate impression of peremptoriness is liable to be created.

Juncture

Given the preference for avoiding the use of elided weak forms, the general evenness of stress, and the tendency to simplify complex consonant clusters, this is not a feature of English likely in itself to cause special problems.

Orthography and punctuation

There is no direct influence on Indian learners of English from the rather different alphabetical systems used to record Indian languages. Semi-phonetic spellings are encountered with the usual frequency, and there is sometimes some uncertainty in the use of capital letters, which are not distinguished in any Indian script.

Indian scripts possessed only the equivalent of the full stop before the introduction of English typography. The whole battery of commas, colons, question marks, and the like are now freely used in writing Indian scripts, although not always very systematically. A similar uncertain use of punctuation may be detected in Indian learners of English, who have particular problems in the use of inverted commas. Since true reported speech is not a construction characteristic of most Indian languages, it is quite common to find punctuation of this type:

*She said that 'Rakesh was not feeling well.'

Grammar

General

The following section has been compiled on the basis of the contrasts between English and Hindi, as the most prominent representative of the Indo-Aryan languages. For those concerned with speakers of the Indian languages most prominently represented in the United Kingdom, it may be observed that what is said about Hindi applies equally to the virtually identical Urdu, and almost without exception to the very closely related Panjabi. Much will also hold true of Gujarati, though rather less of Bengali, which has evolved many independent patterns. It should be understood that the Dravidian languages of south India have a quite different grammar.

The 'parts of speech' of English and Hindi are broadly similar. Hindi is, however, a more highly inflected language, which in European terms may be compared with Spanish. It has singular and plural noun forms, adjectives placed before nouns, a generally regular system of verb conjugation, which includes simple and progressive, active and passive forms; auxiliary and modal verbs; and past, present, and future tenses (mostly indicated, as in English, by periphrastic compounds involving the use of auxiliary verbs).

Unlike English, Hindi distinguishes masculine and feminine nouns, has common forms for all pronouns, lacks markers of the comparative and superlative forms of adjectives, has no word class corresponding to the English articles, prefers postpositions placed after a noun or pronoun to prepositions, and has as its normal word order one in which the verb is placed finally in a sentence. Some of these differences, as well as some of the apparent similarities, frequently cause problems for Indian learners of English.

Questions and negatives; auxiliaries

1. There is no equivalent of the auxiliary *do* in Hindi. Where no specific interrogative word is used, a question is marked only by its intonation – of a different pattern from English – and word order is unaltered:
    *When you came to India?
    *You like our Indian food?
2. Negatives are formed by putting a negative marker (meaning both *not* and *no*) before the verb:
    *You no(t) like curry?
    The Hindi idiom is to answer yes/no questions by signalling assent or dissent. Assenting to negative questions in the affirmative can cause confusion:
    'You have no objection?' **'Yes.'* (= *I have no objection.*)

3. There is a common question tag, or reinforcer for all questions, irrespective of the subject, like the German nicht wahr?:
   > *You have met Mohan, isn't it?*
4. The principal Hindi auxiliary verb is the verb *to be*. There is no Hindi verb corresponding to *to have*, and its use is often avoided by Indian learners of English:
   > *Your book is lying with him. (for He has got your book.)*

Time, tense, and aspect

A. PAST TIME

Besides a simple past tense, Hindi also distinguishes the past habitual, past progressive, and past perfect, though there are some areas of usage which do not correspond to these tenses in English.

1. The English past progressive may be used inappropriately by analogy with the Hindi past habitual, formed with the present participle and past auxiliary:
   > *We were wanting to go to England.*
2. The simple past may be used where English would prefer the present perfect:
   > *She cooked the food just now. (for She has just cooked the food.)*
3. The past perfect in Hindi is used to refer to past time regarded as separate from the present, without the reference back from one point of time to another implied in English:
   > *They had gone to Delhi this year. (for They went ...)*
4. There is no true reported speech in Hindi, which usually preserves the original tense after past reporting verbs:
   > *He asked that if we are doing this. (for He asked if we were doing this.)*

B. PRESENT TIME

Besides a simple tense, Hindi also distinguishes the present progressive and present perfect. Two common areas of confusion concern the wrong use of the present progressive in English.

1. The present progressive may be used inappropriately by analogy with the Hindi simple present, formed with the present participle and present auxiliary:
   > *He is wanting to study English. (for He wants to study English.)*
2. The present progressive in Hindi is used to say how long a present state of affairs has been going on:

> *How long are you living in England?*
> *She is studying English since six years.*

C. FUTURE TIME

There is a full set of future tenses in Hindi, and these are used much more freely than in English to express the notion of probability:
> *You will be knowing him. (for You must know him.)*

Conditionals

Learners typically use a future tense instead of the present tense in the conditional clause, by false analogy with the Hindi future or present subjunctive:
> *If he will come, then we may go. (for If he comes ...)*

Modal verbs

Hindi has either direct equivalents or quite closely analogous constructions to most English modal verbs. The most serious confusions involve the unfortunate use of an English modal verb, typically *will* or *may*, in imitation of a Hindi present subjunctive in polite forms of requests:
> *You will do this service for me. (for Will you please do ...?)*
> *You may kindly come tomorrow. (for Will you please come tomorrow?)*
> *I may go now. (for May I go now?)*

Compare the use of modal verbs in clauses following verbs of wishing, where Hindi again uses a present subjunctive:
> *He wanted that they should come.*

Non-finite forms

English has both *to do* and *doing* to express the idea of a verbal noun, where Hindi has only a single infinitive. Confusions between the two English forms are particularly common in expressing the idea of purpose, where the Hindi model – of the infinitive followed by the postposition *for* – may be imitated:
> *He went to college for improving his English.*

Word order

Although most Indian languages differ from English in having postpositions in place of prepositions, and place the verb at the end of the sentence, this is not an area of especially serious confusions, except in direct and reported questions (see above).

Articles

The use of the English articles is one of the most difficult points for Indian learners to grasp. Like other Indian languages, Hindi has no equivalent of the definite article, and only the number 'one' to cover some uses of the indefinite. Confusions are consequently very frequent in English, where Indian learners often omit the articles, especially *the*, or substitute *one* for the indefinite article.

Gender, number and case

Hindi nouns are either masculine or feminine, gender being determined by natural sex or, in the case of inanimates, by the form of the noun. Adjectives and verbs frequently agree in gender with the noun they are governed by. Pronouns are not distinguished for gender, and the third person pronouns, *he, she, it*, are represented by demonstratives, also meaning *that* or *this*. Both nouns and pronouns have special cases when followed by a postposition, but neither gender nor case is a serious problem in English for Indian learners.

Plurals of nouns are formed by the alteration of the final vowel or by the addition of endings. But a large group of masculine nouns makes no change in the simple form of the plural, and this may account for the occasional dropping of the final *s* from English plurals.

There are also some differences between Hindi and English in their ideas of what constitutes a plural noun, and this may cause confusions in English. Words like *scissors* and *trousers* are singular in Hindi, whereas some other nouns are treated as plural:

> *The rice are not well cooked.*
> *Her hairs are very long.*

Plural pronouns are often used in Hindi to refer to a single person. When used as actual plurals, the word *people* is often added to them:

> *We people are very lazy.* (for *We are very lazy.*)

Adjectives and adverbs

Adjectives precede the nouns they qualify, in Hindi, as in English, and the two languages have comparable sets of simple adverbs. A few common points of confusion do, however, arise.

1. Hindi has no special forms for the comparative and superlative of adjectives, using instead a simple construction of the type:

   > *The boy is clever from the girl.*

   There is consequently some confusion as to the use of the English comparative and superlative forms, and double forms are common:

   > *He is the most cleverest boy in the class.*

179

2. Hindi does not make the same distinctions between intensifying adverbs as are drawn by the English *more*, *very*, and *too*:
> *I like this music too much. (for ... very much)

3. Both adjectives and adverbs are very frequently repeated in Hindi to give a sense of distribution or emphasis, or both:
> *He cut the bread into little, little pieces. (for ... lots of little pieces)*
> *Please speak slowly, slowly. (for ... rather slowly or ... very slowly)*

Prepositions and particles

Many of the most common errors made by Indian learners of English arise from using the wrong preposition, by analogy with the postposition that would be used in a language like Hindi in a comparable expression. Only a few of the most common confusions can be indicated here:

> *I was angry on him. (for ... angry with him)*
> *They were sitting on the table. (for ... at the table)*

Many verbs having a direct object in English are supplied with a preposition:

> *We reached to that place.*
> *Tell to that boy that he is a cheater.*
> *I asked from him that he should come.*

The final element of phrasal verbs is also liable to confusion:

> *He left off one important point. (for He left out ...)*

A similar source of confusion is provided by reflexive phrasal verbs:

> *'Please enjoy.' 'Oh yes, we will enjoy.' (for 'Please enjoy yourselves.' 'Oh yes, we'll enjoy ourselves.')*

Subordinate clauses

Indian languages are generally less fond of complex subordinate clauses than English, preferring simple parallel constructions. Difficulties are therefore usually experienced by Indian learners of English in handling the more complex types of subordination, including not only indirect speech and the other constructions illustrated above, but also relative clauses, where Hindi favours the construction:

> *Which people lived there, they were all very poor. (for The people who lived there were all very poor.)*
> *All that he was doing, that we liked very much. (for We very much liked all that he was doing.)*

Vocabulary

English loanwords are present in large numbers in all Indian languages, especially in areas connected with modern institutions or technology. This is naturally a great help to Indian learners of English, who will inevitably know a good deal of vocabulary to start with.

Not all such loanwords are, however, immediately transferable back into English, either because their pronunciation has been significantly changed, or because they are now obsolete in British usage, or because they represent distinctively Indian extensions of meaning or fresh coinages. A few examples will demonstrate the types of difficulty which may arise. The names of the months are all borrowed from English, but their pronunciation has often been significantly altered: *'farvari'* for *February*; *'a'prail'* for *April*; *'a'gast'* for *August*; *'ak'toober'* for *October*, etc.

Similarly, a hotal is not the simple equivalent of the English *hotel*, but also includes cafés and restaurants. A furlong, now restricted to the race-track in Britain, may be used to indicate a short distance anywhere, for instance, down the road to the next crossing, i.e. *crossroads*. The roof of a room is its *ceiling*, and the back garden of a house is where one is invited to go by one's host with the words: 'Now I will show you my back side.'!

Culture

In spite of changes in recent times, and the influence of the cultures of the surrounding societies upon communities of speakers of Indian languages settled outside the subcontinent, the traditional Eastern respect for the teacher and for the written word is still a prominent characteristic of learners from India and the neighbouring countries. An emphasis on formal discipline and written work is perhaps the one best calculated to meet preconceived attitudes, which may find it harder to cope with the necessary emphasis on everyday colloquial usage. Teachers may find it hard to elicit responses from female learners, unless they are in an all-female class.

Samples of Hindi and Urdu

A passage of Hindi printed in the Nagari script

एक दिन बेगम साहृबा के सिर में दर्द होने लगा । उन्होंने लौंडी से
कहा — जा कर मिरज़ा साहब को बुला ला । किसी हकीम के यहाँ से दवा
लायें । दौड़, जल्दी कर । लौंडी गयी तो मिरज़ाजी ने कहा — चल, अभी आते
हैं । बेगम साहृवा का मिज़ाज गरम था । इतनी ताब कहाँ कि उनके सिर में
दर्द हो और पति शतरंज खेलता रहे । चेहरा सुर्ख हो गया । लौंडी से कहा —
जा कर कह, अभी चलिए, नहीं तो वह आप ही हकीम के यहाँ चली जायेंगी ।

A direct transliteration and word for word translation

ek   din begam sāhabā ke sir   meṅ dard hone lagā.
One day Begam Sahiba -'s head in   pain to-be began.

unhoṅne lauṅḍī se   kahā – jā-kar   mirzā sāhib ko
Her-by   maid   from said 'having-gone Mirza Sahib to

bulā lā.   kisī   hakīm ke yahāṅ se   davā
call bring. Some doctor -'s house from medicine

lāeṅ.   daur, jaldī kar.   lauṅḍī gayī to
(he) may-bring. Run, haste make.' Maid   went then

mirzājī ne kahā – cal abhī   āte haiṅ. begam
Mirzaji by said 'Go, just-now (we) come.' Begam

sāhabā kā mizāj garm thā. itnī   tāb   kahāṅ
Sahiba -'s temper hot   was. So-much patience where

ki unke sir   meṅ dard ho aur pati   shatranj
that her head in   pain be and husband chess

kheltā rahe.   cehrā surkh ho gayā. lauṅḍī se
playing remain. Face red   became. Maid from

kahā – jā-kar   kah, abhī   calie,   nahīṅ to
said 'Having-gone say, "Just-now let-him-go, not   then

vah ap hī   hakīm ke yahāṅ jāeṅgī.
she herself doctor -'s house will-go."'

An idiomatic translation of the Hindi passage

One day Begam Sahiba started to have a headache. 'Go and call Mirza
Sahib,' she told the maid, 'and ask him to get me some medicine from a

doctor's. Run along, hurry!' When the maid went to him Mirzaji said, 'Off you go, I'm just coming'. Begam Sahiba was furious. How could she put up with having a headache while her husband went on playing chess? Her face flushed. She told the maid to go and tell him to leave straightaway, otherwise she'd go to the doctor's herself.

Urdu version of the same passage in Perso-Arabic calligraphy

ایک دن بیگم صاحبہ کے سر میں درد ہونے لگا تو ماما سے کہا جا کر مرزا جی کو بلالو۔ کسی

حکیم کے یہاں سے دوا لا دیں۔ دوڑ جلدی کر۔ سر پھٹا جاتا ہے۔ ماما گئی تو مرزا جی نے کہا

چل ابھی آتے ہیں۔ بیگم صاحبہ کو اتنی تاب کہاں کہ ان کے سر میں درد ہو اور میاں شطرنج

کھیلنے میں مصروف ہوں۔ چہرہ سرخ ہو گیا اور ماما سے کہا جا کر کہہ کہ ابھی چلیے ورنہ

وہ خود حکیم صاحب کے پاس چلی جائیں گی۔

A direct transliteration and word for word translation

ek   din begam sāhiba ke sar   meṅ dard hone lagā
One day Begam Sahiba -'s head in   pain to-be began,

to   māmā se   kahā jā-kar   mirzā-jī ko bulā
then maid   from said 'Having-gone Mirzaji to call

lo. kisī hakīm ke yahāṅ se   davā   lā
get. Some doctor -'s house from medicine bring

deṅ.   dauṛ jaldī kar.   sar   phaṭā jātā
(he) may-give. Run haste make. Head split   going

hai. māmā gaī to   mirzā-jī ne kahā cal abhī
is.' Maid   went then Mirzaji by said 'Go just-now

āte haiṅ. begam sāhiba ko itnī   tāb   kahāṅ
(we) come. Begam Sahiba to so-much patience where

ki un-ke sar meṅ dard ho aur miyāṅ   shatranj
that her   head in   pain be and husband chess

khelne meṅ masrūf hoṅ. cihra surkh ho   gayā
playing in   occupied be. Face red   became

aur māmā se kahā jā-kar   kah ki abhī
and maid   from said 'Having-gone say that "Just-now

caliye   varna   voh khud   hakīm sāhib ke
let-him-go otherwise she herself Doctor Sahib -'s

pās calī jāeṅgī.
side will-go-off."'

An idiomatic translation of the Urdu version

One day Begam Sahiba started to have a headache. 'Go and call Mirzaji,' she then told the maid, 'and ask him to get me some medicine from a doctor's. Run along, hurry! My head is splitting'. When the maid went to him, Mirzaji said, 'Off you go, I'm just coming'. How could Begam Sahiba put up with having a headache while her husband was engrossed in playing chess? Her face flushed, and she told the maid to go and tell him to leave straightaway, otherwise, she'd go to the doctor's herself.

(From *The Chess Players* by Prem Chand)

Speakers of West African languages

Philip Tregidgo

Distribution

The languages of West Africa are too numerous and diverse for detailed regional listing. Within each state many different mother tongues are spoken, often unrelated one to another and mutually quite unintelligible. Even those which have achieved some status as a *lingua franca* within a given area tend to have more than one dialect, and any written literature will be of recent origin. Many languages are spoken only within very small areas, and many have never been written down at all.

Introduction

From an English language teaching point of view, it is more useful to classify the states of West Africa according to their official second language (English or French). The second language is the language of government and, to a large extent, of education, subject to local policy. It is also the medium of a growing African literature, since French, and particularly English, command greater prestige and a far wider market than any of the mother tongues. For these reasons, the choice of English or French as an official second language tends to have a stronger influence on English teaching materials and methods than the mother tongue of pupils or teacher.

A large proportion of the population are of limited education, and understand only a few words of English, or none at all. Those who have had an elementary education may use English only occasionally, and with severely limited competence. Even the highly educated elite do not necessarily speak it in the home, and may seldom read it, except in the press and at work.

The status of pidgin English is controversial. Each anglophone country has its own dialect of pidgin, used to some extent as a popular *lingua franca*, and pidgins in general are attracting increasing attention academically. (There is a degree course in Cameroon pidgin currently on offer at Leeds University.) But pidgin English is strongly opposed by most West African intellectuals, and it has little official recognition. It will not be considered here, though it will be reflected in many of the features of

185

pronunciation and grammar to be referred to. (Note that much of the strangeness of written pidgin derives from its spelling, which is adapted to suit the pronunciation.)

The anglophone states of West Africa include Nigeria, Ghana, Sierra Leone, and The Gambia (all former British colonies), and also Liberia, which has historical links, now tenuous, with the USA. In Cameroon, English has, in theory, equal status with French, but in practice only two of its five provinces (about 25 per cent of the population) are anglophone.

The francophone states (apart from Cameroon) comprise Mauritania, Mali, Niger, Chad, Senegal, Guinea, the Ivory Coast, Bourkina Fasso (formerly Upper Volta), Togo, and Benin. Here the education system shows a strong French influence, and English, learnt by some as a third language, tends to be spoken with a French accent. These anglophone and francophone countries cover the whole of West Africa except for Guinea-Bissau (formerly Portuguese Guinea). Arabic is not learnt except to some extent for religious purposes among Islamic peoples, chiefly in the sub-Saharan areas.

The most important of the mother tongues in anglophone West Africa (apart from English in Liberia) are as follows:

Nigeria: Hausa and Fulani in the north, Yoruba in the southwest, Ibo in the southeast. Hausa is probably the most important and highly developed of all West African languages. It is somewhat related to Arabic, and has a long literary tradition. It is Ibo speakers, however, who have contributed most to modern Nigerian literature in English.

Ghana: The Akan group of languages (mainly Twi and Fante) in Ashanti and the south, Ga in the area of Accra, Ewe (usually pronounced *evay*) in the southeast, Dagbani and others in the north.

Sierra Leone: A little English in Freetown, but mainly Krio in the west, Temne and others in the north, and Mende (= Mande, Mandingo) in the south.

The Gambia: Mende, Wolof, and others. In 1982 the country was merged with the surrounding francophone state of Senegal under the name Senegambia.

Liberia: A little English in Monrovia, but mainly a variety of other languages.

Although the influences of these many first and second languages are very diverse, it *is* possible to talk about typical West African problems in the learning of English. These may be partly due to the interference of certain broad features that are common to many West African languages, such as tonality and a comparatively simple vowel system, partly also to the incipient development of English as a *lingua franca*, and partly to common cultural features. The ensuing analysis applies particularly to Nigeria and Ghana, which (especially the former) make up the heavy nucleus of West African English teaching.

Phonology

General

West African languages tend to have fewer vowels than English, and fewer final consonants and consonant clusters. Thus many English vowels are not differentiated by West Africans, and many mid and final consonants sound indistinct. In addition, most West African languages are both tonal and syllable-timed. These features tend to give West African English a jerkiness, both in timing (with unnaturally regular syllables, and not much variation of emphasis) and in intonation (with ups and downs, but not much overall pattern).

Vowels

1. /iː/ and /ɪ/ often sound identical, both being pronounced short, and sometimes further confused with /eɪ/: *ship* for *sheep*, or sometimes *shape*.
2. /e/ and /ɜː/ are very often identical: *bed* and *bird*. The /ɜː/ phoneme causes particular problems, and may be further confused with /ɑː/: *bird* and *barred*.
3. /æ/, /ɑː/ and /ʌ/ are confused: *cat, cart*, and *cut*. In some areas /æ/ and /ʌ/ are confused with /e/: *bat* and *but* with *bet*.
4. /ɒ/, /ɔː/ and /əʊ/ are confused: *rod, roared*, and *road*.
5. /ʊ/ is confused with /uː/: *pull* and *pool*.
6. /ə/, like /ɜː/, causes great difficulty, not only in itself, but also (more especially) because West Africans do not generally weaken the vowels of unstressed syllables. As a result they tend to pronounce words as they are spelt, making a clear difference, for example, between the sounds of *policeman* and *policemen*; *-ence* and *-ance*, etc. The indefinite and definite articles are pronounced approximately /ɑː/ and /deɪ/, and *-er* endings are pronounced /ɑː/.
7. No distinction is made in vowel length. All vowels tend to be pronounced short. This increases the confusion between voiced and voiceless final consonants, as in *write* and *ride*.

Consonants

1. /ð/ and /θ/ are usually pronounced /d/ and /t/: *day* for *they*; *tin* for *thin*; *tree* for *three*, etc.
2. /ŋ/ is commonly pronounced /n/ or /ŋg/: '*singin*' for *singing*.
3. In some areas /l/ and /r/ are confused: '*rolly*' for *lorry*, and there may be widespread confusion between, for example, *grass* and *glass*; *play* and *pray*, etc.

187

4. Voiced final consonants tend to be devoiced and the preceding vowel shortened: *write* for *ride*; *rice* for *rise*; *rope* for *robe*; *picks* for *pigs*, etc.

5. Consonant clusters cause difficulty, especially where final, when some consonants tend to be omitted: *nest* for *next*; *knees* for *needs*; *fat* for *fact*, etc.

   Final clusters such as *film, months, asked, helps*, etc. cause special problems, and the same sort of difficulty occurs at junctures such as *five big towns*. For these reasons there is often a general indistinctness in the consonants of continuous speech, which hinders comprehension more than inaccurate vowel pronunciation.

Influence of spelling on pronunciation

As has already been mentioned, vowels that should be pronounced weak are very commonly given the full form implied by the spelling. It may also be the influence of spelling that causes such words as *tongue, among, money, stomach, love, other* and *touch* to be pronounced with /ɒ/ or /ɔː/ instead of /ʌ/. Pronunciation faults also affect spelling, of course, especially following the successful use of direct method teaching in primary schools: *the order one; in other that* (confusion of *order* and *other*); *The sun bent my skin*, etc.

Rhythm and stress

West African languages are typically syllable-timed, which strongly affects the rhythm of West African English. Stress-timed speech is totally unfamiliar. For the same reason, West Africans have great difficulty with the rhythms of English verse. Even apparently regular iambs sound strangely staccato in West African speech, and the more irregular feet of some English verse, including nursery rhymes, causes special difficulty, which cannot be cured by such advice as 'Say it naturally'.

   Contrastive emphasis, as in *I did it* and *I did it*, or in cases like *Did you say the green book or the red book?* also needs special attention, and this involves intonation, as well as stress.

Intonation

West African languages are typically tonal, i.e. each lexical item, even of a single syllable, will have a fixed tone or sequence of tones, irrespective of its context. Thus the concept of a particular tune applying to a whole utterance, and being capable of variation for the sake of emphasis or attitude is quite strange. The intonation of West African English is largely limited to a rise for yes/no questions and for pauses within the sentence, and a final fall for statements and *wh*-questions. Other patterns are rarely heard except among the highly educated. A further difficulty arises when an African name with its fixed intonation has to be fitted into an English sentence, since it is almost impossible to avoid a solecism in either English or the mother tongue.

Punctuation

The hyphen and the dash are not well understood and are often confused. In some areas a comma is often used incorrectly before reported speech:
> *He said that, he doesn't want to come.*

Other common mistakes, e.g. overuse of capitals, commas between complete sentences (often incorrectly linked with *also, however*, etc.) are, of course, not confined to West Africa.

Grammar

General

It would be difficult for even a specialist to make valid and useful generalisations about the grammar of West African languages, but every teacher of English in West Africa quickly notices the recurrence of certain types of mistake. The following selection is very widespread, though the part played by mother tongue interference is not always clear, and regional variations are certainly found.

Verbs

1. The regular endings and the use of auxiliaries in the simple present and past cause frequent problems:
   > *She want to speak English, but she don't know how.*
   > *He doesn't goes to school.*
   > *He didn't came back.*
2. The infinitive form after *make, let, see* and *hear* also causes problems:
   > *He makes me to do it.*
   > *He makes me does it.*
   > *I saw him did it.*
3. Similar mistakes are common when verb phrases are reduced after conjunctions:
   > *I didn't see anything or heard anything.*
   > *He made me sit down and told him about it.*

   Either/or questions produce similar errors:
   > *Do you make it by hand, or you use a machine?*
4. Choice of an appropriate tense form causes many problems. Progress-

189

ive forms are used fairly aptly on the whole, except with certain stative uses of, e.g. *have, think,* and *see*:
> **I was having no money.*
> **I am thinking you are wrong.*
> **I am not seeing anything.*

5. The present perfect is frequently misused, or not used:
> **I have seen him yesterday.*
> **I am a teacher since 1980.*

6. The past perfect, too, is not generally understood, and tends to be used in place of *used to*:
> **In the old days we had travelled on foot.*

   Used to itself is often used in the present for habitual action:
> **That boy use to tell lies.* (for *That boy tells lies.*)

7. *I will* and *I am going to* (or in pidgin *I go,* e.g. *I go kill him*) tend to be overused when the contracted form *I'll* would be more apt.

Modal verbs

Modal verbs and related forms are used fairly well on the whole, though epistemic uses (e.g. *That must/may/can't be true*) are not well understood.

   Must and *is to* tend to be overused at the expense of *have to*:
> **I can't come as I must take an exam.*
> **Nowadays all children are to go to school.*

Needn't is often followed by *to*:
> **You needn't to say that.*

Nouns and articles

1. The difference between countable and uncountable nouns is not well understood, and many uncountables are wrongly classified:
> **We had a rain this morning.*
> **He gave me some informations.*

   Similar mistakes occur with other nouns, e.g. *firewood, food, luggage, advice, furniture, news, equipment, help, dress, property, land, luck, permission.*

2. Other mistakes with articles may or may not be related to countability:
> **This is goat.* (Names of animals in particular tend to be treated as proper nouns.)
> **This instrument is called thermometer.*
> **He has written some book.*

3. *Some* often occurs after negatives:
> **I don't want some.*

4. The definite article is often wrongly used or omitted with names and titles:
> *Do you want to speak to Minister?*
> *He goes to Roman Catholic School.*
> *the South Africa; the Tema Harbour*, etc.

5. Expressions of quantity are often misused, e.g. *much*:
> *They don't have much children.*
> *Yes, I can eat much.*
> *It is much interesting.*

6. *Little* and *few* are also confused, and the negative effect of omitting *a* is not understood:
> *There are a little eggs.*
> *Give me few more oranges.*
> *There are a few mosquitoes, so we do not suffer from malaria.*

7. *Too* and *enough* are often not understood:
> *This stew is too good!*
> *He ran too fast to catch the bus.*
> *The roads are bad, so there are enough accidents.*

8. *So* is often wrongly used without *that*; and comparative forms without *than*:
> *In the southwest there is so much forest.*
> *The library contains more books.* (for *The Library contains quite a lot of books.*)

Subordinate clauses

A. CONDITIONAL

Tense forms in conditional sentences cause problems:
> *If I tell him, he would beat me.*
> *If it would have not happened, he would not be killed.*

B. TIME CLAUSES

These have similar tense form problems, and *if* is commonly used incorrectly for *when*, in referring to the future:
> *If the sun sets this evening the meeting will begin.*

C. INDIRECT SPEECH

Sequence of tense rules in indirect speech are not well understood:
> *Jesus told them he will die.*
> *I didn't know you are here.*
> *I hope you would come.*

191

Indirect questions are not distinguished from direct ones:
>*I want to know how do you do it.*
>*He asked her that, will you marry me.*

D. CONCESSIVE

Though clauses tend to be followed by *but* in the main clause; and *however* clauses cause word order difficulties:
>*Although it is difficult, but I can do it.*
>*However it is difficult, I will do it.*

E. RELATIVE

Relative clauses commonly cause problems, especially the repetition of pronouns:
>*That is the man I saw him.*

Pronouns

1. *He* and *him* are often used for human females and for animals:
   >*I greeted my sister when he came.*
2. Reflexive pronouns are often used in place of *each other*:
   >*They greeted themselves.*
3. In continuous writing there is a tendency to avoid pronouns (and other anaphoric devices) in an effort towards completeness and clarity, and the result often sounds wordy and repetitive.

Vocabulary and culture

Where English is a second language as opposed to a foreign language, it becomes to some extent the property of the non-native user; it is adapted to his or her own purposes, and reflects his or her own culture. Africans themselves have often resisted this notion, especially in the presence of a British teacher, and claim to want to learn standard British English. The fact remains that in West African countries English has already been adapted in certain characteristic ways; in pronunciation, in vocabulary and general expression, even in certain marginal points of grammar; and many teachers will find difficulty in deciding how far to go in 'correcting' certain features in order to make them conform to the British norm. Should one, for example, accept a *storey-building*; *He has travelled* (for *He is away*); *We are tight friends*; *They were making noise*, etc., all of which are commonly used in West African English? Should one try to reduce the degree of formality in letter writing, or in greetings, which is ingrained in West African culture? Such questions remain highly debatable.

West African languages are rich in proverbs and colourful sayings. Africans tend in consequence to be unduly attracted to English proverbs and sayings, and to mistake them for idioms, to be used as often as possible.

The reading of fiction and biography for pleasure is comparatively rare. Most reading is done for educational or self-improvement purposes, at a very slow pace, and with excessive use of the dictionary. Books chosen tend to be very dry and didactic. Choice of suitable fiction is not easy. African students are often totally unfamiliar with European objects, attitudes, interests, worries and conventions, and from this point of view, twentieth century fiction is often less suitable than, say, Dickens. The rapid expansion since the 1950s of a genuinely African literature in English suggests a possible solution, but the language of much of it is too difficult at junior secondary level, and the content is sometimes controversial.

Swahili speakers

Neville Grant

Distribution

TANZANIA, KENYA, UGANDA, MOZAMBIQUE, ZAIRE, COMORO ISLANDS, Somalia, Rwanda, Burundi, Malagasy Republic, Oman, Zambia.

Introduction

Swahili is the most important language in East Africa, with at least 60 million speakers. Only a minority speak Swahili as their mother tongue: most speak it as a second, third, or even fourth language. Swahili is the national language of Tanzania, one of the four African national languages of Zaire, and the official language of Kenya. It plays a very important role as a *lingua franca* in Eastern and to some extent Central Africa, where it is very widely used both in local trade and international broadcasting. It is used in a number of newspapers, and has a growing literature.

Recent research indicates that Swahili was emerging as a separate language as early as the ninth century, and that it probably originated from around the Tana River estuary in Kenya. But as trade developed, the language spread both up and down the East African coast, and into the interior. Its literary history dates back at least to the early eighteenth century, from which a great deal of traditional tenzi (epic poems) have survived. The name Swahili comes from the Arabic word sawāḥil, meaning *coasts*, and the language contains a number of words of Arabic origin. However, the language is essentially African.

Swahili belongs to the Bantu family of languages, which are spoken by most Africans south of a line drawn roughly from Douala in Cameroon in the west, eastwards to the north of Lake Victoria; and from the east of Lake Victoria across to Brava in Somalia. Apart from Swahili, the Bantu languages include Nguni languages (Zulu, Xhosa, Ndebele, and Swati, etc.); the Shona group; Sotho-Tswana; the many languages of Zambia, Malawi and Tanzania; and many languages spoken in Kenya and Uganda, of which Gikuyu/Kamba and Luganda are the best known. Swahili is not completely typical of Bantu languages (see below), but it is the most widely spoken language in black Africa, and it shares with the other Bantu languages all their most outstanding structural and morphological characteristics. Because of this, many if not most of the observations made about Swahili in this chapter may be applied, *mutatis mutandis* to other Bantu languages.

There are about twenty different dialects of Swahili: the most important are Kiunguja, the dialect of Zanzibar; Kimvita, the dialect of Mombasa; and Kiamu, the dialect of Lamu Island in Kenya. The Kingwana dialect, widespread in Zaire, is based on Kiunguja, which has come to be regarded as the standard form of Swahili.[1]

Bantu languages share *inter alia* the following characteristics:

1. *Noun class system* In any Bantu language almost all noun forms consist of a prefix plus stem. The prefix will act as a marker, indicating what class the noun is in:

   mtu = person   watu = people
   kiko = a pipe   viko = pipes

   The number of noun classes varies slightly from one Bantu language to another. Swahili has some fifteen noun classes, rather fewer than most other Bantu languages.

2. *Concord* In Bantu languages the noun dominates the sentence. The other words in the sentence are brought into concordial relationship with the noun by means of affixes called *concords*. Two examples of Swahili will suffice:

   Kisu kile kikubwa kimevunjika. (lit. *knife – that – big – is broken*) = *That big knife is broken.*

   Visu vile vikubwa vimevunjika. (lit. *knives – those – big – are broken*) = *Those big knives are broken.*

3. *Agglutination* All Bantu languages have an agglutinating morphological structure. Here is a Swahili example:

   wameshindwa
   wa = *they*
   me = tense/aspect marker
   shinda = stem of the verb kushinda *to conquer*
   w = passive marker
   (meaning *They have been conquered.*)

4. *Sound systems* Bantu languages have a very similar sound system:
   – Most Bantu languages are tonal: tonality is virtually absent from most dialects of Swahili.
   – Phonemically the Bantu languages are also remarkably similar. Most of them have the same five vowel phonemes (see below), and no diphthongs. The consonant systems are also very similar,

---

[1] For more information on the various dialects of Swahili, see *Swahili Language Handbook* by Edgar C. Polomé (Centre for Applied Linguistics, 1967).

except that some of the southern Bantu languages have borrowed some Khoisan 'click' sounds, and Swahili has borrowed some Arabic sounds for words of Arabic origin.

These then are some of the salient defining characteristics of Bantu languages. It will be seen that the main differences between Swahili and the other Bantu languages lie in the few words of Arabic origin it has borrowed, together with some consonants, its lack of tonality, and in the smaller number of noun classes that it contains. In all other respects, Swahili may be regarded as a typical Bantu language, and the comments that follow about Swahili speakers' difficulties in learning English will therefore be applicable to a very large extent to speakers of other Bantu languages as well.

Phonology

General

The main differences between Swahili and English are as follows:
— Swahili has only five vowels, in contrast to the 22 of English.
— English has 24 consonants; Swahili has 28.
— Swahili speech alternates vowels with consonants, and contains virtually no consonant clusters.
— In Swahili, all utterances and syllables end in a vowel sound.
— The two languages have very different systems of word stress.
— The intonation patterns are somewhat different.

Vowels

The vowel sounds represent the biggest single problem area for Swahili speakers learning English. The five vowels of Swahili are as follows:

/i/
/e/   These are slightly higher than their nearest equivalents in
/u/   English.

/a/   This sound is shorter, higher, and further forward than its nearest English equivalent.

/o/   This sound is somewhere between the English /ɒ/ and /əʊ/.

Virtually all English vowel and diphthong sounds may therefore cause problems. The tendency is for Swahili speakers to deploy the Swahili sound that they perceive as being nearest to the target English sound, and this problem is compounded by the notoriously misleading orthography of English. The problem may be summarised conveniently by this diagram:

Swahili phonemes	English phonemes (RP)	Key words
/i/	/iː/	*bead*
	/ɪ/	*bid*
	/ɪə/	*beard*
	/eɪ/	*bade*
/e/	/e/	*bed*
	/eə/	*bared*
	/ʌ/	*bud*
	/æ/	*bad*
	/ɜː/	*bird*
/a/	/ɑː/	*bard*
	/aʊ/	*bowed*
	/aɪ/	*bide*
	/ɒ/	*bod*
/o/	/ɔː/	*board*
	/əʊ/	*bode*
	/ɔɪ/	*buoyed*
	/ʊ/	*bull*
/u/	/ʊə/	*boor*
	/uː/	*booed*

The author is indebted to Dr H. F. Grant for a version of the diagram above. Another version (featuring General American) appears in Polomé (1967).

The English phoneme /ə/ is omitted from this diagram, as it has no equivalent in Swahili and requires special attention. In practice Swahili speakers tend to assign to it the sound value most strongly implied by the orthographic symbol that represents it, e.g. *again* might be pronounced /æɡeɪn/.

Specific sound contrasts causing difficulties include:

/iː/ and /ɪ/	*leave* and *live*
/æ/ and /e/	*band* and *bend*
/æ/ and /ʌ/	*rag* and *rug*
/æ/ and /ɑː/	*hat* and *heart*
/ɑː/ and /ʌ/	*heart* and *hut*
/ɪ/ and /e/	*bit* and *bet*
/ɜː/ and /ʌ/	*bird* and *bud*
/e/ and /ɜː/	*lend* and *learned*
/ɒ/, /ɔː/ and /əʊ/	*cot, caught,* and *coat*
/e/ and /eɪ/	*edge* and *age*
/ʊ/ and /uː/	*full* and *fool*
/æ/ and /ɜː/	*tanned* and *turned*

197

Consonants

All the English consonants have their rough equivalents in Swahili, except /r/, which in Swahili is an alveolar trill, not unlike a rolled Scottish /r/. In addition there is a certain amount of dialectical variation in Swahili, which can cause problems that are not easily predictable. There may also be influences on the speaker's English from his or her first language, if this is not Swahili. Predictable problems include:

1. /l/ and /r/ are often confused by those who speak Swahili as a second or third language: *load* for *road*.
2. /h/ is sometimes dropped: *eat* for *heat*.
3. /θ/ and /ð/ occur in Swahili words derived from Arabic, but not in other Bantu languages. Such words and sounds are avoided in some dialects: the sounds /t/ or /s/ may be used for /θ/, and /d/ or /z/ for /ð/: *useful* for *youthful*; *breeze* for *breathe*, etc.
4. The following sound contrasts are not made in some dialects of Swahili, and other Bantu languages, and confusion can arise:
   /g/ and /k/: *engaged* and *encaged*
   /b/ and /p/: *bride* and *pride*
   /dʒ/ and /tʃ/: *judge* and *church*
   /t/ and /d/: *train* and *drain*
5. /s/ replaces /ʃ/ in some dialects of Swahili, which can carry over into English: *sew* for *show*.
6. In Zairian Swahili and in other Bantu languages, /g/ is devoiced to /k/, and /z/ to /s/: *lock* for *log* and *peace* for *peas*.
7. Also in Zairian Swahili, /d/ and /l/ may be used in free variation, as may /l/ and /r/; even sometimes /b/ and /w/.

Syllabic intrusion and addition

Consonant clusters are much rarer in Swahili than in English, and Swahili speakers therefore tend to separate out the consonants in a cluster with 'intrusive' vowel sounds. In addition, Swahili speakers tend to add an extra vowel to utterances ending in a consonant:
   /ekɪsplaneɪʃon/ for *explanation*
   /sɪtɪrenɪθɪ/ for *strength*

Influence of spelling on pronunciation

Since there is a regular correspondence between sound and orthographic symbol in Swahili, the unwary learner is easily misled by the irregularities of English spelling. The problems are fairly predictable:

1. Silent letters may be pronounced, e.g. in *honour* and *sign*.
2. Incorrect sound values will be assigned to words that are oddly spelt,

e.g. *'orainge'* for *orange*: *'biskwit'* for *biscuit*, etc. Words with a silent letter are a common problem, e.g. *thumb*.

Rhythm and stress

Swahili is a syllable-timed language, whereas English is a stress-timed language. In consequence, Swahili speakers tend to give every syllable in English almost equal stress.

Weak forms in English tend to be overstressed, and may be given their strong pronunciation.

Apart from the Arabic loanwords, which are stressed on the antepenultimate syllable (e.g. 'thamani = *value* and ka'dhalika = *likewise*), Swahili, in common with all other Bantu languages, stresses the penultimate syllable of a word. Carried over into English, this can lead to distortions in words like *photo'graphy*, *hospital'ity*, *ci'garette*, etc.

Intonation

In Swahili the typical intonation pattern is a low fall, which is carried over into English even where English uses a rise. As a result it is not always clear if a Swahili speaker is, for example, asking a question in English.

Grammar

General

From the description of Bantu languages above, it will already be apparent that there are radical differences between the grammatical systems of English and Swahili. The noun class system, noun dominance, and agglutination have already been referred to. Swahili also has a number of extremely economical inflectional devices for signalling a great variety of grammatical meanings.

Aliweka kalamu mezani. (= *He (or she) put the pen on the table.*)

A	li	weka	kalamu	meza	ni
third person sing. pronoun marker	simple past tense marker	verb: *put*	noun: *pen*	noun: *table*	location marker

Swahili does not have anything quite like the English auxiliary verb system for asking questions, indicating tense and modality, etc. In Swahili there are no articles, and there is no gender marking. English prepositions have no exact equivalent in Swahili, which uses locative forms attached to the noun, as in the example above (**mezani**), various class concords, and a variety of multi-purpose prepositional inflections and particles.

Word order – S-V-O, S-V-IO-O – is more or less the same (in statements, but not in questions), but in Swahili, as in all Bantu languages, aspect is at least as important as tense, and this leads to a wide variety of confusions in using verbs in English.

Questions and negatives; auxiliaries

1. The auxiliary *do* has no equivalent in Swahili, and tends therefore to be misused, or omitted:
    *He not leave yesterday.
    *He leave yesterday?
    *Why the boys hid behind the trees?
2. Sometimes *do* is used unnecessarily:
    *Every morning I do get up and I do have my breakfast.
3. Yes/no questions are marked only by a change of intonation, and orthographically by the question mark:
    *The work it is finished?
4. Questions with a question word follow either the pattern 'statement + interrogative', or the pattern 'interrogative + statement':
    *He arrived when?
    *Why you are late?
5. In Swahili, negative forms are usually indicated by verb inflection:
    anakwenda = *he is going*
    haendi = *he is not going*
6. *No* and *not* tend to be used interchangeably:
    *He is no going to the mosque today.
    *There is no any rice in the market.
(See also the section 'Articles and determiners'.)

Time, tense and aspect

Arguably, aspect plays as important a part in verb formation as time, and this can lead to a number of problems. Time is indicated by the following tense markers (infixes):
1. -na-: Present progressive tense
    Watoto wanasoma. (= *The children are reading. / The children read.*)
Swahili uses adverbials to differentiate between present progressive and simple present, and the two tenses are thus confused in English:
    *They are going to school every morning.

Also affected are verbs of perception, and non-conclusive verbs, such as *know*, *like*, *have*, and *understand*:

I am seeing many different colours in that khanga.

I am having no news from home.

Another very common error is the omission of the *s* on the third person singular form of the simple present:

The boy love to play football.

In subordinate clauses -na- can also be used as a marker to indicate the present time in the context. When carried over into English, this results in many tense errors, in direct and reported speech:

The students realised that the school is on fire.

One day she was told that her mother is ill.

2. -li-: Simple past

   Nilikwenda mjini jana. (= *I went to town yesterday.*)

It will be observed that the stem of the verb – in this case kwenda – remains unchanged, and this too results in error when carried over into English:

I go to town yesterday.

Sometimes the auxiliary *did* is seen as equivalent to the tense marker -li-, and an unnecessary auxiliary intrudes:

I did go to town yesterday.

Other problems in using the simple past in English include:

– Use of the regular suffix for irregular verbs:

   leaved for *left*

   finded for *found*, etc.

– Inflecting question and negative forms:

   Did they went to town?

   The man did not died.

– Using the simple past instead of the present perfect:

   We finished the exercise. (for *We have finished the exercise.*)

– Using the simple past instead of the past perfect, which does not exist in Swahili:

   Before he came to Nairobi, he never saw an aeroplane.

– Using the present instead of the past for the 'unreal past':

   You have better go soon.

   It is time we return to school.

3. -ka-: Subsecutive

   Nilikwenda mjini nikamwona Moyo. (= *I went to town, I then see Moyo.*)

The infix -ka- indicates that one action follows another, and is part of a sequence of actions. Attempts to transfer this convention to English lead to further tense errors, as well as either the omission of the conjunction *and* or, alternatively, the failure to commence a new sentence. What may be perceived as a punctuation error is often, more seriously perhaps, an attempt by the writer to superimpose Swahili syntax on English:

> *I went to the market I buy some fruit.*

4. -ta-: Future (in relation to the time of reference)

> **Nitakwenda mjini kesho.** (=*I shall go to town tomorrow.*)

The *shall/will* future forms tend to be used in English as direct equivalents of this infix -ta-, including occasions when these future forms are not used in English:

> *Don't go until he will come.*
> *Unless he will come soon, he will miss the bus.*

The -ta- infix is also used in Swahili in contexts that in English require *would*:

> *I wish he will hurry up.*
> *Mwajuma said she will tell the headmaster next day.*

Note here that the tense marker stays the same in reported speech. It should be added that Swahili conventions in using reported speech lead to other errors in English, too:

> *He said that, I shall go to town tomorrow.* (for *He said he would go to town the next day.*)

Note that the intrusive comma as well as the unchanged person and tense forms are all results of direct translation from Swahili.

ASPECT

Like other Bantu languages, Swahili uses different markers to indicate the way an action is visualised. Among these markers are:

1. -me- This infix indicates an action that has been completed, the results of which are still relevant, and thus may be seen as parallel to one use of the present perfect in English:

> **Wanangu wamefika.** (= *My children have arrived.*)

However its use does not correspond exactly with the English usage:

> **Chumba kimechafuka.** (= *The room* is *untidy.*)
> **Tumesikia.** (= *We understand.* / *We have heard.*)

This may account for Swahili speakers occasionally using the present perfect tense instead of the simple present tense in such contexts.

Conversely Swahili speakers very frequently fail to use the present perfect in sentences like *He has worked there since 1980*. The Swahili convention is to use the -na- infix:

> *He is working there since 1980.*

Another common error is the confusion of *since* and *for*:

> *He has worked there since six years.* or *He is working there since six years.*

2. -ki- In contrast with the -me- infix, the -ki- infix indicates an action
    happening simultaneously with another action, but not completed:
    > **Tuliwaona watoto wakisoma.** (lit. *We saw them the children
    > they reading.*)

    Attempts to make parallel constructions in English lead to errors
    such as:
    > *The women pounded the grains and sifting them.*
    > *He walked slowly and carrying a heavy basket.*
    > *He slept meanwhile his sister was working* (where *meanwhile*
    >   may be an attempt to convey the sense of the -ki- infix).

    -ki- is also used as a conditional marker:
    > **Mungu akipenda.** (= *If God wills.*)

    Since there is no equivalent in English, Swahili speakers may use a
    variety of different tenses in a conditional clause.

Modal verbs

Modality is usually expressed by means of verb inflection, and a wide
variety of errors are made:
- The use of *can* and *will* for *could* and *would*:
    > *Ali promised he can help them the following week.*
- Confusion of *may* and *might*; *would* and *should*.
- Faulty construction:
    > *I can be able to help.*

Other verb forms

1. The verbal noun form in Swahili is the same as the infinitive form.
    This leads to many problems:
    > *They succeeded to finish the work.*
    > *They stopped to talk.* (for *They stopped talking.*)
    > *They made him to work hard.*
2. Verbs that are transitive in English may be intransitive in Swahili:
    > *At the party they enjoyed very much.*
    > *She needed some rice, so she went to the market and bought.*
3. Verbs of prohibition, prevention and denial in Swahili must be
    followed by a verb with a negative inflection:
    > *He prevented him not to go.*
    > *He denied that he did not know him.*
4. In Swahili verbs may be transferred into the passive by means of
    inflection:
    > **kupiga** = *to beat*
    > **kupigwa** = *to be beaten*

The Swahili convention is so different from English that many problems arise:
> *Our school is difficult to be reached.*
> *This water is good to be drunk.*

5. Question tags are very commonly misused. Swahili has a simple tag sivyo? (= *not so?*):
> *You have seen the headmaster, didn't you?*

6. Answers to negative questions can also lead to a complete breakdown in communication. The Swahili words ndiyo and siyo are often roughly translated as *yes* and *no*. More accurately, they signal assent and dissent: *It is (not) as you say.* So the answer to a negative question might be misleading:
> 'So you don't want to go to the dance?' 'Yes.' (= *Yes, I don't want to go.*)

Non-verb sentences

These are common in Swahili, e.g. location markers may be taken to imply predication:
> Kikapu kiko jikoni. (lit. *Basket – it – there – kitchen – in/at*) = *The basket is in the kitchen.*

Miscellaneous

All the following errors are attributable to Swahili interference:
> *I forgot my book at home.*
> *It was last week when I came to Tabora.*
> *Clinics are not enough.* (for *There are not enough clinics.*)
> *In my family we are many.*

Articles and determiners

There are no definite or indefinite articles in Bantu languages, and there are many problems as a result:
1. The omission of articles:
> *Where is pen I gave you?*
2. The use of the wrong article:
> *Please close a door.*
3. Confusion of *a* and *an*:
> *That is an useful book.*
4. Misuse of the definite article with proper nouns:
> *the President Nyerere*
> *River Tana is long.*

Other very common errors include:
1. Confusion of *few/ a few, little/ a little*:
    **Because of the rain, there were a few at the match.*
2. Use of *all* for *both*:
    **All my parents come from Mombasa.*
3. Confusion of *much/many, few/little*:
    **She has much clothes.*
    **There is few rice in the basket.*
4. Confusion of *no* and *not*:
    **There is no any / no enough food.*
5. Confusion of *some* and *any*:
    **Has he some petrol? He hasn't some petrol.*

Nouns

Bantu language noun class systems are so different from English that many problems arise, including:
— Misuse of uncountable nouns:
    **informations, equipments, breads, a cattle, an advice*, etc.
— Using a plural verb form with a singular noun:
    **This news were good.*
— Using plural nouns in the singular:
    **a trouser, a scissor*, etc.
— Failure to use or misuse of the Saxon genitive, which does not exist in Swahili:
    **the door's handle   the house of my friend*
— Confusion of nouns and adjectives (often through faulty phonology):
    **wealth* and *wealthy, difficult* and *difficulty*, etc.

Pronouns

The biggest single problem is the failure to distinguish between masculine and feminine forms, which are not marked in Swahili or other Bantu languages:
    **She loved his husband.*
Another major problem is the redundant use of pronouns, a feature of Swahili:
    **Kukubo he has brought the food.*
    **Have you brought it the food?*
The reply to this question sometimes omits the object pronoun infix:
    **I have brought.*
Emphatic forms are sometimes used inappropriately:
    **Myself, I have arrived.*
    **Myself travelled to Mombasa.*

Adjectives and adverbs

Adjectives, or descriptives, follow the noun in Swahili, and the order of adjectives in English can cause problems. But the main problem areas are in complex adjectival patterns:

> Mtoto wangu ni mrefu sawa na wako. (= *My child is tall as yours.*)
>
> Nyumba hii kubwa kuliko ile. (= *This house big than that [one].*)

There is no inflection for comparative and superlative forms, which are signalled by phrases like kuliko or kupita, and this leads to many errors:

> *This house is very big than that one.* (The intensifier sana is being used as the equivalent of *more.*)
>
> *This house is more bigger than that one.*
>
> *He was the very interesting man I have met.*
>
> *This is the best book than all the others.*

Apart from the difficulties with phrasal verbs, noted above, other problems with adverbs include:

1. Omission of adverbs:
> 'Are they coming later?' *'I don't think.' (so omitted)
>
> *I worked as I could.*

2. Faulty comparative constructions, as with adjectives:
> *They are walking slowly more than me.*
>
> *I am working hard as you.*

3. Faulty adverb formation:
> *They ran away cowardly.*

Other similar errors include *fastly, hardly (for hard), quick (for quickly), loudly and aloud being used interchangeably.

Prepositions and particles

The systems used in Swahili are very different from English and therefore cause great problems.

1. Omission:
> *She explained them the exercise.*
>
> *He arrived ten o'clock.*
>
> *She replied me that she doesn't know.*

2. Use of unnecessary prepositions:
> *They requested for help.*
>
> *What time did you reach at Tanga?*

3. Use of incorrect prepositions. One major problem is that Swahili has a locative suffix (ni), the meaning of which varies according to the context. As a result English prepositions of location are likely to be confused:

>mezani (= *at, to, on, by, from the table*)
>nyumbani (= *at, to, in, by, from the house*)
>mwituni (= *at, to, in, by, inside, from, near the forest*)

There are other problems, one of the more significant being the multi-purpose preposition **katika**, which can mean *in, into, out from, up into, up from, on,* and *while*. It also has other idiomatic uses.

Another multi-purpose preposition is **kwa**, which can mean *with, on, to, from, for, as a result of,* and *during*:

>kwa miguu (= *on foot*)
>kwa kisu (= *with a knife*)

Among the many common errors are:

>*to arrive to school*
>*to drive with a car*
>*to be full with water*
>*to meet at London*
>*to look to the board*
>*to walk till the college*
>*to stay to evening*
>*to enter for the hall*
>*to go for leave*

All English phrasal verbs are likely to cause problems. Their nearest equivalent in Bantu languages are the 'prepositional verbs' which, by inflection, express a wide and subtle variety of relationships that are in some ways comparable to, but not coincident with, the prepositional and adverbial particles used in English. Many errors result:

>*They put off the fire.*

Other verbs are given unnecessary particles:

>*They accompanied with his sisters.*
>*We discussed about politics.*

Subordinate clauses

A. RELATIVE

The equivalent of the English relative pronoun in Swahili is the connective, **amba**, which inflects to show concordial agreement:

>Hiki ni kikapu ambacho nilikinunua. (= *Here is the basket which I bought.*)

One feature of this structure is that the subordinate clause includes the object pronoun infix -ki-, so that the literal translation of the sentence is:

>*This is the basket which I bought it.*

The inclusion of the subject or object pronoun is a common error:

>*The girl who I married her is very beautiful.*
>*The people that they came from Lesotho settled in Zambia.*

B. CO-ORDINATION AND SUBORDINATION

The main conjunction in Swahili is na (= *and*), which is used mainly as a connective in phrases. Also common are co-ordinating conjunctions such as juu ya hayo (= *in addition*), kwa hivyo (= *because of this*), etc. Their equivalents in English are sentence connectors rather than conjunctions, and this leads to sentences like:

> *She missed the bus therefore she was angry.
> *The pupils did the exercise meanwhile the teacher was marking.
> *She was exhausted. Even though she continued to work.
> *He worked hard because of this he was made a prefect.

Patterns of subordination can also cause problems. The all-purpose intensifier sana is translated directly into English to produce sentences like:

> *The chest is too heavy that I cannot lift it.
> *The chest is very heavy that I cannot lift it.

The equivalents of *although* (ingawa) and *but* (lakini) are both used in a concessive sentence:

> *Although it was late but they went on working.
> *Despite they were cold, but they worked hard.

Vocabulary

The following tend to be confused or misused, either because they each have only one equivalent in Swahili, or because of semantic overlap, or for other reasons:

to borrow / to lend	to rest / to have a holiday
to rise / to raise	to see / to find
to rob / to steal	to send / to bring
to stay with / to keep	to leave / to give up
to escort / to see someone off	to wear / to put on (clothes)
to bath / to bathe	to cheat / to deceive / to tell lies
to refuse / to deny	
to like / to love	to follow / to accompany
to prefer / to like	to meet / to find / to discover
to do / to make	to hurt / to pain
to reach / to arrive	to lay / to lie
to discover / to invent	to say / to tell
to learn / to teach	to take place / to take part
to think / to hope	to convince / to persuade
to wound / to hurt / to injure / to damage	to attend / to attend to
to refuse / to forbid	to win / to beat
	to take off / to put off

newspaper/magazine	*every time / all the time*
fault/mistake	*wonderful/strange*
arm/hand	*leg/foot*
very/too/so	*all/both*
job/work	*in time / on time*

The following examples of East African idiomatic English are in common use, though many are of arguable acceptability:

> *on my side* ... (= *in my opinion* ...)
> *on the side of* ... (= *as regards* ...)
> *somehow* (= *rather*)
> *to school* (vb), e.g. *I schooled in Moshi* (= *to go to school*)
> *brotherisation* (= *nepotism*)
> *menu* (= *programme*)
> *to foot* (= *to walk*)
> *to help myself* (= *to urinate*)
> *today morning* (= *this morning*)
> *yesterday night* (= *last night*)

Culture

Anyone who has taught in Africa will agree that the students are a pleasure to teach. They want to learn, and if this chapter may seem to imply that they find it hard to do so, or make many errors, then such an inference is completely wrong. Africans are born linguists: they may well have to know several African languages (and not all of them Bantu), before they learn English, and their success in learning English, given the many difficulties, is quite remarkable.

The visiting teacher who hopes to teach in Africa would do well to remember the following points:

1. The good teacher is also a good learner, of both the culture of the host country and one of its languages. If students and fellow members of staff form the impression that you are anxious to learn, they will be that much more welcoming. Even if you regard yourself as a poor linguist, do try to learn whatever the main local language is. It is enjoyable, it helps you to teach more effectively, and above all, it helps you to form worthwhile relationships with people from the host country.

2. Find out as quickly as possible about local etiquette. Note particularly how people greet each other, and take leave of each other, and try to act in a similar way. It is widely felt that Europeans tend to be far too preoccupied with the job in hand to bother to observe basic rules of courtesy. For example, in Britain or the USA it would not be considered unusual to start a conversation: 'Hello. Look, about that

209

timetable. When ... ?' In such a situation the main focus of interest is the timetable, not the person being addressed. In many parts of the world, including Africa and the Middle East, such a brisk approach would be seen as very rude. It is very important to start off any such conversations with enquiries about the person's health, family, etc., in a manner that shows you are really interested.

3. Many gestures and mannerisms acceptable in European societies are considered rude in many African countries. For example, in many African societies, greeting a person with a strong handshake and a steady gaze may be thought offensive. On the other hand, shaking hands is much more common than it is in Britain, even with someone whom one sees fairly often. Most finger gestures should be avoided, particularly the vertical 'come here' beckoning with the forefinger.

4. A visitor who sits down uninvited is showing normal courtesy, not undue familiarity. Unexpected visitors should always be welcomed, no matter how pressing one's prior engagements. This may partly explain why guests at a party often arrive late, although it should be added that in many African societies guests are not expected to arrive on time.

5. Find out about local attitudes to dress. On the coast, or in Muslim areas, great care should be taken to avoid causing offence. For example, women should dress carefully and arms and legs should be reasonably covered. Men too need to exercise some care. There is a common belief among young European males that very casual dress indicates informality, and therefore friendliness. Often, however, it has the opposite effect. Except on very informal occasions, shorts are usually considered distasteful at best. Short shorts are definitely unacceptable. In a few countries, notably Tanzania, shorts are actually forbidden.

A sample of written Swahili with a word for word translation

Hapo kale   paka hakukaa   katika nyumba za watu; alikaa
Here formerly cat   did-not-stay place houses of men; he-stayed

mwituni au maguguni tu.   Paka mmoja alikuwa rafiki ya sungura
in-forest or in-bush   only. Cat one   he-was friend of hare

wakatembea   pamoja, na paka akastaajabia   werevu wa
and-they-wandered together, and cat   and-he-admired cleverness of

rafiki yake; lakini siku moja funo   akagombana   na
friend his; but   day one duiker and-he-argued-together with

sungura akamwua   kwa pembe zake. Sasa kwa kuwa rafiki
hare   and-he-him-killed with horns his. Then of   to-be friend

yake amekufa paka akafuatana   na   yule   funo.
his he-is-dead cat and-he-accompanied with this (the) duiker.

An idiomatic translation

A long time ago the cat did not live in men's houses: he lived only in the forest or in the bush. A certain cat was the friend of a hare and wandered about with him; the cat admired the cleverness of his friend, but one day, a duiker quarrelled with the hare and killed him with a thrust of his horns. Since his friend was dead, the cat began keeping company with the duiker.

(From *An Introduction to Languages and Language in Africa* by Pierre Alexandre)

Acknowledgement

The author would like to thank Said El-Gheithy of the City Literary Institute, London, for his comments on an early draft of this paper.

Bibliography

Alexandre, Pierre (1972) *An Introduction to Languages and Language in Africa.* Translated by F. A. Leary. Northwestern University Press and Heinemann Educational Books.
Ashton, E. O. (1944, 13th impression 1966) *Swahili Grammar.* Longman.
Doke, C. M. (1967) *The Southern Bantu Languages.* Dawsons of Pall Mall for the International African Institute.
Greenberg, J. H. (1966, 2nd edn) *The Languages of Africa.* Mouton.
Ladefoged, Peter *et al.* (1971) *Language in Uganda.* Oxford University Press.
Myachina, E. N. (1981) *The Swahili Language.* Routledge and Kegan Paul.
Ngara, E. A. (1982) *Bilingualism, Language Contact and Planning (Proposals for language use and language teaching in Zimbabwe).* Mambo Press.
Ohannessian, Sirarpi, and Kashoki, Muhanga E. (1978) *Language in Zambia.* International African Institute.
Perrott, D. V. (1951) *Teach Yourself Swahili.* The English Universities Press Ltd.
Polomé, Edgar C. (1967) *Swahili Language Handbook.* Center for Applied Linguistics.
Polomé, Edgar C, and Peter Hill (eds) (1980) *Language in Tanzania.* Oxford University Press for the IAI.
Welmer, William E. (1973) *African Language Structures.* University of California Press.
Whitely, Wilfred H. (1969) *Swahili (The rise of a national language).* Methuen.
Whitely, Wilfred H. (ed.) (1974) *Language in Kenya.* Oxford University Press.

Japanese speakers

Ian Thompson

Distribution

JAPAN, Korea, Hawaii.

Introduction

Japanese is probably related to Korean, and possibly to Manchurian, Mongolian and Turkish too. It is not related to Chinese. In modern Japan everyone understands and can speak an approximation to the standard language, though wide dialectal variety exists.

Japanese and English speakers find each other's languages hard to learn. One reason for this is that the broad constituents of sentence structure are ordered very differently in the two languages. The following fragment from a Japanese magazine, translated word for word into English, illustrates the learner's problem:

> *Listener called one as-for, midnight at waking study doing be expectation of person (focus-particle) nucleus being reason is-probably.*

or, less exotically:

> *It must mean that the audience consists of people who are presumably staying up studying late at night.*

In addition to the difficulties posed by great grammatical, lexical and phonetic disparity, Japanese speakers' attitudes to language in general are heavily coloured by two aspects of their own tongue. Firstly, 'respect language' is so finely graded that an out-of-context fragment of dialogue can tell the eavesdropper a great deal about the age, sex, relationship and relative status of both speakers; even a transcript bereft of such vocal clues as voice quality and articulation reveals a sensitive choice of vocabulary and grammar. Students of English are therefore anxious about whether they are being sufficiently (or excessively) polite, and many cannot bring themselves to say *you* to strangers, or to call their teacher by name. Secondly, Japanese has enormous numbers of words which are pronounced the same but written differently – sometimes twenty in a group – so that the Japanese speaker trusts eyes before ears. It is worth noting, also, that eloquent, fluent speech is not highly rated in

Japan; indeed, it is often distrusted. Tentativeness is preferred to assertiveness, hesitancy to momentum. Japanese abounds in what are to European ears 'unfinished' utterances, and the Japanese have an amazing ability to hear the unspoken word and to sense changes in atmosphere and human relationships.

Given these striking differences between Japanese and English attitudes to language, it takes the student a good while to tune in. An added barrier to adaptation is the tension associated in Japan with language learning – though women find it easier to relax in the language class than men.

Phonology

General

Japanese has a rather limited phonetic inventory, both in number of sounds and in their distribution. There are only five vowels, though these may be distinctively short or long. Syllable structure is very simple (generally 'vowel + consonant', or vowel alone). There are few consonant clusters. Japanese learners therefore find the more complex sounds of English very hard to pronounce, and they may have even greater difficulty in perceiving accurately what is said. Often a student can say quite a complicated sentence with faultless grammar and choice of words, yet would be unable to understand the same sentence if it was said to him or her. In order not to embarrass the speaker, Japanese listeners often nod sagely even when they understand scarcely a word.

In Japanese speech, lip and jaw movement tend to be minimised, and many social situations demand soft speech. Many speakers prefix utterances with an indrawn hiss as a sign of modesty. These features may be carried over into English.

Vowels

Some of the most noticeable problems for Japanese learners are:
1. /ɔː/ and /əʊ/ are both pronounced as a long pure /oː/, causing confusion in pairs like *caught* and *coat, bought* and *boat.*
2. /æ/ and /ʌ/ are both pronounced as /a/, causing confusion in pairs like *lack* and *luck, match* and *much.*
3. /ɜː/ becomes /aː/: *tarn* for *turn.*
4. /ə/ becomes /aː/, or else is replaced by the short vowel suggested by the spelling: /kɒmpoːzaː/ for *composer.*
5. Diphthongs ending in /ə/ are pronounced with /aː/ instead. /ðeaːfoaː/ for *therefore.*

213

6. /ɪ/ and /ʊ/ are devoiced (whispered) in some contexts, making them difficult for an English listener to hear.
7. /uː/ is unrounded. Practice may be needed in words like *who, too, usual.*

Consonants

Some of the most noticeable problems are:

1. /l/ and /r/ are both pronounced as a Japanese /r/ (a flap almost like a short *d*), causing confusion in pairs like *glamour* and *grammar, election* and *erection.*
2. /h/ may be pronounced as a bilabial *f* /ɸ/ before /uː/: '*foo*' for *who.* Before /iː/, /h/ may sound almost like /ʃ/ (so that *he* and *she* are confusingly similar).
3. Conversely, /f/ may be pronounced almost like /h/ before /ɔː/: *horse* for *force.*
4. /θ/ and /ð/ do not occur in Japanese. They may be pronounced as /s/ and /z/ or /ʃ/ and /ʤ/: *shin* for *thin*; *zen* for *then.*
5. /v/ may be pronounced as /b/: *berry* for *very.*
6. /g/ may be pronounced /ŋ/ between vowels: '*binger*' for *bigger.*
7. /n/ after a vowel may disappear (with nasalisation of the vowel), or may become /m/ or /ŋ/, depending on context: *sing* for *sin.*
8. /t/, /d/, /s/ and /z/ often change before /ɪ/ and /iː/ as follows:
    /t/ becomes /tʃ/: '*cheam*' for *team.*
    /d/ becomes /ʤ/: *jeep* for *deep.*
    /s/ becomes /ʃ/: *she* for *see.*
    /z/ becomes /ʤ/: '*jip*' for *zip.*
9. /t/ and /d/ often change before /ʊ/ and /uː/ as follows:
    /t/ becomes /ts/: '*tsoo*' for *two.*
    /d/ becomes /ʤ/ or /z/: '*dzoo*' for *do.*

Syllable structure and word-linking

English consonant clusters are difficult for Japanese learners, and they often tend to break them up by inserting short vowels, which also serve to 'round off' final consonants. So for instance *table* may be pronounced /teburu/; or *match* /matʃi/. Students find it hard to shed this 'rounding-off' vowel and link when a vowel begins the following word: this is particularly noticeable when the final consonant is /n/ or linking /r/. A good deal of practice may be required in this area.

Rhythm, stress and intonation

The Japanese are very good at hearing and repeating stress and intonation patterns, but there are only limited parallels between the prosodic

systems of the two languages. Prosodic near-universals common to both
include:
- raising the whole pitch-range of the voice when embarking on a new
  topic of conversation and lowering it to signal a coming end;
- broadening the pitch-range to show interest and involvement. Japanese questions, both *wh-* and *yes/no*, usually have a rise on the
  utterance-final question particle ka; the question-tag particle ne tends
  to rise to show uncertainty and fall to show confirmation and
  agreement.

However, many of the attitudinal colours painted by English
intonation patterns find expression in Japanese by adverbials and
particles. And Japanese does not share the English use of intonation to
highlight information structure (for instance, to distinguish information which speaker and listener share from information which is
new to the listener).

English intonation and sentence-stress patterns therefore have to be
consciously learnt and practised, but Japanese students are particularly receptive to clear explanations of how these features work.
They quickly learn word stress, the only areas of difficulty being:
- compound nouns such as *water-pollution control*;
- words borrowed into Japanese with an accent pattern that conflicts
  with the English stress pattern, such as rekoodo (*a 'record*), Peruu
  (*Pe'ru*).

Summary

The following transcription will give some of the flavour of the vowels,
consonants, syllable structure and word-linking features of a Japanese
accent:

> The team who usually win have lost this year. They'll have to
> make a bigger effort in future.
>
> [//za tʃiːmu ɸɯː jɯːdʒɯari ʔwiĩ habu rosto dʒisu ʔjiaː//zeiru
> habu tsuː meiku a biŋaː ehoːto iĩ çɯːtʃaː//]

Orthography and writing

Japanese learners do not generally have great difficulty with English
spelling or handwriting, perhaps because of the training involved in
mastering Japanese characters. (And Western script is familiar to most
Japanese, even those who have learnt no English, from its frequent use in
rōmaji transliterations.)

Grammar

Word order

Japanese is a 'subject–object–verb' language. Qualifier precedes qualified, topic precedes comment and subordinate precedes main. What
correspond to English prepositions follow the noun, and so do particles
meaning *too, either, only* and *even.* Subordinating conjunctions follow
their clause; sentence particles showing interrogation, affirmation, tentativeness and so on follow the sentence. Modal verbs follow lexical verbs.
All adjectivals, however long, precede their substantive.

The following examples will illustrate Japanese word order:

Watakushi wa nani mo iwanakatta no ni,　　hen na
I-as-for　　what-also　　said-not　　although, strange-being

koto o　　　　yutta yoo ni omowarete　　komarimashita.
thing (object) said　way-in thought-being troubled.

(= *I'm upset because people think I said something strange, when I said
nothing at all.*)

Kono 1000- gata no nyuusen de　　haisha ni naru
This　1000- type- of enter-service-at scrap-to　become

yotei datta 100-gata wa,　　amari no ninki ni
plan　was　100-type-as-for excess-of popularity

haisha ni dekizu ni iru.
scrap-to　cannot.

(= *This type 100, due to be scrapped when the type 1000 came into
service, cannot be withdrawn because of its great popularity.*)

Verbs

The Japanese verb is a very self-contained entity: except for the copula **da**
(= *be*) every verb can stand as a sentence on its own, requiring neither
subject or object to be expressed:

　　　Wasureta. (= *I've forgotten it.*)

This can lead students to leave out pronoun subjects and objects in
English.

Like English, Japanese expresses tense, voice and other meanings
through changes in the form of the verb. However, Japanese has
one-word verb forms, with no auxiliary verbs, so that students find
English verb phrases difficult to construct. The Japanese verb does not
change for person or number, so students easily forget the English
third-person singular *-s.*

The use of *do* in questions and negatives causes problems. (Japanese questions of all types are marked by clause-final **ka**, with no change of word order; negation is shown by a change in the verb form.) Students may have special difficulty with embedded questions such as *It depends whether* ... or *It's a question of how far* ...

Tenses

Broadly speaking, Japanese students have the same difficulties as other learners with the complex English tense/aspect system. Problems encouraged by Japanese grammar include the use of the present for the future:

> *I see her tomorrow.*

and occasional confusion between progressive and perfect forms.

Indirect speech maintains the tense of the original, leading to mistakes in English:

> **Kakenai to yutta.** (lit. *write–cannot–with–said*) = *She said she cannot write it.*

Unreal conditionals are not formally distinct from real conditionals in Japanese, and herein lies a major problem for students, for even when they have mastered the mechanics of forming unreal conditionals and wishes in all their complexity, the problem of concept remains: there is no neat Japanese peg to hang it on. So learners will need careful explanations of the meanings involved in structures such as these.

Passives

Japanese has a suffixed passive, but its range of use differs from English. Inanimate subjects take a passive verb less readily in Japanese, so students may find it difficult to construct sentences like *Our house was built 200 years ago* or *The parcel was sent last week*. On the other hand, a Japanese passive can be used in some cases where it is not possible in English:

> *He was stolen his money.* (for *He had his money stolen.*)
> *She was died her husband.* (for *Her husband died.*)

A difference in the way underlying voice is expressed in English and Japanese leads to mistakes with the expressions *easy to* and *difficult to*:

> *I'm easy to catch cold.*
> *This pen is difficult to write.*

The passive is also used in a wholly active sense to show respect and reserve:

> *When were you come to Japan?*

217

Complementation

Verbs and clauses are nominalised in Japanese in a very simple way, by placing after them one of the particles koto or no. The Japanese – no less than any other nationality – find confusing the choice exemplified in:

I'd like you to go.
I object to *your going.*
I'm surprised at the fact that you're going.
It's a good idea for you to go.

Nouns

A large class of Japanese nouns of Chinese origin can also function as adjectives and adverbs (depending on the following particle). This can lead to mistakes in English:

*Tokyo is very safety city.
*We should eat more nourishment diet to avoid ill.

Nouns compound freely, placing the elements in much the same order as in English; the tendency of Romance-language speakers to split and link (**scheme of insurance of employees of bank*) is not shared by the Japanese.

The English stylistic taboo against repeating nouns does not hold in Japanese:

*My sister's friends sometimes telephone my sister early in the morning.

Number and the use of articles

Many nouns referring to people may take one of a number of plural suffixes (depending on degree of respect), but if the context makes plurality clear the noun goes unmarked, as do virtually all nouns not referring to people. Therefore, as no element in the Japanese sentence regularly shows plurality, and since the distinction between count and mass (countable and uncountable) is not recognised, number and countability pose major problems. Many Japanese learners achieve really creditable proficiency in all aspects of written English, except for articles and the number–countability problem:

*In Japan, industrial product is cheap. Because we have an economic growth. But vegetable is so expensive. Because we Japanese have a few lands.

Surprisingly little material exists for teaching plurals and articles. It is a difficult area, and perhaps a tedious one, but many Japanese feel inhibited in speaking because they have not been trained to make instinctive choices of article and number. Typical article errors at an elementary level are:

> *We used to live in the big house in suburb of Fukuoka. A house was built of the wood.*
> *Oh, that's a shrine; people say some prayers there.*
> *I usually spend Sunday by a river; the people who work in office need to relax in some countryside.*

Pronouns

English personal pronouns have various equivalents in Japanese. For instance, *you* is anata, kimi, omae, kisama, the addressee's name or title, or a kinship term, among other forms of address. Each word carries precise implications of age, relationship, status and attitude, and the lack of choice in English often embarrasses the Japanese.

Typical errors of pronoun choice in English include using *he* or *she* about a person present, instead of the name; and addressing somebody by their name plus a third-person verb. Examples of other problems:

> 'Do you get a lot of snow in Hokkaido?' *'Yes, I do.'*
> *To make omelette, first I crack two eggs ...*
> 'Do you ever write poetry?' *'Yes, I wrote it yesterday.'*

Possessive pronouns, unless emphasised or contrasted, go unexpressed in Japanese:

> *She washed face and cleaned teeth.*

English indefinite pronouns involve the same difficulties (in particular, the choice between *some* and *any*) as for other learners.

Relative pronouns do not exist in Japanese. Nouns (and pronouns) may be modified by complex phrases which come before the noun or pronoun, rather on the following lines:

> there in visible house living people (= *the people who live in the house you can see over there*)
> twenty years ago together school-to went friend (= *a friend I went to school with twenty years ago*)
> Tokyo in born I ... (= *I, who was born in Tokyo, ...*)

Adjectives and adverbs

Japanese has a class of 'adjectives' which behave largely like verbs: they can be inflected to show tense and condition:

> yokatta (= *was good*)
> yokattara (= *if it's good, if you like*)

This can lead students to treat English adjectives like verbs, at least to the extent of omitting the copula *be*:

> *That film good.*

Many of these Japanese adjectives are 'subjective', referring to the speaker's or hearer's feelings. So a Japanese learner may ask *Is Japanese food delicious?*, meaning *Do you find Japanese food delicious?* To take another example, the Japanese adjective **kowai** tends to mean *I/you/we are afraid* or *you are frightening*; with a third-person subject it will mean, not *he/she is afraid*, but *I/you/we are afraid of him/her.* This naturally leads to confusion in students' use of parallel English adjectives.

The grammar of Japanese nouns can lead to the misuse of English nouns as adjectives, as mentioned above:

> *This is democracy country.*

A number of English verbs can be followed by adjectival complements (for instance *look, sound, turn*). The Japanese equivalents have adverbial complements:

> *It looks tastily.*
> *It sounds strangely.*
> *It burned bluely.*

Japanese does not distinguish between gradable and non-gradable adjectives, so students may use adverbs of degree and emphasis inappropriately:

> *It was very enormous.*
> *I'm absolutely tired.*

Comparative and superlative inflections do not exist in Japanese. A common mistake is:

> *I intend to work hard more than last term.*

Words answering the questions *Where?* and *When?* are nouns in Japanese; *top* and *up* are the same word; **mae** means *the front* or *ago*:

> *I like here.*
> *She is in upstairs.*

Japanese has an impressive inventory of devices for injecting vagueness and tentativeness into utterances, which gives rise to overuse of *perhaps, rather, a little* and *such.*

Determiners

Troublesome pairs of quantifiers include *whole/all, all/every, several / any number of, far / a long way, long / a long time, much / a lot of, much/many, a bit / quite a bit, far/distant.*

Infelicitous collocations can also arise:

> *I have quite many English friends.*

Much/many and *little/few* in Japanese can be predicative:

> *Mountain is many. So vegetables field is few.*

Conjunctions and complex sentences

English and Japanese conjunctions do not always have simple one-to-one equivalents. *And*, for instance, corresponds to at least eleven different

Japanese forms, depending on whether they connect nouns, adjectives, verbs or clauses. Taking one common *and* equivalent, namely Japanese *to*, and turning it back into English, we find *and, with*, quotation marks, *when, if, whenever, as, to* and *from*. Another Japanese structural word, mo, corresponds variously to *also, both ... and, (n)either ... (n)or, whether ... or, even, if, though, -ever, as much as*, or prosodic emphasis. Japanese students can therefore be expected to have more trouble than Europeans in mastering the meaning and use of English conjunctions.

Japanese clause-conjunctions often double as postpositions or particles. Perhaps because of this, Japanese students do not always appreciate the clause-combining role of English conjunctions, and there is a strong tendency to use them with one-clause sentences:

> *I am working very hard. Because I want to succeed an exam. But I am afraid I can't succeed it. So I must be more diligence.*

Vocabulary

Three factors aid the Japanese in learning the vocabulary of English:
1. Japanese itself has an enormous lexicon, much of it phonetically opaque, so that the meaning becomes clear only when the word is seen – assuming the learner knows the Chinese characters that constitute it. The Japanese are therefore accustomed to and skilled at learning vocabulary.
2. There are very few bad Japanese–English / English–Japanese dictionaries in Japan, and there are many excellent ones.
3. A surprising number of English words are used – though often in barely-recognisable form – in everyday speech and especially in the blandishments of television commercials and in popular magazines. On the supermarket shelves only those products that are traditionally Japanese – **sake**, chopsticks, **miso** and so on – have Japanese trade names. 'Western' goods carry quasi-English names: Lion toothpaste, Pokari Sweat after-exertion drink, Cabstar light vans. There are even a few false friends, like **konsento** (= *electric socket*), and telescopings such as **ensuto** (= *stopping the engine*) and **masukomi** (= *mass communications*), which students use on the innocent assumption that they are current outside Japan.

Of the many lexical pitfalls that yawn before the student, many lie on the border between vocabulary and grammar. Japanese distinguishes differently from English between state and action verbs, so that **okiru** means *get up* and *be up*; **kiru** means *put on* and *wear*. *Can* co-occurs with some verbs where English rejects it:

> *If you come to Japan, I think you can enjoy.*

Though Japanese has equivalents for *walk, fly* and *drive* it prefers *go (by) walking, go by plane* and *go by car* when reaching one's destination is the main interest. *Come* and *go* are always seen from the *speaker's* viewpoint:

'*Are you coming to my party?*' **'Yes, I'm going.'*

The same applies to *bring*, which has the added complication of corresponding to three Japanese forms according to whether it means *bring a thing, bring an inferior or equal being*, or *bring a superior being* – a feature shared by *take* in its sense of *accompany, bring with you*. *Receive* and *accept* can be confused, and *get* is no easier for the Japanese than for anyone else.

The verb yameru can mean *refrain, give up . . . -ing* or *give up the idea of*; hence such brave attempts as:

**Please give up smoking on the coach.*
**I've given up getting married.*

Itadakimasu – said before eating – and a large number of similar crystallised expressions have no neat English equivalent, which is the source of much embarrassment and perplexity. Many are subtle variants of *I'm sorry to . . . you* and *Thank you*. The Japanese, like the English, are embarrassed about giving and receiving compliments.

Hiroi and its opposite semai mean not only *wide* and *narrow* but also *spacious* and *cramped*. **England is very wide country* is usually intended to mean that as England is fairly flat you can see a long way.

Translation problems may lead students to confuse *interesting* and *funny, funny* and *out of sorts, important* and *carefully, careful* and *dangerous*.

Style

A problem with the written work of Japanese students is that though spelling, organisation and grammar may be faultless, overuse of abstract nouns and the invoking of unfamiliar images may result in incomprehensibility to the English reader. Abstraction is respected in Japan. There is a great tradition of poetry that uses simple concrete vocabulary to step outside itself, and a huge stock of abstract nouns, largely composed of two- or three-character compounds. Some of these have come into being during the last hundred years as equivalents to words current in Western European languages; some of them were born of a civilisation utterly remote from that of the West.

The language classroom

All Japanese nowadays do three years, 90 per cent do six years and about 50 per cent do at least eight years of English at school and college; but in addition a large number go to private schools in the evening and on Saturday afternoon – in addition to their regular studies – so as to do better in the subjects that will one day bring them success in the university entrance examination, where English looms large. Parents often insist that the private school should stick rigidly to the syllabus followed in the main school, so that listening, pronunciation, role play and language games sadly have no place. English-language broadcasts, newspapers and books are widely available, so that no-one need feel cut off from contact with English, but going abroad on holiday to a first-language, English-speaking country is expensive and – given the short Japanese annual holidays – impracticable for most people.

The traditional Japanese regard for authority and formality is in tune with teacher-dominated lessons where much heed is paid to the 'correct' answer, learning of grammar rules and item-by-item (rather than contextualised) vocabulary. The four performance skills are ranked as follows: writing, reading, speaking, listening; and what listening there is tends to be testing, where the student ticks off the approved answer in a multiple-choice set. Chokuyaku (word-for-word translation of real English into bizarre Japanese) is much favoured. At least in middle and high schools, covering the age-range twelve to eighteen, the foregoing still prevails; but in many universities and private language schools new methods are eagerly adopted – though some run counter to national temperament.

The Japanese do not care to be 'put on the spot' in public; getting it wrong can be a cause of real shame, especially in front of classmates who are younger or socially inferior (in the Japanese sense). A spontaneous answer is rare; long thought or a discreetly whispered conference with a compatriot usually precede the student's response. The Japanese tend not to air their private opinions in public, which means that 'What do you think of . . .?' topics of discussion can be full of long and painful silences. The non-Japanese teacher easily misinterprets embarrassment as inability to speak. The uninhibited, even aggressive participation in multi-national discussions by many Europeans may affront the Japanese sense of propriety, yet the student will often bottle up this unease for weeks, giving away no hint of it.

Chinese speakers

Jung Chang

Distribution

PEOPLE'S REPUBLIC OF CHINA, TAIWAN, HONG KONG, MACAO, SINGAPORE, MALAYSIA; there are also large communities of Chinese speakers throughout southeast Asia, Oceania and North and South America. About one fifth of the world's population are native speakers of Chinese.

Introduction

The Chinese language, or the Han language, as the Chinese call it, is a collection of numerous dialects which may be classified into eight dialect groups (sometimes referred to as different languages): Northern Chinese (also known as Mandarin), Wu, Hsiang, Kan, Hakka, Northern Min, Southern Min, and Yueh (i.e. Cantonese). While the last four dialects are the mother tongues of most Chinese speakers outside China, Northern Chinese is the native dialect of over 70 per cent of the Chinese population at large, and is the basis of modern Standard Chinese, which is the accepted written language for all Chinese, and has been promoted as the national language.

The Chinese dialects share not only a written language but also important basic features at all structural levels. The problems discussed in this chapter are by and large common to speakers of all dialects.

Chinese and English belong to two different language families (Sino-Tibetan and Indo-European), and have many structural differences. Difficulties in various areas at all stages of English language learning may be expected.

Phonology

General

The phonological system of Chinese is very different from that of English. Some English phonemes do not have Chinese counterparts and are hard to learn. Others resemble Chinese phonemes but are not identical to them in pronunciation, and thus cause confusion. Stress, intonation and juncture are all areas of difficulty. In general, Chinese speakers find English hard to pronounce, and have trouble learning to understand the spoken language.

Vowels

1. There are more vowel contrasts in English than in Chinese, so English vowels are closer to each other in terms of position of articulation than Chinese vowels. This means that more effort is required to distinguish them.
2. The contrast between /iː/ and /ɪ/ has no equivalent in Chinese. Learners confuse pairs such as *eat* and *it*, *bean* and *bin*.
3. The same applies to /uː/ and /ʊ/, leading to confusion, for instance, between *fool* and *full*, *Luke* and *look*.
4. /æ/ does not occur in Chinese. Learners tend to nasalise it. It may also be confused with /ɑː/, /ʌ/ or /e/, so that a word such as *cap* might be pronounced /kæp/, *carp*, *cup* or '*kep*'.
5. /ɒ/ has no equivalent in Chinese. Learners sometimes make it sound like /ɔː/, /aʊ/, /ʊ/ or a front vowel. So for instance *shot* might be pronounced *short*, *shout* or /ʃʊt/.
6. /ʌ/ is sometimes replaced by /a/, which is a close approximation to a Chinese phoneme.
7. Chinese diphthongs are usually pronounced with quicker and smaller tongue and lip movements than their English counterparts. Learners therefore make these sounds too short, with not enough distinction between the two component vowels.

Consonants

1. In the three pairs of stops /p/ and /b/, /t/ and /d/, /k/ and /g/, the unaspirated group /b/, /d/ and /g/ are voiced in English but are on the whole voiceless in Chinese. Chinese students tend to lose the voiced feature in speaking English.
2. /v/ is absent from most Chinese dialects. As a result, it is sometimes treated like /w/ or /f/: *invite* may be pronounced '*inwite*'; *live* pronounced '*lif*'.
3. Many Chinese dialects do not have /n/. Learners speaking these dialects find it difficult to distinguish, for instance, *night* from *light*.
4. /θ/ and /ð/ do not occur in Chinese. /θ/ is likely to be replaced by /t/, /f/ or /s/, and /ð/ by /d/ or /z/. So for example *thin* may be pronounced *tin*, *fin* or *sin*; *this* may be pronounced '*dis*' or '*zis*'.
5. /h/ tends to be pronounced as a heavily aspirated velar fricative (as in Scottish *loch*), which approximates to a Chinese consonant.

6. Most Chinese dialects do not have /z/. The usual error is to substitute /s/: *rise* may be pronounced *rice*.
7. /dʒ/, /tʃ/ and /ʃ/ are distantly similar to a group of three different Chinese consonants. Many learners' pronunciation of these is therefore heavily coloured and sounds foreign.
8. Some southern Chinese find /l/ and /r/ difficult to distinguish, leading to the kind of mistake caricatured in jokes about 'flied lice', etc.
9. Final consonants in general cause a serious problem. As there are few final consonants in Chinese, learners tend either to add an extra vowel at the end, or to drop the consonant and produce a slight glottal or unreleased stop: *duck*, for instance, may be pronounced /dʌkə/ or /dʌʔ/; *wife* may be pronounced /waɪfuː/ or /waɪʔ/.
10. /l/ in final position is particularly difficult: it may be replaced by /r/, or followed by /ə/, or simply dropped: *bill*, for instance, may be pronounced *beer*, /bɪlə/ or /bɪʔ/.

Consonant clusters

1. Initial consonant clusters are lacking in Chinese, and cause problems. The common error is to insert a slight vowel sound between the consonants, pronouncing *spoon*, for instance, as '*sipoon*'.
2. Final clusters are even more troublesome. Learners are likely to make additional syllables, or to simplify the cluster (for instance, by dropping the last consonant). So *dogs* may be pronounced /dɒgəz/ or /dɒg/; *crisps* may be pronounced /krisiːpuːsiː/ or /krisiːpuː/.

Rhythm and stress

Reduced syllables are far less frequent in Chinese than in English. Moreover, these syllables in Chinese are usually pronounced more prominently than in English, and undergo fewer phonetic changes. Thus learners tend to stress too many English syllables, and to give the weak syllables a full rather than reduced pronunciation:

> 'fish 'and 'chips (with *and* stressed and pronounced /ænd/)
> 'The 'capital 'of 'Britain 'is 'London. (with both *the* and *of* emphasised)

When students try to reduce the accent on the English weak forms, they sometimes find them so hard to pronounce that they omit them: 'fish 'chips.

Intonation

Pitch changes in Chinese are mainly used to distinguish meanings of individual characters (the 'tones'); sentence intonation shows little variation. The English use of intonation patterns to affect the meaning of a whole utterance is therefore difficult for Chinese to grasp. Unfamiliar with these patterns, Chinese learners tend to find them strange and funny. Some add a tonic value (often a high falling tone) to individual syllables. Thus their speech may sound flat, jerky or 'sing-song' to English ears.

Juncture

The monosyllabicity of basic Chinese units leads to learners' separating English words rather than joining them smoothly into a 'stream of speech'. This contributes to the staccato effect of a Chinese accent. Learners need considerable practice in this area.

Orthography; reading and writing

Spelling

The writing system of Chinese is non-alphabetic. Chinese learners therefore have great difficulty in learning English spelling patterns, and are prone to all sorts of errors. Common mistakes include:
1. Failure to apply standard spelling conventions:
     dinner spelt **diner*   *eliminate* spelt **eliminat*
2. Problems arising from the lack of hard and fast spelling rules in English:
     *docter   **patten*   **liv*   **Wenesday*   **anser*
3. Mistakes resulting from learners' incorrect pronunciation:
     campus spelt **compus*   *swollen* spelt **swallen*
     around spelt **aroud*   *sincerely* spelt **secerly*
4. Omission of syllables:
     *unfortually   **determing*   **studing*

Reading and writing

Alphabetic scripts present Chinese learners with quite new problems of visual decoding. The way the information is 'spread out' in each word seems cumbersome for a reader used to the compact ideograms of Chinese. Individual words may take a relatively long time to identify, and (since words take up more space than in Chinese) the eye cannot take in so much text at a time. Chinese learners therefore tend initially to have slow reading speeds in English relative to their overall level of proficiency.

Alphabetic handwriting, on the other hand, presents no serious problems for Chinese learners.

227

Grammar

General

There are certain similarities between the syntactic structures of English and Chinese, yet the divergence is vast. It is advisable not to regard anything as a 'basic' point which students 'ought to know'.

Parts of speech

Parts of speech in Chinese are not always formally distinguished. There is no established comprehensive grammatical classification, and the same word may often serve different structural functions. As a result, learners have to try hard to remember the set classes of English words and their functions in a sentence. They may fail to distinguish related words such as *difficult* and *difficulty* in terms of their parts of speech, or to appreciate the fact that certain functions in a sentence can only be fulfilled by words from certain classes:

> *She likes walk.
> *I have not son.
> *He is not doubt about the correct of his argument.
> *It is very difficulty to convince him.

Verb forms

Chinese is a non-inflected language. What English achieves by changing verb forms, Chinese expresses by means of adverbials, word order and context. English inflection seems generally confusing and causes frequent errors:

1. Subject–verb concord:
   > *Everybody are here.
   > *Biling and Baoying has a shared kitchen.
2. Irregular verb formation:
   > *strided   *hurted   *flied   *blewn
3. Structure of complex verb forms:
   > *The window was breaking by the wind.

Time, tense and aspect

1. Chinese expresses the concept of time very differently from English. It does not conjugate the verb to reflect time relations. Learners have serious difficulty in handling English tenses and aspects. Errors like these are common:
   > *I have seen her two days ago.
   > *I found that the room is empty.

> ** My brother left home since nine o'clock.*
> ** She will go by the time you get there.*

2. Some students have the false impression that the names of the tenses indicate time. For example, they think that the 'present tense' indicates 'present time'. They therefore find puzzling utterances like:
   > ** There is a film tonight.*
   > ** The play we just saw tells a tragic story.*
3. Progressive aspect causes difficulty:
   > ** What do you read? (for What are you reading?)*
   > ** I sit here for a long time.*
4. Certain conventions in using tenses cannot be explained semantically, which causes problems. In adverbial clauses indicating future time, for example, learners do not necessarily appreciate why the 'present' tense is required:
   > ** We shall go to the country if it will be a nice day tomorrow.*
   > ** She will submit the paper before she will leave the college.*

Verb patterns

1. Often transitive verbs are used as intransitives, and vice versa:
   > ** He married with a charming girl.*
   > ** She talked a few words with one of the passengers.*
2. Patterns of complementation cause difficulty even for advanced learners:
   > ** I suggest to come earlier.*
   > ** The grass smells sweetly.*
   > ** Most people describe that he is handsome.*
   > ** She told that she'd be here.*
3. It is particularly difficult for the Chinese to differentiate between the use of an infinitive (with or without *to*), a present participle, a past participle and a gerund. One frequently hears mistakes like:
   > ** I was very exciting. (for excited)*
   > ** I'm sorry I forgot bringing your book.*
   > ** You'd better to come earlier.*
   > ** She's used to get up at seven.*
4. Adjectives and verbs are frequently identical in Chinese. Thus the verb *be* tends to be dropped when followed by predicative adjectives:
   > ** I busy.*
   > ** She very happy.*

Auxiliaries; questions and negatives

Chinese does not use auxiliaries to form questions and negatives. The insertion of *do/don't*, etc. presents problems:

> *How many brothers you have?*
> *I did not finished my work yesterday.*

Question tags meaning *Is that so?*, *Is that right?* are used very commonly in Chinese. These are often converted to an all-purpose *is it? / isn't it?* in English:

> *He liked it, is it?*
> *You don't read that sort of books, isn't it?*

Modals

Certain meanings of English modals have direct equivalents in Chinese modals and can be readily understood. But other meanings which have no Chinese counterparts are problematic. For instance, *should* as in *I think you should take up writing* is easy as it corresponds to a Chinese modal, *yīnggāi*. But *should* is more difficult in the utterances below since it has no straightforward Chinese translations:

> *It's strange that you should say this.*
> *We should be grateful if you could do it.*

On the whole, English modals indicate a wider range of meaning and feeling than their Chinese counterparts. Chinese learners therefore tend not to use them as frequently as they should, and may fail to express the nuances that English modals convey. Compare:

> *This can't be true.*　　　*I might come.*
> *This is definitely not true.*　*I'm probably coming.*

One point needs particular mention here. Communication in English requires appropriate polite forms of instructions, invitations, requests and suggestions, in which modals play a central role. Not being able to use modals (and associated patterns) adequately, Chinese students often fail to comply with the English conventions, and may appear abrupt. For example, they may say such things as:

> 1. *Please read this article.*
> 2. *We hope that you will come and have lunch with us to-morrow.*
> 3. *You come and sit here please.*
> 4. *I suggest that you have a word with him.*

when it would normally be more polite to say:

> 1. *You may like to read this article.*
> 2. *We were wondering whether you could come and have lunch with us tomorrow.*
> 3. *Would you come and sit here, please?*
> 4. *You might want to have a word with him.*

Even advanced learners are sometimes unable to appreciate the shades of meaning involved in the use of different modals:

> *Can you do me a favour?* (for *Could . . .*)
> *I need to finish the report today.* (for *I must. . .*)

Subjunctives

Chinese does not differentiate subjunctive from indicative mood. Learners are therefore likely to replace the former by the latter in English:

> *If I am you, I shan't go.*
> *I suggest that this applicant may be considered at the next meeting.*
> *I wish you can come.*
> *It's time that we should leave.*

Articles

There are no articles in Chinese. Students find it hard to use them consistently correctly. They may omit necessary articles:

> *Let's make fire.*
> *I can play piano.*

or insert unnecessary ones:

> *He finished the school last year.*
> *He was in a pain.*

or confuse the use of definite and indefinite articles:

> *Xiao Ying is a tallest girl in the class.*
> *He smashed the vase in the rage.*

Gender

There is no gender distinction in the spoken form of the Chinese pronouns: for example, *he*, *she* and *it* share the same sound. Chinese learners often fail to differentiate them in spoken English:

> *I've a brother, and she's working in a factory.*
> *Look at the actress over there. I know him.*
> *Julie is a good director. His films are very engrossing.*

Number

Plurality is rarely expressed in Chinese. -*s* tends to be dropped:

> *I have visited some place around York.*
> *I've seen a lot of play lately.*

This is particularly true in speech, where there is already a problem with the pronunciation of final consonant clusters.

The countable/uncountable distinction

Chinese students sometimes find the English concept of countability hard to grasp. For example, *furniture, equipment, luggage, news*, etc. can all be counted in the Chinese mind. Hence such errors as:

231

Chinese speakers

> *Let me tell you an interesting news.*
> *She's brought many luggages with her.*

Pronouns

English uses pronouns much more than Chinese, which tends to drop them when they may be understood. Pronouns such as those in bold type in the following sentences sometimes disappear under the influence of Chinese:

> The teacher came in with a big book in **his** right hand.
> I bought the book before **I** left the shop.

In personal pronouns, Chinese does not make the distinction between the subjective case (e.g. *I*) and the objective case (e.g. *me*). In the possessive, it does not distinguish the adjectival (e.g. *my*) from the nominal (e.g. *mine*). Students sometimes choose the wrong category of pronouns in English:

> *I am like she.*
> *The book is my.*

Word order

A. QUESTIONS

Chinese word order is identical in both statements and questions. Inversion in English interrogative sentences may be ignored or may be applied wrongly:

> *You and your family last summer visited where?*
> *When she will be back?*
> *What was called the film?*
> *Would have she gone home?*

B. INDIRECT QUESTIONS

Chinese uses inset direct questions in indirect questions. This sometimes leads to errors such as:

> *He asked me what does she like.*
> *She wondered where was her father.*

C. INVERSION IN GENERAL

Not only interrogatives, but also other sentences with inverted word order are error-prone:

> *Only by doing so they could succeed.*
> *He was unhappy, so I was.*

Postmodifiers

Noun modifiers in Chinese, no matter whether they are words, phrases or clauses, come before the nouns they modify. So English post-modifiers often hinder comprehension. In production, errors like these emerge:

> *This is important something.
> *This is a very difficult to solve problem.
> *That is the place where motion pictures are made there.

Position of adverbials

Chinese adverbials usually come before verbs and adjectives in a sentence. A learner is very likely to say, for instance:

> 1. *Tomorrow morning I'll come.*
> 2. *This evening at seven o'clock we are going to meet.*

when it is more natural in English to say:

> 1. *I'll come tomorrow morning.*
> 2. *We are going to meet at seven o'clock this evening.*

Conjunctions and compound sentences

A common mistake is to duplicate conjunctions, as their Chinese equivalents usually appear in pairs:

> *Although she was tired, but she went on working.
> *Because I didn't know him, so I didn't say anything.

Prepositions

The use of English prepositions is highly idiomatic and difficult for learners. Errors of all kinds are common:

> *What are you going to do in this morning?
> *I go York in May.
> *He is suffering with cold.
> *The text is too difficult to me.

Vocabulary

False equivalents

English and Chinese words overlap a great deal in meaning. However, apart from some nouns, they rarely produce exact equivalents. The rough Chinese counterparts given to learners are therefore to a large extent false equivalents, which often lead to 'Chinglish' or even nonsensical errors.

233

For example, *allergic* and *sensitive* can both be translated into one Chinese expression mǐngǎn. Thus:

*I have grown allergic to the usage of English.

Similarly, the false equivalent of *until*, zhídào, leads to this sentence:

*He took a rest until he had finished his work.

when the intended sentence is:

He did not take a rest until he had finished his work.

'Small verbs'

'Small verbs' such as *be, bring, come, do, get, give, go, have, make, take, work* are characterised by the range of distinctive meanings each of them possesses and by the ease with which they combine with other words to form special expressions, many of which are highly idiomatic. These verbs do not have equivalents in Chinese and are very difficult to handle. Students tend to avoid using them. For instance, a Chinese learner is likely to say:

1. *Please continue with your work.*
2. *He finally yielded.*

instead of:

1. *Please get on with your work.*
2. *He finally gave in.*

Lack of command of such items leads to various errors:

*The plane takes up easily. (for *takes off*)

*They've worked forward this plan. (for *worked out*)

Idiomatic expressions

Idioms are as difficult for the Chinese as for any other language learners. One area that needs special attention is that of social interaction, where Chinese and English typically employ different expressions to fulfil the same function. For instance, three common Chinese greetings translate directly as:

Have you eaten?

Where are you going?

You have come.

(And Chinese students are indeed frequently heard to use these expressions in greeting English people!)

Other examples include:

*Did you play very happy? (for *Did you have a good time?*)

*Don't be polite. (for *Make yourself at home.*)

*Please eat more. (for *Would you like a little more?*)

Culture

Traditional Chinese culture places a very high value on learning. An English language teacher can expect to find his or her pupils admirably industrious and often in need of dissuasion from working too hard.

A related view in many Chinese students' minds is that learning needs serious and painstaking effort. Activities which are 'pleasurable' and 'fun' are rather suspect as not being conducive to proper learning. Teachers who have adopted an approach involving 'learning while having fun' should be prepared to show its validity.

Teachers are highly respected in Chinese culture, and are typically regarded as being knowledgeable and authoritative. Out of respect, Chinese students are usually not as ready to argue or to voice opinions in class as European students.

Regarding methods of learning, a salient feature of Chinese education is rote memorisation. One reason for this is that all the basic written units of Chinese, the characters, have to be learned by heart individually. This method plays a significant part in the way English is learned in China, and may predispose some Chinese students to spend considerable time on memorisation at the expense of practice.

Sample of written Chinese

Transliteration of Chinese text with a word for word translation

利戎：
　来信收到了，谢谢你的问候。没有早些回信，
请原谅！

lirong:
lirong:

```
lai    xin   shou dao le, xiexie ni de  wen hou. meiyou zaoxie
come letter receive,      thank your  regard.   not    earlier

hui   xin,   qing   yuanliang!
return letter, please forgive!

ni   jinlai   shenti zenmeyang? xuexi shunli  ma?
you recently body   how?        study smooth [interrogative]?

yiding   xiang wangchang yiyang guo de hen  yukuai
certainly as    usual      same  live  very happy
```

ba?
[particle inviting confirmation]?

   wo hen hao, zuijin   you le
   I   very well, recently have [particle indicating change of state]

nupengyou, jiao shizhu, hen mei.
girl-friend,   call shizhu, very beautiful.

zuotian   shi chuxi,   wo qu ta jia   li,
yesterday be new year's eve, I   go her home in,

he ta quanjia   yikuair guo nian.   ta jia
with her whole family together spend new year. her home

keting   de tianhuaban, jiaju   he qiang shang
sitting-room of ceiling,   furniture and wall- on

daochu   gua zhe   ge zhong
everywhere hang [particle indicating state] all kind

zhihua,   lipin,   hai zhuang shang le
paper flower, present, also install- on   [particle indicating

                 caise dengpao. shizhu jianyi   zuo youxi,
change of state] coloured bulb. shizhu suggest play game,

ba   yanjing meng qilai
[particle introducing fronted object] eye   cover

mo liwu.   wo mo dao de hen hao, shizhu didi de
feel present. I feel-get   very good, shizhu brother

ye   bucuo. wo wanr de hen kaixin, zhidao tian kuai liang
also not bad. I   play   very happy, until   sky soon light

cai zou. lin   zou shi dajia yue hao xinnian diertian   lai
only go. near leave time all   agree   new year second day come

wo jia.   zhen xiwang ni ye neng lai!
my house. really wish   you also can   come!

   xiexie ni qing wo he didi   xiatian dao ni   jia   zuoke.
   thank you invite me and brother summer to   your home visit.

women yiding   lai.   wo zai guowai xuexi de jiejie neishihou
we   definitely come. my abroad   study   sister that time

ye huilai le,   wo xiang
also return [particle indicating change of state], I   think

wenwen, ta   nengbuneng gen women yikuair lai?
ask,   she can-not-can with us   together come?

bu duo xie le, qing daiwen   quanjia
no more write, please on my behalf ask all family

hao. pan   zaori huixin!
well. look forward to early return letter!

zhu ni   xinnian kuaile!
wish you new year happy!

cimin   yijiubasi nian yuandan
cimin   1984   year new year's day

An idiomatic translation

New Year's Day, 1984.

Dear Lirong,

Thank you for your letter, and thanks for the regards. I'm sorry that I didn't write earlier. Please forgive me!

How have you been recently? Is everything going well with your studies? Are you enjoying life as usual?

I'm very well. I've got a girl-friend now. Her name is Shizhu. She's very beautiful. Yesterday was New Year's Eve. I went to her place and spent the evening with her family. The sitting-room of her house was decorated with all sorts of paper flowers, presents and coloured lights, hanging from the ceiling, the furniture and the walls. Shizhu suggested that we play a game. We were to take down presents with our eyes covered and to keep the first ones we got. The one I got was very good, so was the one Shizhu's brother got. I had a lovely time and didn't leave until nearly dawn. Before I left we all agreed to meet at my house on the second day of the New Year. I really wish you could be here!

Thank you for inviting my brother and me to stay with you in the summer. We would love to come. My sister who is studying abroad will be back by then. I wonder whether she could come with us?

I'll stop here for now. Please give my regards to your family. I'm looking forward very much to hearing from you soon.

A Happy New Year to you.

Cimin

Vietnamese speakers

P. J. Honey

Distribution

VIETNAM, Cambodia, Laos, Thailand, France, USA, Australia.

Introduction

Scholarly opinions differ about the origins of the language. Although more than half the words used in modern Vietnamese are borrowed from Chinese, the grammatical structure is different from Chinese. There are three principal dialects which become mutually intelligible after relatively short exposure. Vietnamese is monosyllabic and non-inflecting, and possesses six tones. The earliest writing comprised ideograms, either Chinese characters or others developed from these. This character writing was replaced during the late nineteenth and twentieth centuries by a romanised script, termed quốc-ngữ, devised by Christian missionaries during the seventeenth century. Today very few Vietnamese can any longer read or write characters.

Because their mother tongue has no inflections, differentiates words by tone, and makes great use of syntax and particles for grammatical purposes, Vietnamese find a language like English, which is so dissimilar to their own, very difficult to learn.

Phonology

General

The structure of the Vietnamese syllable is 'consonant–vowel–consonant'. However, the first or third of these three parts, or both first and second, may be absent. Examples of Vietnamese syllables:

cam   am   ca   a

Each syllable has a prosody of one of a set of six tones, which imparts a sing-song quality to spoken Vietnamese. Moreover, these tones preclude the use of clause- or sentence-ending intonation, making it difficult for the foreign listener to determine when the speaker has completed an utterance by any criterion other than pause.

Vietnamese tones

Five of these six tones are indicated in the romanised script by five diacritical marks, the absence of a diacritic indicating the sixth. These tones are:

1. High rising: commences at a mid–high pitch and rises sharply. It is indicated by an acute accent above the vowel, e.g. bá (= *to embrace*).

2. High level: commences at about the same mid–high pitch as the preceding tone and maintains the same constant level. Has no diacritic, e.g. ba (= *three*).

3. Low falling: commences at a low pitch and falls even lower. It is marked by a grave accent above the vowel, e.g. bà (= *grandmother*).

4. Fall rise: commences at a mid–low pitch, sinks lower, and then rises again. It is marked above the vowel by a question mark without a dot, e.g. bả (= *poison*).

5. High creaky: commences at a mid–high pitch, is broken by a glottal stop, and ends on a slightly higher pitch, the whole being marked by glottalisation or 'creak'. It is marked by a tilde above the vowel, e.g. bã (= *residue*).

6. Low creaky: enunciated at a low pitch with heavy glottalisation or 'creak'. It is marked by a full stop written underneath the vowel, e.g. bạ (= *random*).

Vowels

The highly complex Vietnamese vowel system possesses eleven pure vowels and many more diphthongs and triphthongs. Most of these vowels are positionally free but some are bound, having only a restricted possibility of occurrence. For example the centralised vowel written â is found only before a following consonant, never in the open position: ân, bắt. While most of the diphthongs and triphthongs are immediately recognisable as such from the spelling, some are not. The vowel in the word ác is simple, but that in the word ách is a diphthong, the vowel quality being determined by the consonant cluster ch.

Although it is apparent from the spelling that the vowel in the word chia is a diphthong and that in dưới is a triphthong, such is not the case in the word deo, which is not a diphthong but a triphthong. The complexity of the vowel system and the vagaries of the quốc-ngữ script, fixed in the Vietnamese mind, give rise to considerable confusion when the learner faces English spelling.

Pure vowels are relatively few in English, but Vietnamese will frequently have recourse to the nearest Vietnamese pure vowel in pronouncing what they wrongly perceive to be a pure vowel in English: lo /lô/ for *low*; me /mê/ for *may*.

Certain pairs of Vietnamese diphthongs are distinguished only by the length of the constituent vowels: e.g. may /mai/ meaning *to sew* and mai /ma-i/ meaning *tomorrow;* nau /nau/, *to take refuge*, and nao /na-u/, *to make a disturbance.*

Similar diphthongs occur in English, but the length of the constituent vowels is immaterial, being merely an exponent of the individual speaker's accent, and does not affect meaning. This frequently causes difficulty to Vietnamese learners, who hear a difference which is meaningful in Vietnamese and do not associate a word spoken by one English teacher with the same word spoken by another teacher having a different accent.

Consonants

The Vietnamese consonant system is very different from that of English, and there is considerable variation between dialects. Vietnamese learners can be expected to have particular difficulty with some or all of the following sounds: /f/, /θ/, /ð/, /z/, /ʃ/, /ʒ/, /tʃ/, /dʒ/. Note:
1. The closest Vietnamese equivalent to /f/ is bilabial.
2. Vietnamese learners tend to pronounce final stops (/p/, /t/, /k/) unexploded in all contexts.
3. The bilabials *m* and *b*, in initial position, are frequently pre-voiced, that is to say voicing commences before, not simultaneously with, the opening of the lips. Many Vietnamese so pronounce them in English.
4. Initial *t* is unaspirated in Vietnamese, producing a sound which can be confused with English /d/. However, there is also a strongly aspirated initial /tʰ/, written *th* in Vietnamese, which learners may produce as the equivalent of English *th* (/θ/ or /ð/).
5. Initial *g* is frequently pronounced laxly without full closure, which gives it a guttural sound. It is often so pronounced by Vietnamese speaking English.

Consonant clusters

Many English consonant clusters are not found in Vietnamese, which gives rise to mistakes. The most prevalent is the omission of inter-consonantal *s*: *'abtrak'* for *abstract*; *'kaptn'* for *capstan*. Final *s*, when following a consonant, is frequently omitted too. Such mistakes persist and are very difficult to eliminate.

Stress and tone
(See also notes on Vietnamese tones above.)

Being monosyllabic and tonal, Vietnamese is unable to express stress by tone, as in English, because this would affect existing syllabic tone. Each individual syllable is pronounced with its characteristic tonal pattern, without which it would be unrecognisable. In compound words comprising two or more syllabic units, each syllable retains its own distinctive tone. Vietnamese learning English invariably encounter difficulty over stress. Their first inclination is to give full stress to each syllable of a polysyllabic word. For example, while they experience little difficulty in saying *black bird*, they find it impossible to say *blackbird* with the stress upon the first syllable only. It is this which imparts a typical 'staccato' quality to Vietnamese English, even in speakers who are otherwise fluent. The Vietnamese ear is trained to identify each of the set of six tones instantaneously, yet Vietnamese learners find English intonation patterns, whether in monosyllables or longer utterances, difficult to hear and often impossible to imitate correctly. Take, for example, the replies in the following exchanges:

> '*I beg your pardon.*' '*Yes?*' (high level tone)
> '*Are you going to?*' '*Yes.*' (mid falling tone)

Other contexts in which *Yes* is spoken with still other tones readily come to mind. Because none of these is identical with a Vietnamese tone, it is not immediately recognisable. This difficulty becomes even greater when the meaningful patterns of tone and stress extend over groups of words, sometimes imparting different meanings to utterances comprising the same English words:

> *Do you?* (mid + high level tone; equal stress – a simple interrogative)
> *Do you?* (mid + low fall rise tone; unstressed + stressed – asking whether you, not other people, do)
> *Do you!* (high + low tone; stressed + unstressed – expressing surprise and interest that you do)

Orthography and punctuation

Spelling

Modern Vietnamese spelling is entirely phonetic and poses no problems for native speakers. Vietnamese are, therefore, surprised at first by the complexity of English spelling, but they appear to experience no more trouble with it than other foreign learners.

Punctuation

Before the introduction of the quốc ngữ script, Vietnamese was written in characters or ideograms and used no form of punctuation similar to the Western system. Even when the quốc ngữ script was invented by Christian missionaries in the mid-seventeenth century, it was employed only for the printing of prayer books and catechisms and so remained unknown to all but a few Vietnamese. Only when this romanised script was universally adopted in the early part of the present century did most Vietnamese encounter punctuation, since when it has constituted a continuing source of difficulty. French rather than English punctuation conventions were adopted in Vietnam, but even today there is no unanimity among Vietnamese over what constitutes correct punctuation. Learners of English tend to use Vietnamese punctuation conventions which, though generally correct, do differ in some respects from those of English. Direct speech is normally indicated not by quotation marks but by a dash:

  – Thế thì dễ mặc tôi. (= '*In that case leave it to me.*')

Quotation marks are used in Vietnamese, but they are usually of the French kind (« ... »).

A very common mistake of Vietnamese writers is the failure to insert a comma at the end of a subordinate clause. This fault is frequently carried across into the writing of English. Generally speaking, punctuation is not accorded the same importance in Vietnamese education as it is in England and consequently the notions of punctuation among Vietnamese learners of English tend to be somewhat hazy.

Grammar

General

For Vietnamese learners, especially if they are unfamiliar with some other polysyllabic inflecting language, English poses considerable problems because it is so very different from their mother tongue. They are faced for the first time with words of more than one syllable and, moreover, with words which may change their form in response to the requirements of grammar. They have to contend with a system of spelling which is often very far from the strictly phonetic quốc-ngữ script of their own language, and with intonation that is not inherent in each single syllable but can spread over whole clauses or sentences. All of these novel features are likely to cause initial confusion, and some learners require a lengthy period to adjust to them.

The following remarks are not exhaustive but seek to draw attention selectively to individual features of English which Vietnamese learners find especially puzzling and to the types of error they are most likely to make.

Word order

Vietnamese, being non-inflecting, relies on word order and function words alone to signal functional meaning. That is why word order is of the greatest importance. Moreover, Vietnamese rarely uses the verb *to be*, a phenomenon which grammarians explain by stating that Vietnamese adjectives contain their own verbs:

> **Người này già.** (lit. *person – this – old*) = *This person is old.*
> **Sách ấy hay.** (lit. *book – that – good*) = *That book is good.*

With other verbs the customary Vietnamese word order is: 'subject + verb + object':

> **Tôi đọc sách.** (lit. *I – read – books*) = *I read books.*
> **Anh viết thư.** (lit. *elder brother – write – letters*) = *You write letters.*

Vietnamese word order greatly influences the Vietnamese speaker of English and deserves comment. It follows the English order in the following:

– Positive statements:
> *I write letters.*
> *The person (is) old.*

– Adverbial expressions of place:
> *He works in a factory.*
> *Put this on the table.*

– Word-group modifiers of nouns:
> *The man dressed in black is a stranger.*

– Indirect objects:
> *I gave him a book.*
> *I bought a book for him.*

– Relative clauses:
> *The man who called is my friend.*

– Questions asked with interrogative words:
> *Which books are yours?*
> *Who came here?*

– Interrogative: 'statement + question tag':
> *You do speak French, don't you?*
> *He is tired, isn't he?*

In other instances the Vietnamese word order differs. See in particular the following section.

Questions and negatives; auxiliaries

The commonest question form, expecting a yes/no answer, offers the hearer the choice by inserting the word có (= *have*) before the verb and không (= *(or) not*) at the end:

> Anh có viết thư không? (lit. *elder brother – have – write – letter – (or) not*) = *Do you write letters?*
>
> Người này có già không? (lit. *person – this – have – old – (or) not*) = *Is this person old?*

The affirmative response is có and the negative không.

Vietnamese does not ask questions by inversion, that is to say by asking *Do you?*, *Does he?*, etc.

The negative word in Vietnamese precedes the verb or adjective:

> Người này không già. (lit. *person – this – not – old*) = *This person is not old.*
>
> Anh không viết thư. (lit. *elder brother – not – write – letters*) = *You do not write letters.*

One of the commonest Vietnamese mistakes is to omit the copula or auxiliary verb:

> *This person not old.*
> *You not write letters.*

Time, tense and aspect

While it is possible to express time in Vietnamese, with some precision when necessary, the language is without the often complex structure of tenses and moods found in some Western tongues. Vietnamese employs aspect rather than tense, expressing whether the action of the verb is future, past or present progressive by preceding it with one of the three words sẽ, đã, đang:

> Cô sẽ đi về nhà. (lit. *aunt – future marker – go – return – house*) = *You (female) will return home.*
>
> Anh đã mua sách. (lit. *elder brother – past marker – buy – books*) = *You (male) bought books.*
>
> Mời ông ngồi chơi, tôi đang viết thư. (lit. *invite – grandfather – sit – relax – I – present progressive marker – write – letters*) = *Do take a seat, I'm writing letters.*

More frequently, though, time is not directly expressed but is understood from the context, or from time expressions such as *today, last night, next year* and so on.

Vietnamese, like Chinese, find English tenses difficult to understand, and this is the area in which they make most mistakes of all. Particularly difficult for them to master are tenses expressed by auxiliary verbs. For example:

English: *I'll be going to school tomorrow.*
Vietnamese: **Mai tôi đi học.** (lit. *tomorrow – I – go – study*)
Vietnamese speakers very frequently use the present tense in English, translating literally from Vietnamese:

*Tomorrow I go to school.

Still more puzzling for a Vietnamese are sentences such as *I am going to school tomorrow, I am going to go to school, I was going to school tomorrow*, etc. Accustomed as they are to the simplicity of the Vietnamese expression of time, they often find English quite incomprehensible.

Non-finite forms

Undoubtedly one of the most persistent mistakes made by Vietnamese speakers of English is the incorrect use of the infinitive in utterances which require a gerund:

*He suggested to go on holiday.

*He considered to call on you.

*She delayed to buy a new dress.

Even Vietnamese who have spoken English fluently for years continue to be puzzled by this use of the gerund and persist in using the infinitive.

Position of direct and indirect object

In a restricted number of instances Vietnamese uses the same word order as English to express the direct and indirect object:

Tôi đánh nó một trận đòn. (lit. *I – strike – he – one – volley – cane*) = *I gave him a caning.*

Most instances employ a second verb in what is termed a 'verb series', and by far the commonest such verb is **cho**, meaning *to give*. When so used, **cho** is frequently rendered in English by *for*:

Tôi mua cho nó một quyển sách. (lit. *I – buy – give – he – one – classifier – book*) = *I bought him a book.*

Or: **Tôi mua một quyển sách cho nó.** (lit. *I – buy – one – classifier – book – give – he*) = *I bought him a book.* or *I bought a book for him.*

Use of it *as subject*

English makes wide use of the impersonal *it* as subject of a sentence, as in *It is raining, It is cold, It is necessary*, etc. There is no equivalent usage in Vietnamese, which normally identifies a subject or expresses the idea in a different way. In statements about the weather Vietnamese uses **trời** (= *heaven*) as the subject. In other cases the Vietnamese subject is verbal:

Nói tiếng ta thì dễ lắm. (lit. *speak – language – us – then – easy – very*) = *It is very easy to speak Vietnamese.*
Cần phải đi. (lit. *must – should – go*) = *It is necessary to go.*
These structures are reflected in the English mistakes of Vietnamese learners.

The passive voice

Use of the passive voice is relatively rare in Vietnamese, very much rarer than in most European languages. This does not appear to be due to a conscious effort on the part of speakers of Vietnamese to avoid the use of passive forms, nor is it anywhere stated by teachers of Vietnamese to be desirable. It would seem to be a natural characteristic of Vietnamese expression.

The English passive is sometimes rendered in Vietnamese by use of the word do, which means *through the agency of*. Do stands directly before the perpetrator of the verb's action:

Quyển sách này do ông Nguyễn Văn Vinh viết. (lit. *classifier – book – this – through the agency of – grandfather – Nguyễn – Văn – Vinh – write*) = *This book was written by Mr Nguyễn Văn Vinh.*

It is characteristic of Vietnamese learners of English that they avoid using passive forms, and it is sometimes hard to convince them that English passives entail no special difficulties. They also tend to equate Vietnamese do with the English word *by*, which they are, in consequence, liable to misuse.

Articles

The English definite and indefinite articles *the, a, an* have no exact parallels in Vietnamese, which uses a type of word termed classifier, the word for *one* or a deictic adjective to make similar distinctions in nouns:

cái nhà (lit. *classifier + house*) = *the house*
một cái nhà (lit. *one + classifier + house*) = *a house*
nhà này (lit. *house + this*) = *this house*

There is a further complication in that not all Vietnamese words occur with classifiers, and sometimes the presence or absence of a classifier distinguishes between two different but homophonous nouns:
– differentiated by classifier:

đường (noun) = *sugar*
con đường (classifier + noun) = *the road*

– unclassified:

năm (noun) = *year*
một năm (lit. *one – year*) = *one year* or *a year*

Vietnamese learners are aware that English sometimes uses a definite article, sometimes an indefinite article, and sometimes no article at all, but since the English system is different from their own, they are frequently at a loss to know which to use. Hints such as checking whether a noun is countable or uncountable are of some help, but mistakes are frequent. Typical are errors such as the following:

* *I'd like to become doctor, not dentist.*
* *I'm tired so I'm going to the bed.*
* *I hope that you will hear a good news.*
* *I like to eat in restaurant.*

Vietnamese personal pronouns

The system of personal pronouns in Vietnamese is extremely complex. Indeed, readers of this chapter may have been puzzled by the inclusion of such words as *grandfather, aunt, elder brother* and so on in the word-for-word rendering of some of the examples given. There is no set of general personal pronouns such as the English *I, you, he, she, they* which may be used freely without external non-linguistic connotations.

Vietnamese makes use of plural markers and specific personal pronouns to express an exclusive/inclusive distinction. For example, chúng tôi (plural marker + *I*) expresses the exclusive *we*: that is to say, it includes the speaker and others but it excludes the listener. Chúng ta (plural marker + *we*) expresses the inclusive *we*: that is to say the speaker, possibly others, and the listener:

> Chúng tôi không muốn đi. = *We (but not you) didn't want to go.*
> Chúng ta được mời = *We (including you) have been invited.*

Certain pairs of pronouns for *I* and *you* indicate the relative social status of the speaker and listener and, since Vietnamese society holds old age in high esteem, there are respectful pronouns used of older people. Kinship terms (e.g. *grandfather, aunt, uncle, elder sister*, etc.) are widely used as personal pronouns and are qualified for plurality by plural markers. The use of one such term out of a possible choice will be determined by such extra-linguistic factors as status, familiarity, age and so on. There is also a very precise system of teknonymy – the use of kinship terms within the extended family – to refer to oneself, the listener, or the person spoken about. For example:

> Xin chị đừng bùôn vỉ em. (lit. *beg – elder sister – don't – sad – because – younger sister*) = *Don't you (female older) be sad on account of me (younger sibling).*
> Con đi với mẹ ra phố hàng Bạc. (lit. *son or daughter – go – with – mother – out – street – goods – silver*) = *I (son) will go with you (mother) to Silver Street.*

In recent years further complications have been introduced by political developments. For example the new pronoun **đồng chí** (= *comrade*) has been introduced and the connotations of some existing pronouns have changed.

Adjectives and adverbs

Vietnamese adjectives follow nouns or pronouns:

> **những người già** (lit. *plural marker – person – old*) = *old people*
>
> **cái nhà rộng** (lit. *classifier – house – spacious*) = *the spacious house*

This may lead to mistakes.

The English use of *the* followed by an adjective, as in *the rich, the poor, the young* is particularly puzzling to the Vietnamese.

Adjectival comparison

In the *-er than / more than* type of comparison, the Vietnamese word order is: 'subject – adjective – more than – object of comparison':

> **Ông Bình già hơn tôi.** (lit. *Grandfather – Binh – old – more – than – I*) = *Mr Binh is older than me.*

In the *not as ... as* type of comparison Vietnamese word order is: 'subject – not – adjective – equal to – object of comparison':

> **Ông Bình không già bằng tôi.** (lit. *Grandfather – Binh – not – old – equal to – I*) = *Mr Binh is not as old as I am.*

The preceding type of comparison may also be expressed in Vietnamese by the word order: 'subject – adjective – not – equal to – object of comparison':

> **Ông Bình già không bằng tôi.** (lit. *Grandfather – Binh – old – not – equal to – I*)

Adverbial expressions of time

In English adverbial expressions of time usually occur at the ends of sentences, as in *He went home yesterday* or *I shall leave tomorrow.* Vietnamese almost invariably places such expressions at the beginning of the sentence:

> **Ngày mai tôi đi nghỉ mát.** (lit. *day – morrow – I – go – rest – cool*) = *I go on my holidays tomorrow.*

Adverbial expressions of place: There is/are

Normally, adverbial expressions of place in Vietnamese parallel the English word order, for example:

248

Ông ấy chờ trong phòng khách. (lit. *grandfather – that – wait – in – room – guest*) = *He is waiting in the sitting room.*

Nó học ở nhà. (lit. *he – study – is at – house*) = *He is studying at home.*

In sentences commencing with *There is/are*, however, the word order changes to: 'adverb of place – have – subject':

Trong buồng có nhiều người Anh. (lit. *inside – room – have – many – person – English*) = *There are lots of English people in the room.*

Verb + particle

Vietnamese regularly uses what are termed 'verb series' to express the equivalent of the English verb + preposition or adverbial particle, and the parallel is sometimes exact:

mau lên (lit. *quick – go up*) = *hurry up*

ngồi xuống (lit. *sit – go down*) = *sit down*

In cases such as these, of course, the Vietnamese speaker experiences no difficulty. The remainder pose great difficulty, and he finds himself guessing – usually incorrectly – at the English word. A typical mistake is **I had a tooth off at the dentist.* (for *I had a tooth out . . .*). Again, English uses the same verb with different prepositions or particles to express quite different meanings: *Chop the tree down, Chop the tree up, Look after this for me, Look into this for me.* Indeed, a number of English words regularly occur with a relatively large number of different particles: *give in, give out, give away, give off, give up*, etc. A very frequent error in Vietnamese English is the use of an incorrect particle after a verb, and the laughter provoked by the sometimes comic effect of such a mistake makes Vietnamese speakers very nervous about this usage.

Subordinate clauses

English commonly begins sentences with subordinate clauses introduced by conjunctions such as *because, although, even if.* The main clause of the sentence then follows:

Because he was too young, he could not go.

Even if I had a ticket, I wouldn't go.

When expressions of this kind are used in Vietnamese, it is usual for the main clause to be introduced by a balancing word:

Vì nó trẻ quá, nên không đi được. (lit. because – *he – young – too much* – therefore – *not – go – can*)

Nếu tôi có vé, tôi cũng không đi. (lit. if – *I – have – ticket – I –* also – *not – go*)

249

Indeed, Vietnamese frequently omits the subordinating word and uses merely the balancing word in the main clause:

> Nó trẻ quá, **nên** không đi được. (lit. *he – young – too much – therefore – not – can – go*)

In consequence, it is not unusual for Vietnamese speakers to introduce these balancing words into the main clause of such sentences in English, particularly the word cũng (= *also*), which has a wide range of occurrence:

> **Even if I had a ticket, I would also not go.*

Culture

Teachers will find few problems arise in dealing with Vietnamese students. Most Vietnamese will be reasonably familiar with Westerners, usually French or Americans, except for the young who were born after 1975, and even they will have heard about them. I have yet to hear of a Vietnamese who took offence at anything a Western teacher did or said. People usually find Vietnamese friendly, cheerful, well-behaved, intelligent and very eager to learn.

A sample of written Vietnamese

Emperor Duy Tan

Quốc ngữ script

Vào mùa đông năm 1944 ít lâu trước lê Giang-Sinh, một buổi tối tôi đang ngồi đọc sách trong phòng thì có tiếng gõ cửa. Tiếng gõ cửa hơi lạ. Một số những bạn bè thỉnh thoảng tìm tôi vào buổi tối gõ cửa khác, quen thuộc, mà tôi nhận ra. Thực ra lúc bấy giờ những tiếng gõ cửa vào ban đêm chưa làm tôi lo sợ, những hoạt động của tôi và bạn bè còn rất giới hạn và chưa có gì nguy hiểm.

Tôi đứng lên, mở cửa. Trước ngưỡng cửa hiện ra một người đàn ông Việt-Nam khoảng 40, hay 45 tuổi, cao lớn, khoác chiếc áo lạnh dày, khuôn mặt ông hoàn toàn xa lạ đối với tôi. Tôi cố moi trong trí nhớ xem có người quen biết nào lâu năm không gặp lại, nay đến tìm tôi, nhưng tuyệt nhiên không tìm thấy một nét quen thuộc nào. Tôi nhìn người đàn ông lạ chờ đợi. Người đàn ông lạ tự giới thiệu :

– Thưa ông, tôi là Vĩnh-San.

A word for word translation

enter-season-winter-year-1944-little-long-before-festival-Christmas,-one-period-night-I-time-marker-sit-read-book-in-room-then-have-

noise-knock-door. noise-knock-door-slightly-strange.
one-number-plural marker-friends-periodically-seek-I-enter-period-
night-knock-door-different, know-belong-which-I-accept-out.
True-out-time-that-hour-plural marker-noise-knock-door-during-night-
not yet-make-I-worry-fear, plural marker-action-of-I-and-friends-still-
very-limit-and-not yet-have-anything-dangerous.

I-stand-rise, -open-door. before-threshold-door-appear-out-one-
person-sex-male-Vietnam-approximately-40, -or-45-years of age-tall-
big,-wear-classifier-coat-cold-thick, frame-face-grandfather-strange-
relatively-with-I. I-try-extract-in-memory-see-have-person-know-know-
any-long-year-not-meet-again,-now-arrive-seek-I,-but-absolutely-not-
seek-see-one-feature-know-belong-any. I-look-person-sex-male-strange-
wait-wait.
person-sex-male-strange-self-introduce:
– respected-grandfather, -I-to-be-Vinh-San.

An idiomatic translation

One night in the winter of 1944, not long before Christmas, I was reading
in my room when there came a knock on the door. The knock itself was a
little unusual. Numbers of my friends used, from time to time, to call on
me at night and knock, but differently, with familiar knocks which I
recognised. In fact, at that time, the sound of a night-time knock at the
door had not yet begun to alarm me. My own activities and those of my
friends were still very restricted and no danger attached to them.

I stood up and opened the door. On the threshold was a Vietnamese
man of some 40 or 45 years of age, tall in stature, and clad in a thick
winter coat. His face was completely unknown to me. I cudgelled my
memory, seeking to recall some acquaintance whom I had not seen for a
long time and was now coming to call on me, but I failed completely to
recognise even a feature of the man's face. I stared at the stranger and
waited.

The stranger introduced himself. 'I am', he said, 'Vinh-San'.

(From *Ben Giong Lich Su 1940–1965* by L. M. Cao Van Luan)

Thai speakers

David Smyth

Distribution

THAILAND

Introduction

Thai (formerly called 'Siamese') is a member of the Tai family of languages which are dispersed over a wide area of Asia, from northern Vietnam to northern India. Thai is the national language of Thailand, and as such is spoken by forty million people. Distinct dialects of Thai are spoken in the north, northeast and south of the country, but the language of the Central Region is regarded as the standard and is used both in schools and for official purposes throughout the country.

Thai, like Chinese, is a tonal language, with the meaning of each syllable being determined by the pitch at which it is pronounced. Thai has five tones – mid, low, high, rising and falling. It is a non-inflected language and much of the lexicon is monosyllabic; polysyllabic words do exist, although the majority of these are foreign borrowings, particularly from the classical Indian languages, Sanskrit and Pali.

Thai is written in an alphabetic script that was ultimately derived from Indian sources. It is written across the page from left to right; words are not separated as in most European languages, and where spaces do occur in the script, they very often correspond to some form of punctuation in English, such as a full stop or comma.

Phonology

General

There are significant differences between the phonological systems of Thai and English. In Thai, there are 21 consonant phonemes and 21 vowel phonemes. In the Thai consonant system, the aspirated voiceless stops /p^h/, /t^h/ and /k^h/ are distinct phonemes and not simply allophones (varieties) of /p/, /t/ and /k/ as they are in English. English has more fricatives than Thai, and Thais tend to have difficulty in producing these (e.g. /θ/, /ð/, /v/, /z/, /ʃ/ and /ʒ/). Vowel length is significant in Thai with a distinction made between long and short vowels.

Thais speak English with a 'Thai accent' because they try to fit every English word into the Thai phonological system. While this is to some extent true of every foreign accent, there does appear to be a peculiar reluctance among many Thai speakers to shed their accent. In Thailand, this can be explained perhaps by peer group pressure and not wanting to show off; but as numerous English loanwords (including brand names of thousands of consumer goods) have passed into everyday Thai, it has also become a perfectly legitimate strategy to pronounce English words in a Thai way, and to do otherwise would merely be pretentious. This process is further reinforced in early English lessons, where teachers may provide a transliteration of English words in Thai script to help pupils with the new alphabet, and English–Thai dictionaries produced in Thailand frequently provide a similar transliteration of English words as a pronunciation guide. As a result, English consonants and vowels are frequently pronounced as their nearest Thai equivalents.

Some of the more common features of a 'Thai accent' in English are:
- Stress on the final syllable of words.
- Problems in articulating certain final consonants and consonant clusters.
- A staccato effect, deriving from:
  a) a tendency to assign tones to syllables;
  b) a tendency to give equal weight and timing to each syllable;
  c) glottal stops before initial vowels;
  d) insertion of a short vowel /ə/ between certain initial consonant clusters;
  e) reduction of consonant clusters at the end of words to single consonants.

Vowels

iː	ɪ	e	æ	eɪ	aɪ	ɔɪ
	ɔː	ʊ	aʊ	əʊ		
uː	ʌ	ɜː	ə	eə		aɪə
						aʊə

Shaded phonemes have equivalents or near equivalents in Thai and should therefore be perceived and articulated without great difficulty, although some confusions may still arise. Unshaded phonemes may cause problems. For detailed comments, see below.

Thai speakers

1. /æ/ is frequently pronounced as a long vowel, /æ:/.
2. Diphthongs /eɪ/, /əʊ/ and /eə/ are frequently pronounced as long pure vowels, /e:/, /o:/ and /æ:/ respectively.
3. English words ending in a vowel frequently have the final vowel lengthened to accommodate the stress placed on the final syllable.

Consonants

p	b	f	v	θ	ð	t	d
s	z	ʃ	ʒ	tʃ	dʒ	k	g
m	n	ŋ	l	r	j	w	h

Shaded phonemes have equivalents or near equivalents in Thai and should therefore be perceived and articulated without great difficulty *when they occur as initial consonants*. Unshaded phonemes may cause problems. For detailed comments see below.

1. In pronouncing English initial consonants for which there is no rough equivalent in Thai, Thai speakers are likely to make the following substitutions:

   English: /v/   /θ/   /ð/   /ʃ/   /z/

   Thai approximation: /w/ /t/ /s/ /d/ /t/ /s/ /tʃ/ /s/
2. Many of the shaded consonants will cause great problems of articulation for Thai speakers when they occur as *final consonants*. Thai has only eight final consonant phonemes and no final clusters. As a result, English final consonants and consonant clusters are frequently subjected to a radically different pronunciation. Such transformations are not random, however; some typical changes undergone by single final consonants are:

   English: /d/ /θ/ /ð/ /s/ /z/ /ʃ/ /ʒ/ /tʃ/ /dʒ/   /v/ /f/   /l/

   Thai approximation: /t/   /p/   /n/
3. /g/ and /dʒ/ are often pronounced as unvoiced consonants by Thai speakers when they occur at the beginning of a word.
4. Although /r/ exists in Thai, it presents a problem to many Thai speakers even in their own language, where they may often substitute /l/. This strategy is invariably carried over when speaking English.
5. The glottal stop is a phoneme in Thai.

Consonant clusters

English has a much wider range of consonant clusters than Thai, and consonant clusters do not occur at the end of words in Thai at all. Among the initial two-segment clusters which do not occur in Thai are: /dr/, /fr/, /fl/, /fj/, /tw/, /sl/, /sw/, /sm/, /sp/, /sk/, /st/.

In pronouncing English words where such clusters occur, Thais tend to insert a short vowel, sometimes even creating another fully stressed syllable:

> *smoke* becomes '*sa-moke*'
> *frown* becomes '*fa-rown*'

A similar process operates with English three-segment initial clusters:

> *screw* becomes '*sa-crew*'
> *strike* becomes '*sa-trike*'

There is, however, a Thai equivalent to initial /kr/ and /tr/.

It is not uncommon, especially in Bangkok, for Thai speakers to drop the second segment of a two-segment consonant cluster at the beginning of a Thai word. Thus words like plaa (= *fish*) and khray (= *who?*) are frequently pronounced '*paa*' and '*khay*'. Thais who 'reduce' Thai words like this will often carry the process over into English, and say '*bake*' for *brake* and '*fee*' for *free*; and the '*lice*' is usually '*fied*' in Thailand, rather than '*flied*'!

English final clusters present the Thai speaker with a problem and usually some way of 'reducing' them to single manageable final consonants is sought. Usually, the first segment of the cluster is retained and the rest dropped:

> *pump* becomes '*pum*'
> *perfect* becomes '*perfec*'
> *lunch* becomes '*lun*'

Rhythm and stress

Every syllable in Thai carries a certain fixed tone. Thais tend to give equal weight and timing to each syllable and this, together with the fact that tonal pitch is located on single syllables (instead of groups of syllables, as it is in English) produces a rather staccato effect when transferred to English. The single most common mistake of Thai speakers is to stress the final syllable of polysyllabic English words, as in *but'ter, *cof'fee, *shop'ping, and so on. More complex uses of stress, for example to alter meaning or to convey attitudinal meaning, are likely to present problems even to advanced learners.

Intonation

Intonation patterns in Thai are very different to those of English. Being a basically monosyllabic language, Thai has a sharp up-and-down pitch contour. Although questions in Thai are frequently marked by 'question words' at the end of a sentence which have an inherent rising tone, this does not automatically facilitate the reproduction of English question contours. Particular attention should be paid to the intonation of polite requests; Thai uses a whole series of untranslatable words or 'particles' at the end of sentences to perform some of the functions fulfilled by intonation in English. When translating from Thai to English, the polite particles used in requests are obviously omitted, leaving a rathe: brusque imperative if the speaker has been too literal.

Juncture

In Thai, it is impossible to produce new consonant clusters from the junctures of final and initial consonants; the glottal stop before initial vowels also tends to preclude a link between final consonant and initial vowel. Thai speakers are likely to be unaware of the phonetic changes that take place in English through juncture (e.g. *would you* /wʊdʒə/; *get back* /ge(p)bæk/) unless these are specifically pointed out.

Influence of spelling on pronunciation

Thais learning English obviously make numerous mistakes in pronouncing new words because of the considerable mismatch between spelling and pronunciation in English. Typical problems which persist even among fairly advanced learners are:
1. Uncertainty as to when *th* is pronounced /θ/ and when /ð/ (assuming of course that the speaker can productively differentiate between the two sounds).
2. Uncertainty as to when *s* is pronounced /s/ and when /z/.
3. Failure to make a reduced pronunciation of the unstressed vowels in words such as *common, problem, police, possible, breakfast*.
Conversely, the Thai spelling of common English loanwords reinforces a non-English pronunciation, which then assumes a legitimacy which learners sometimes find hard to defy when dealing with the word in an English context!

Orthography and punctuation

Spelling and writing

Thai is written with an alphabetic system which runs across the page from left to right. There is no distinction between upper and lower case. The position of vowel symbols varies, with some written above the consonant, some below, some to the left and some following on the right

— and some surrounding the consonant on three sides! Thai words are not separated by spaces, and the spaces that do occur in Thai writing generally correspond to punctuation marks in English. Thai numerals are also different, although Arabic numerals are widely used nowadays and most literate people are familiar with them. Equally, many people with virtually no knowledge of English will have some familiarity with the Roman alphabet.

Punctuation

Essentially, there are no punctuation marks in Thai; spaces between groups of words are used to indicate pauses. Sometimes Thai books are printed with Western punctuation marks, but these are really redundant. Punctuation presents quite a problem to Thai learners; errors of omission are frequent, while the concept of what constitutes a sentence may prove an obstacle.

Grammar

General

The grammatical structure of Thai is very different to that of English. Plurals of nouns and verb tenses are frequently unmarked, and when they are marked, it is by the addition of particular structural words rather than by inflection. Thai adjectives and adverbs can also function as verbs, while the Thai pronominal system is more complex and makes different distinctions to that of English. One of the few broad areas of similarity is the order of words in a sentence; but although Thai sentences tend to follow a 'subject + verb + object' pattern, it is very common for the subject to be omitted if it can be clearly understood.

Auxiliaries; questions and negatives

There are no auxiliary verbs in Thai.
1. In Thai, a sentence is transformed into a question by the addition of a question word which is placed at the end of the sentence. Since the question word has no equivalent in English, Thai speakers will often simply substitute a rising intonation in an otherwise literal translation:
    He go? (Note also the uninflected verb.)
2. More specific questions such as *When?*, *Why?* and *How?* have close Thai equivalents, but since certain of these can occur either at the beginning or the end of the sentence, the learner is likely to produce sentences like:

257

> **When he go?*
> **He go when?*

How many? is frequently used to the exclusion of How much? and the verb is often omitted also:

> **How many price of that shirt?*

3. Negatives in Thai are formed by putting the negative word mây in front of the verb. Confusion sometimes arises as to whether this word should be translated as *no* or *not*:

> **He not go.*
> **He no go.*

Time, tense and aspect

The Thai verb has no inflected forms; a single word pay (= go) covers not simply *go* and *goes* but also *went, was going, has gone, is going, will go, would go* and so on. Usually situation and context preclude any ambiguity, but where there is a possibility of misunderstanding arising, structural words are added, usually immediately in front of the verb, to clarify the time-reference. In normal narrative, it is usually quite enough to use simply the verb with no pre-verb modifier.

Verb inflections and complex verb phrases present a formidable obstacle to Thai learners, and many prefer to use the unmarked base form of the English verb rather than attempt a more difficult form which they feel will more than likely be incorrect. (However, a Thai who appears to be using the base form of a verb in speech may actually be having problems with pronunciation rather than grammar. He or she may be trying to say, for instance, *cooked* or *arranged*, but failing to pronounce the *-ed* at the end of the cluster.) This is obviously a major area in which Thai speakers are at a disadvantage compared with European learners of English, and this should be borne in mind when teaching classes of mixed nationalities.

Articles

There are no articles in Thai, and errors of confusion between indefinite and definite articles, as well as when to omit articles, occur frequently:

> **He is very nice man.*
> **What the food you like?*
> **The buffaloes are the important animals in Thailand.*

Adjectives and adverbs

Adjectives and adverbs in Thai occur after the noun or verb which they modify. They also function as verbs meaning *to be* (the Thai equivalent of *to be* is not used as a copula with adjectives). Thus the expression rót dii

(= *car-good*) can be considered as either a phrase (*a good car*) or a sentence (*the car is good*). As a result, the verb is often omitted in English sentences:

> **This car not good.*
> **This food very tasty.*

In Thai, there is no distinction between adjective/adverb pairs as there is in English (e.g. *good/well, fast/quickly, clear/clearly*). Thai learners tend to overuse the adjectival form in English:

> **You speak Thai very good.*

The comparative and superlative degrees of adjectives and adverbs in Thai are formed by the addition of *more than* and *(the) most* respectively, immediately after the base word. As a result, the English suffixes *-er* and *-est* are frequently disregarded by Thai learners:

> **This dress is beautiful more than that one.*
> **I work the most hard of my brothers.*

Nouns

Thai nouns have neither gender nor case, nor is there any distinction between singular and plural forms. Context is generally sufficient to indicate whether a noun has singular or plural reference, but in instances where it is important to be more precise, Thai employs 'pluraliser words' which occupy a fixed position in relation to the noun, or exact numerical descriptions. Thai learners make frequent errors in using the singular form of an English noun (the unmarked form) where a plural should be used:

> **I have many friend.*

Numerical expressions in Thai are more complex than in English, and involve the use of a special 'noun classifier'. *Two cars* and *five girls* would be expressed in Thai as:

car	*two*	*vehicle*
girl	*five*	*person*
(noun) +	(number) +	(classifier)

The Thai pattern seldom causes interference beyond the initial stages, although failure to pluralise a noun after a number is very common:

> **I have five brother.*

Pronouns

The pronoun system of Thai is considerably more complex than that of most European languages, with a wide range of words to indicate relationships of both hierarchy and intimacy. Kin terms and personal names are widely used as first and second person pronouns to signal intimacy. English pronouns present problems for the Thai learner, because the two languages make different distinctions in both gender and number. Thus, the Thai first person pronoun can distinguish between masculine and feminine, whereas the most commonly used third-person pronoun does not, leading Thai learners frequently to use *he* and *she* interchangeably in English:

> *My girlfriend, he is very nice.*
> *The policeman she chased me.*

(Note also the duplication of noun and pronoun which occurs commonly in spoken Thai.)

The same third-person pronoun not only does not distinguish gender – it does not distinguish number either, resulting in confusing statements like:

> *My American friends are in Thailand. I will meet him at the hotel.*

or worse:

> *My sisters study at university. He work very hard.*

Thai pronouns do not have separate forms to indicate subject or object functions; nor is there a possessive pronoun in Thai. Possession in Thai is expressed in the terms 'noun + *of* + noun/pronoun', although the Thai word for *of* is optional and frequently omitted. This can lead to mistakes like:

> *house of my father* or *house of father*

It is very common in Thai to omit the subject from a sentence if it is perfectly clear who or what is being talked about. This frequently means that pronouns are discarded in Thai sentences, and the habit is sometimes carried over into English:

> *My brother was angry when came home.*

Prepositions

Most English prepositions have near Thai equivalents and are relatively easy for Thai learners to grasp. More difficult are English 'verb + preposition' or 'adjective + preposition' combinations which have a single-word Thai verb equivalent. This leads to errors such as:

> *I angry you.*
> *We interest / are interested it.*
> *He frighten / is frightened you.*

Subordinate clauses

Thai learners inevitably experience difficulty in producing the correct verb tenses in complex sentences with subordinate clauses. Relative clauses present a further problem in that Thai has only one relative pronoun, and *who* and *which* in particular are frequently confused:

> *My friend which I met . . .*

Conditional clauses in Thai frequently omit the Thai word for *if*, and this is sometimes carried over into English. Other typical sentence constructions arising from a literal translation from Thai include:

> *Although ... , but ...*
> *Because ... , therefore ...*

Vocabulary

Traditionally, Sanskrit and Pali have been used for coining new words in Thai; however, the influx of western technology and consumer goods has resulted in a considerable number of English loanwords being adopted into the Thai lexicon. Such borrowings are given a Thai pronunciation which Thai learners often find difficult to shed when using the word in English. Apart from these loanwords, there is no similarity between the Thai and English lexicons, and the Thai learner has none of the advantages of the Western European learner who can draw on a knowledge of Latin and Germanic roots to increase vocabulary. The fact that many Thais with very little communicative competence in English nevertheless seem to have an extensive English vocabulary is largely due to traditional methods of education, which put great emphasis on rote learning at the expense of developing communication skills.

Culture

Generally speaking, Thais have a very positive attitude towards learning English. Competence in the language is not only intrinsically desirable; it is also believed to be, not without good reason, the key to a more prosperous life. Most of the top jobs require a sound knowledge of the language, and tens of thousands of parents make considerable financial sacrifices each year so that their offspring can move from the provinces to the big cities, or from the big cities to overseas, in order to gain a better facility in the language. There even appears to be a certain social prestige attached to simply attending English classes, for many people with little need for English and little real interest appear to be willing to part with considerable sums of money to register for courses from which they will gain little benefit and to which they feel even less commitment!

English has been regarded as essential for national development, and has thus been a compulsory element in the secondary school curriculum for many years. However, the quality of language education provided varies enormously; in Bangkok, expensive private schools often provide English at the primary level, and with competent teachers and sometimes native speakers on their staffs, their pupils can be very fluent speakers by the time they leave school. Children from a rural background face a severe handicap by comparison, for the best teachers have traditionally gravitated towards the capital, where the pay and conditions are better. The American presence in Thailand during the Vietnam war to some extent broadened the audience for English (and all its associated riches), but, by and large, English remains an activity of the urban minority, and this is reflected in the kinds of opportunities open to foreigners who wish to teach English in Thailand.

The teacher is traditionally a highly respected and respectable figure, and a class in Thailand is likely to have definite ideas about what is and what is not appropriate 'teacher behaviour'. Most things are a matter of common sense, although the Thailand-bound teacher would be well advised to find out something about cultural *faux pas* in general, from such sources as travel books, tourist guides or more specialised works. One area where Westerners do sometimes offend is in the matter of dress: appearance is very important in Thai society and a failure to adapt to this (and other cultural values) can seriously undermine the effectiveness of the teacher and even create latent hostility. When it comes to actual teaching, provoking participation can be a serious problem. Students are used to receiving knowledge passively and may feel threatened by a more active communication-oriented approach; alternatively, they may feel that they are learning nothing once the blackboard examples of grammatical rules give way to 'chaotic conversation classes'. The Western teacher should also bear in mind that Thai society is a very hierarchical one in which seniority in years is, *per se*, worthy of respect. Thus in classes of mixed ages, it is important to make sure that older learners are not in any way made to lose face (e.g. by leaving a long pause after a question which the learner cannot answer, brushing aside pedantic questions as irrelevant, etc.). If this happens, the individual is likely to boycott further classes, while the whole class is likely to feel 'unhappy' and will hence be less co-operative.

A sample of written Thai

Type-written Thai

ประชากรทางภาคใต้มีลักษณะแตกต่างจากประชากรทางภาคอื่นบ้างในทางผิว พรรณและรูปร่างหน้าตากับสำเนียงภาษา ส่วนความเป็นอยู่และอาชีพนั้นส่วนใหญ่ก็คือ การกสิกรรม แต่มีข้าวน้อยกว่าภาคกลาง มีผลไม้มากซึ่งพอจะเป็นรายได้ดีถ้าการขน ส่งสะดวก หาตลาดได้ไกลๆ ผลิตผลที่เป็นรายได้ขึ้นหน้าขึ้นตากว่าผลไม้คืออยางพารา ซึ่งปลูกกันมากในจังหวัดตอนใต้และเหมืองแร่ดีบุกในบางท้องที่

A direct transliteration

prachaakǫǫn thaang phâak tâay mii láksanà tạạktàang càak prachaakǫǫn thaang phâak ừụn bâang nay thaang phǐwphan lậ rûuprâang
nâataa kàp sǎmniang phaasǎa sùan khwaam pen yùu lậ aachîip nán
sùan yày kǫ̂ khụụ kaan kàsikam táạ mii khâaw nǫ́ǫy kwàa phâak
klaang mii phǒnlamaáy mâak sǔng phǫǫ ca pen raaydâay dii thâa
kaan khǒn sòng sadùak hǎa talàat dâay klay klay phalìtphǒn thîi pen
raaydâay khûn nâa khûn taa kwàa phǒnlamáay khụụ yaang phaaraa
sǔng plùuk kan mâak nay cangwàt tǫǫn tâay lậ mǔangrậạ diibùk nay
baang thǫ́ǫngthîi

A word for word translation

people way region south have characteristic different from people way
region other somewhat in way of complexion and shape face eyes with
sound of language. as for way of life and profession part big is agriculture
but have rice little than region middle. have fruit much which sufficient
will be income good if carrying sending convenient, find market far far.
product which is income rise face rise eye (more) than fruit is Para rubber
(tree) which grow together much in province part south and mines tin in
some areas.

An idiomatic translation

The people of the south differ somewhat from the people of other regions
in their complexion and physical appearance and in their language. As far
as their way of living and occupations are concerned, they are mainly
involved in agriculture. But there is less rice than in the Central Region.
There is a lot of fruit, sufficient to bring in a good income if trans-
portation is convenient and markets can be found over a wide area.
Products which bring in a more noticeable income than fruit are the Para
rubber tree, which is grown in the southern provinces and the tin mines in
some areas.

The cassette

On the accompanying cassette, speakers of the various languages referred to in the book were recorded:
1. talking informally about themselves;
2. telling the story shown in the picture strip below;
3. reading aloud the text which follows (which is designed so as to test for a number of common pronunciation mistakes).

Picture story

The picture story is reproduced by kind permission of the ARELS Examination Trust.

Transcript of reading passage

If you're going shopping, John,
could you get me these few things, please?

Three kilos of green beans,
six tins of mixed pickles,
ten red or yellow peppers,
a bag of apples,
half a carton of large tomatoes,
a pot of hot coffee,
four sorts of corn,
a cookery book,
a bunch of bananas and some butter,
two tubes of that useful new glue,
some first early potatoes,
eight paper plates,
a whole Dover sole,
five kinds of light white wine,
a pound of brown flour,
some olive oil and cooking foil,
some beer, not too dear,
some pears to share,
some ham to cure, if you're sure it's pure,
and a measure of orange juice,
and a chunk of Dutch cheese, cut thick or thin.

Thanks very much, John.